Documenting Irish Feminisms

The Second Wave

Linda Connolly and Tina O'Toole

 The Woodfield Press

This book was typeset for
THE WOODFIELD PRESS
17 Jamestown Square, Dublin 8
www.woodfield-press.com

Design: cover and typography Petra Stone

A catalogue record for this title is available from
The British Library

ISBN 0-9534293-5-0

Acknowledgement: the research project on which this book is based – the Irish
Women's Movement Project – was subvented by Cycle 1 of the Higher Education
Authority's Programme for Research in Third Level Institutions.

Printed in Ireland by
ColourBooks, Dublin

COMMISSIONING EDITOR
Helen Harnett

HOUSE EDITOR
Elina Talvitie

Contents

Also published by The Woodfield Press

The Gore-Booths of Lissadell
DERMOT JAMES

Differently Irish: A Cultural History Exploring Twenty Five years of Vietnamese-Irish Identity
MARK MAGUIRE

Royal Roots – Republican Inheritance: The Survival of the Office of Arms
SUSAN HOOD

The Politics and Relationships of Kathleen Lynn
MARIE MULHOLLAND

St Anne's – The Story of a Guinness Estate
JOAN USSHER SHARKEY

Female Activists: Irish Women and Change 1900–1960
MARY CULLEN & MARIA LUDDY (eds)

W & R Jacob: Celebrating 150 Years of Irish Biscuit Making
SÉAMAS Ó MAITIÚ

Faith or Fatherhood? Bishop Dunboyne's Dilemma
CON COSTELLO

Charles Dickens Ireland: An Anthology
JIM COOKE

Red-Headed Rebel: A Biography of Susan Mitchell
HILARY PYLE

The Sligo-Leitrim World of Kate Cullen 1832–1913
HILARY PYLE

John Hamilton of Donegal 1800–1884
DERMOT JAMES

The Tellicherry Five: The Transportation of Michael Dwyer and the Wicklow Rebels
KIERAN SHEEDY

Ballyknockan: A Wicklow Stonecutters' Village
SÉAMAS Ó MAITIÚ & BARRY O'REILLY

The Wicklow World of Elizabeth Smith 1840–1850
DERMOT JAMES & SÉAMAS Ó MAITIÚ
(Now back in print)

Acknowledgements

This book was produced in collaboration with many colleagues both in the university sector and in the wider community. We are indebted to them for their part in creating and maintaining the culture within which this kind of project could develop. An advisory panel was established to help generate the themes of this book and we would like to thank the members of the panel for their support throughout the project's duration: Linda Cardinal, Bríd Connolly, Breda Gray, Orla McDonnell, Carmel Quinlan, Anne Ryan, Anne B. Ryan and Ailbhe Smyth. We would also like to thank our other colleagues on the Women and Irish Society Project at University College Cork (UCC) for their collaboration: Máire Leane, Liz Kiely, Éibhear Walshe and, in particular, Pat Coughlan, whose support throughout was invaluable. Jean Van Sinderen Law, formerly at the Research Office in UCC, also offered help and advice at important stages.

Terri McDonnell of The Woodfield Press was courageous in taking on such a collaborative and creative production, and her professionalism and patience with us was considerable at all stages. We also wish to thank Petra Stone for her expert design work on the book.

We would like to especially acknowledge the immense contribution Róisín Conroy has made to Irish feminist research nationally and internationally by donating her collection of archives to the Boole Library at UCC for public use. This book was, in large part, written with a view to highlighting and encouraging further research into the fascinating documents and sources that Róisín Conroy and others have provided in recent years.

We wish to acknowledge the permission of the Boole Library at UCC, to publish material from the Attic Press/Róisín Conroy Collection, and the Morriset Library, at the University of Ottawa, for allowing us to use material from the Canadian Women's Movement Archive. In a project of this nature, the assistance of archivists and librarians is vital. Most particularly, Carol Quinn, Archivist at the Boole Library, brought her help and significant expertise to bear on the research at many different levels. The help John Fitzgerald, the Librarian at UCC, gave to the project when we first made our submission to the HEA for PRTLI 1 funding was crucial, and we would like to thank him for his continued support. Emer Twomey also provided assistance in the final stages. We would also like to thank, for their assistance: Joan Murphy at the RTÉ Sound Archives; Tonie Walsh at the Irish Queer Archive; the staff at the National Library of Ireland; the Fawcett Library in London; *Women's News* in Belfast; and Lucie Desjardins at the Canadian Women's Movement Archives, Morriset Library. In terms of institutional support, the Sociology Department at UCC provided us with facilities and assistance when conducting the research, and Ciarán McCullagh kindly let us borrow his office when away on sabbatical.

Linda would like to express thanks to the following people for their contribution to the Irish Women's Movement Project programme of events: Sandra Harding,

Sasha Roseneil, Ailbhe Smyth, Margaret Shildrick, Gail Lewis, Breda Gray, Marysia Zalewski, Mary Hickman, Sandra McAvoy, Angela O'Connor, Margaret O'Keeffe, Kathy Glavanis, Niamh Hourigan, Linda Cardinal and Kathleen Lynch. Mary Cullen has been of immense support and help with this book. Her comments on the text were, as always, perceptive and constructive.

Particular thanks are due to Clodagh Boyd for giving us permission to use her unique photographic collection throughout this book, as well as for her enthusiasm for the project. We would also like to thank Derek Speirs for permission to use his photographs. We are grateful to Arja Kajermo and bülbül for permission to use their cartoons, Paula Meehan for permission to publish her poem "The Statue at Granard Speaks", and Kay MacKeogh, who kindly gave us material on trade union activism. We would also like to acknowledge the help of Sara Wilbourne of Cork University Press with the Attic Press book covers, and Catherine Rose of Arlen House.

Tina would like to mention in particular Margaret MacCurtain whose useful advice in the early days of the project, not to mention her infectious enthusiasm for this and other projects, was an inspiration. The contribution of activists themselves to the research process was invaluable, and all of those whose first-hand experience of activism in Ireland and Canada added immensely to both the finished outcome, and our experience of carrying out the research. In particular, thanks are due to Íde O'Carroll, Joan McCarthy, Deirdre Walsh, Nikki Keeling, Helen Slattery, Marie Quiery, Paula Keenan, Claire Hackett, Marie Mulholland, Irene Demczuk, Line Chamberland, and Miriam Smith. I am grateful to all of those who read drafts of various sections, and took the time to provide feedback, including Rosie Meade, Siobhán O'Dowd, Lia Mills, Roz Cowman, and Pat Coughlan. Thanks to everyone at the Institute of Irish Studies at Queen's University Belfast, who provided a vital context for some of this writing to be completed. I would also like to thank my family for their ongoing support.

The house moves, job changes, pregnancy, other research projects, family illnesses, teaching commitments, and other distractions in our lives that coincided with this project at times threatened to overwhelm the project. Special thanks are due to Andy Bielenberg and Benjamin Bielenberg (born 22 November 2004), and to Siobhán O'Dowd for their support and for putting up with the demands of this and other projects.

Linda Connolly and Tina O'Toole,
Cork,
November 2004.

List of Abbreviations

ADAPT   Association for Deserted and Alone Parents
AIM   Action, Information, Motivation
AnCo   Organisation set up in the 1960s to facilitate training in industry, has since been replaced by FÁS
CAME   Clondalkin Adult Morning Education
CAP   Contraception Action Campaign
CSW   Council for the Status of Women, now the National Women's Council of Ireland
CWEI   Cork Women's Education Initiative
CWMA   Canadian Women's Movement Archive
CWRCG   Cork Women's Right to Choose Group
DARG   Dublin Abortion Rights Group
ERA   Equal Rights Amendment
FUE   Federated Union of Employers
GLEN   Gay and Lesbian Equality Network
ICA   Irish Countrywomen's Association
IGRM   Irish Gay Rights Movement
IFI   Irish Feminist Information
IFPA   Irish Family Planning Association
IHA   Irish Housewives Association
ILGO   Irish Lesbian and Gay Organisation
IPPC   Irish Pregnancy Counselling Service
ITGWU   Irish Transport and General Workers' Union
IWLM   Irish Women's Liberation Movement
IWU   Irishwomen United
IWWU   Irish Women Workers Union
LEA   Lesbian Education Awareness
LGBT   Lesbian, Gay, Bisexual and Transgender communities
L.Inc   Lesbians in Cork
LOT   Lesbians Organising Together
MADE   Maynooth Adult Daytime Courses
NAWI   National Association of Widows in Ireland
NGF   National Gay Federation (later National Lesbian & Gay Federation, NLGF)
NLI   National Library of Ireland
NWCI   National Women's Council of Ireland, formerly the Council for the Status of Women
NOW   New Opportunities for Women
PARC   Parents Alone Resource Centre
PLAC   Pro-Life Amendment Campaign

RTÉ	Radió Teilifís Éireann
SLM	Sexual Liberation Movement
SPUC	Society for the Protection of Unborn Children
WIL	Women in Learning
WERRC	Women's Education, Research and Resource Centre (at University College Dublin)
UCC	University College Cork
UCG	University College Galway
UL	University of Limerick
VEC	Vocational Education Committee
WAAG	Women Artists Action Group
WENDI	Women's Educational Network Development Initiative
WIN	Women's Information Network
WIP	Women in Publishing
WPA	Women's Progressive/Political Association
WRC	Women's Representative Committee

Preface

This book originated in a three-year research project entitled The Irish Women's Movement, which was established in the Sociology Department at University College Cork in 1999. The project formed one major strand of an integrated research initiative in the Arts and Humanities in the University that was funded by the Government of Ireland's first Programme for Research in Third Level Institutions (PRTLI 1).[1] The proposal for Women and Irish Society: Understanding the Past and Present Through Archives and Social Research incorporated three collaborate studies: "The Irish Women's Movement Project", which has produced this volume, *Documenting Irish Feminisms*; "The Munster Women Writers Project"[2]; and "Women and Work in Munster 1930–1960".[3]

The Irish Women's Movement Project represents the first time any Irish government has funded a university-led study and analysis of the legacy of feminism and the women's movement in recent Irish history. The women's movement is an important example of a range of social movements that have been neglected in mainstream studies of modern Irish politics, which tend to focus on the state and established politics as the basis of social change. This book maps many of the changes that have occurred in Irish women's lives since the late 1960s, focusing in particular on the role of feminist politics and the women's movement in these developments. The analysis and evidence presented suggests that second-wave feminism is a multifaceted intellectual, political, social and cultural movement that did not just affect women's lives from the 1970s onwards – rather, it is a movement that has had a potent influence on the changing social, cultural and political order that has transformed modern Irish history and society in general in recent decades.

In addition to producing this book, the Irish Women's Movement Project incorporated several other activities. In particular, a basis for linking national and international research, and websites and archives, in the comparative study of women's social movements has been established. In the duration of the project, a detailed bibliography of Irish feminist studies and research was produced and is published on the internet (see the project website www.ucc.ie/wisp/iwm); conferences, workshops, a series of public seminars and a public exhibition were held; an integrated project website was developed; the contents of feminist archives and collections in Ireland were collated and documented; movement photographs, artefacts, symbols and images were recorded and reproduced; an international network of researchers was established; and comparative research was advanced in the field.

This work will continue in the Sociology Department at University College Cork. Institutional links and research partnerships have been established with the Department of Political Science and the Centre for the Study of Women in Politics, at the University of Ottawa, Canada; the Centre for Adult and

Community Education, at the National University of Ireland at Maynooth; the Women's Education, Research and Resource Centre (WERRC), at University College Dublin; and the Sociology Department and Women's Studies Programme, at the University of Limerick.

Although this project has established a strong foundation, it also highlights the need for more recovery work, research and theorising in the field. Fundamentally, we hope that the results of the project will encourage more graduate and under-graduate students to undertake imaginative research on the many aspects of Irish feminism that require new perspectives and critical thinking.

Notes

1 The research environment in Irish universities has been completely transformed over the past five years. Government funding, combined with private matching funding, has supported the HEA Programme for Research in Third Level Institutions (PRTLI) and in the first and second cycles of its operation almost £0.25 billion was allocated on a competitive basis to third-level institutions (see www.hea.ie for details). Although the Government in 2001 postponed the third cycle of this pro-gramme, it is expected to provide a similar scale of funding to cycles 1 and 2.

2 The Munster Women Writers Project compiled a biographical dictionary of writers from the region in the period 1800–2000, both in English and Irish. Collating biographical pieces and biblio-graphical entries for each writer, the project recovered material relating to over 500 writers, which is to be published both in hard cover (forthcoming, Cork University Press) and as an online searchable database. The project team includes Professor Pat Coughlan, Dr Eibhear Walshe and Dr Tina O'Toole, and was based in the Department of English at UCC.

3 This project resulted in the collection of over 40 oral history interviews with women living in counties Cork, Limerick and Kerry. These interviews provide rich ethnographic accounts of women's experiences of diverse kinds of waged work in the 1940s and the 1950s. The project team included Dr Liz Kiely and Dr Máire Leane and was based in the Department of Applied Social Studies, UCC.

Introduction

A central objective of the Irish Women's Movement Project was to produce a comprehensive survey of primary and secondary sources relating to the development of second-wave feminism and the women's movement in Ireland. In recent years, the fact that a growing corpus of documents has become increasingly available to Irish women's movement researchers, both in official library collections and on a more informal basis, has created exciting possibilities in the field. An extensive range of primary materials that have not been available in the public domain since their initial use in political activism were researched in this project. The end result, in this book, is an examination of the development of second-wave feminism in Ireland through the prism of a range of documentary sources that originated from within the women's movement itself (including the minutes of meetings, position papers, flyers, press releases, photographs, artefacts, political art, posters, magazines and other publications as well as banners and other movement objects).[1]

Recent studies have shed light on the development of second-wave feminism in Ireland in relation to the State and mainstream politics (such as Galligan, 1998). However, social movements are collective entities that tend to mobilise both within the state and in civil society. Research based on sources from within the women's movement, such as documents and oral recollections, illuminate how activists themselves have constructed feminist politics in Ireland in a range of institutional (for instance, in the courts and the universities) and non-institutional contexts (for example, in local community groups, consciousness-raising groups and in single-issue campaigns).

Much of this book concentrates on revealing the political nature of second-wave feminism as a social movement – how feminists collectively organised, networked, strategised and effectively mobilised a unique and forceful movement.[2] We use the term "second-wave feminism" to refer to the women's movement that emerged internationally in the late 1960s and early 1970s. This term differentiates it from the early days of feminist activism in the second half of the nineteenth century, when feminists in many countries began first to organise collectively and demand equal opportunities in education, access to the professions, and famously, votes for women. The extensive movement documents studied provide an intimate portrayal of feminist activism, in all its diversity, in the period from the late 1960s to the 1990s. This study also seeks to move existing analyses of the women's movement in Ireland forward by focusing not just on the internal workings of Irish feminism as a multifaceted social movement – rather, it also seeks to connect (or reconnect) feminism more explicitly to the profound social and cultural transformation that has characterised modern Ireland since the 1960s.[3] Movements have a range of potential effects in the social and cultural realm and the extent to which the goals of various feminist campaigns and groups have advanced change in key areas, over time, is addressed in each chapter of this book.

Although major studies of the women's movement have recently appeared in Irish studies, orthodox interpretations of social change in modern Ireland continue to either ignore or else diminish feminism as a minor historical player. The true force and impact of this important movement has been either written out or underplayed in distinguished accounts of social change. Yet, as new sources (in particular, the Attic Press/Róisín Conroy Collection)[4] now reveal, second wave feminists launched and formulated a highly organised collective agenda, which targeted and instigated fundamental change in a wide range of arenas.

A basic premise of this book is that the women's movement is a major consideration in the so-called rapid transformation Irish society has undergone in recent decades. Despite their prevalence in western societies since the 1960s, social movements have been generally neglected in mainstream interpretations of Irish politics and society. In agreement with Crossley (2003: 8) "movements are important because they are key agents for bringing about change in societies." On the other hand, this does not suggest that second-wave feminism and feminists have had an easy time in Ireland. Individual movements are never the only cause of change in a particular arena. However, it is shortsighted to ignore social movements or consider them less important than the family, economy or the state, for example. In addition, knowledge of the prevalence of social and cultural resistance to feminism is as important as feminism itself in any critical account of social and cultural change in the Irish context. For example, the success of the women's movement in decriminalising contraception in the 1970s provoked a backlash in the form of an influential counter-right campaign that was to have a powerful impact on both the women's movement and Irish politics in general throughout the 1980s (see Chapter 2). Neither were second-wave feminist campaigns and agendas always successful or widespread in Ireland. Nevertheless, all these things considered, mainstream interpretations of social change and modernity have undoubtedly underestimated the role of feminism and the women's movement in the ongoing transformation Irish society has experienced since the 1960s.

Following more than three decades of second-wave activism, it is now possible to look back and reflect on the wider impact this phase of feminism has had in Irish society. This study will explore in some depth the influence diverse strands of feminist activism and thought have had, and continue to have, in a number of specific arenas (including reproduction, mainstream politics, community politics, culture and education, for example). Key issues addressed include: the wide-ranging challenge a new wave of liberal, radical and socialist feminist groups, campaigns and services generated in the 1970s; the establishment of reproductive-choice campaigns and services in Ireland; the mainstreaming of feminism in the political arena and the state; the exposure of sexual and domestic violence as a real problem in Irish society from the 1970s onwards; the emergence of lesbian and gay issues and activism in Ireland; developments in social policy and family law; the emergence of feminist thought and ideas in Irish cultural politics and production; the significance of the conflict in Northern Ireland/"the Troubles" in Irish feminist politics; class difference and socialist politics in the women's movement; the expansion of feminist education and research in recent years; the impact of migration on feminist politics; and the challenge locally based community groups pose to the established women's movement.

Social movement analysis is a field of study that can address the cultural as well as the political impact of feminist thought and ideas on society. Giugni (1999: xxiii) suggests: "collective efforts for social change occur in the realms of culture, identity, and everyday life as well as in direct engagement with the State." Movements do not exclusively operate at the level of revolution, mass mobilisation and major legislative change – they also problematise the ways in which we live our everyday lives and call for changes in the private as well as the public sphere.

Irish women's lives, roles and self-image have changed considerably in the last three decades. The average number of children an Irish woman will have today has, for example, significantly decreased since the 1960s. Moreover, it is not unusual for a woman living in Ireland to have her child/children in more than one type of family (see Chapter 3). And increasingly she will choose to work outside as well as inside the home. Although the Irish public have not always readily supported the demands of feminists and the women's movement over the last three decades, the range of questions and debates that were propelled into the public arena by this movement over time have had a wider cultural effect. The women's movement progressively gained a level of attention, through its controversial actions and strategies, which injected a new culture of questioning in a range of spheres (such as intimate relationships, sexuality, family life, marriage, parenting, work and health) from the late 1960s on. In particular, feminist activism brought many issues that were previously hidden and stigmatised in the public sphere into the open for the first time (such as rape, sexuality, abortion, contraception, single motherhood and domestic violence).[5] For example, when the Irish Women's Liberation Movement organised a public meeting in the Mansion House, Dublin, in 1971 it was completely unheard of for a woman to stand up and publicly declare she was an "unmarried mother" – as one woman did. Single motherhood was considered shameful in Ireland at that time and children born outside of wedlock were discriminated against in the law. Domestic violence was widely considered a private issue to be dealt with primarily within "the family", and use of contraception/artificial family planning was illegal.

A fundamental challenge to the cultural conservatism that characterised Irish society for much of the twentieth century emerged from within a whole range of reformist movements that mobilised from the 1960s on, the women's movement being one of the most significant. Second-wave feminist thought and ideas opened up and provoked a wide-ranging questioning of long-established attitudes to women and values that permeated public institutions and private life. This book will demonstrate that the actions of an organised and active women's movement over the last three decades can therefore be said to have contributed to the generation of a new language and cultural space in modern Ireland.

The methodological value of the archives, artefacts and images of second-wave feminism for Irish women's studies and social movement research will be discussed in the rest of this introductory chapter. At the same time, critical questions concerning how the relics of recent feminist movements should be maintained and made accessible are explored. We will argue that although primary archival research is vital for the continued progress of feminist theorising and social movement studies in Ireland, documentary research should be combined with other research methodologies and sources. Biographical material and other publications in the field, including recent studies of Irish feminism based on intensive interviews with activists and oral accounts, were combined with the evidence gathered from the documents surveyed in this research project.[6] Finally, the theoretical standpoint adopted in the study will be explained and a summary of the book will be provided.

The Documents of Second-wave Feminisms

> Archives are political entities and collecting and preserving archival material is a political act.
> (Curnoe, 1989: 237)

Feminist research in Ireland has reached a critical stage in the important task of recovery work. Both public and privately held archives are becoming more available and this is evident in recent Irish feminist recovery projects, such as the compilation of the *Field Day Anthology*, Vols. IV and V[7] (2002), the Women's History Project,[8] and the Munster Women Writers Project.[9] These projects conducted extensive retrieval work and found an array of material documenting women's lives in sources as diverse as state papers, novels and convent records.

The Irish Women's Movement Project is also an innovative recovery project, in the arena of social movement theory and research.[10] A range of movement documents and other sources produced by feminist activists in Ireland, from the late 1960s to the 1990s, were recorded. The research methodology was based on the premise that materials and symbols produced by movement activists *themselves* within feminist groups (i.e. primary sources) can add a great deal more to what is already known about feminist politics from recent academic accounts, based on secondary sources, as well as their links to other social and political movements (such as the labour movement, the Republican movement, the peace/anti-war movement and the international women's movement itself). Furthermore, the records of the Irish women's movement are valuable not only to political activists and scholars interested in understanding social change in Ireland – they are also relevant to the media, community workers, educationalists, and writers, for example.

The most extensive source of new evidence now available in Ireland is archival. The key resource in this project was undoubtedly the Attic Press/Róisín Conroy Collection housed at the Boole Library, University College Cork.[11] This is the first integrated collection in Ireland dedicated entirely to Irish feminism and the women's movement. We also carried out research at the National Library of Ireland, the Irish Queer Archive in Dublin, the collection of *Women's News*

Magazine in Belfast and on a range of smaller collections of material held by individuals, national organisations and community projects. Trinity College, Dublin holds some copies of *Banshee* (the journal of the radical feminist group, Irishwomen United) and some editions of *Wicca* magazine from the 1970s. Documents from these collections as well as the photographic collections of Clodagh Boyd and Derek Speirs are used extensively in this book. Although we endeavoured to recover and research material from groups and individuals nationally, urban and rural, most existing archives derive from Dublin-based feminist groups in the 1970s and 1980s. Locally-based women's groups, for example, have only recently began to preserve and document their histories (see Chapter 7). Some material is available at the Linen Hall Library, the Library of Queen's University Belfast and at the Belfast Institution of Higher Education. However, an archive similar to the Attic Press/Róisín Conroy Collection has yet to be established in Northern Ireland.

Archives and Sources

Irish Collections

The Attic Press/Róisín Conroy Collection, Boole Library, University College Cork (catalogue code: BL/F/AP) was generated and collected by Róisín Conroy as co-founder and publisher at Attic Press and as an activist in the Irish women's movement. The materials were deposited in the Boole Library by Conroy in 1997. The archive covers the years 1963–1991 and contains 133 boxes plus ephemera.

The core sections of the collection relate to the activities of Conroy while working as a librarian within the research unit of the Irish Transport and General Workers' Union (ITGWU), to Irish Feminist Information (IFI) and to Attic Press. There is also a small amount of ancillary material. The collection reflects the various facets of Conroy's career as a librarian and information officer, publisher and campaigner for women's rights.

The collection begins with records of the ITGWU's research unit, where Róisín Conroy worked as an information officer from 1970–1979 and moves on to papers relating to the development and structure of IFI. In 1978 Róisín Conroy and Mary Doran set up IFI as a feminist organisation concerned with the publication and dissemination of information relating to women in Ireland. Over time, IFI organised itself as a company and was overseen by a Board of Directors. Directors included Mary Paul Keane (co-founder of Attic Press), Patricia Kelleher, Gaye Cunningham, Anne Hyland and Pádraigín Ní Mhurchu (IWWU). Records of the Women's Community Press are also preserved. In November 1984 IFI separated its training and publishing functions by launching a feminist publishing house – Attic Press. The archives, which detail the development of both IFI and the setting up and subsequent development of Attic Press, are listed in section 2.1 of the collection's catalogue.[12]

Records relating to international feminist book fairs, women's world festivals and "International Interdisciplinary Congresses" are also contained in this important collection. Talks given by Ailbhe Smyth and Nell McCafferty concerning the history of the feminist movement and the development of the UCD women's studies forum and course can be found among sound archives in the collection.

Papers relating to women's groups and organisations are also present, including the Irish Women's Liberation Movement. These records relate to conferences and seminars as well as the examination of the history of the Irish women's movement. Other women's groups in the collection include the Council for the Status of Women and the Commission on the Status of Women, and there are other records generally relating to forums, seminars and reports. Papers relating to Irish Womenunited can be found in sub-section 6.3. Other groups within this section include the Irish Council for Civil Liberties and the Irish Countrywomen's Association.

Papers relating to campaign issues have been divided into the following categories: employment equality, women's resource centres, Well Woman Centres, women and health, divorce, abortion, contraception, gay rights, one-parent families and prisoners' rights. Correspondence, reports, minutes, research notes, campaign literature, publications and press cuttings can be found among these papers.

One of the campaigns in which Róisín Conroy played a vital role, and which is represented in this collection, was that of the campaign for a Unified Social Welfare Code (section 7.10 of the *Attic Press/Róisín Conroy Collection* catalogue). In 1982 Róisín Conroy took an action to the High Court regarding her inability to qualify for unemployment assistance due to the fact that she was, in law, still considered to be a married woman without any dependant. The High Court eventually ruled in favour of Conroy and the discrimination inherent in the social welfare system had to be rectified by the state.

This archive is a rich source of material documenting the activities of not only Róisín Conroy but also other Irish activists. These include Anne Speed, June Levine, Nell McCafferty, Mary Paul Keane, Mary Doran, Anne O'Donnell, Anne Connolly, Therese Caherty, Patricia Kelleher, Marie McMahon and Ailbhe Smyth (to name but a few). To access the collection and its catalogue contact: Carol Quinn, Library Archivist, Boole Library, University College Cork. Go to: www.ucc.ie and booleweb.ucc.ie for further details.

The Women's History Project produced catalogues of information and a directory of sources relating to the history of women in Ireland. These resources are the outcome of an extensive survey of sources undertaken by the Women's History Project. Currently there are two directories available on the project website: www.nationalarchives.ie/wh/.

The Directory of Sources for the History of Women in Ireland contains information on collections relating to the history of women in Ireland gathered from public and private repositories in the Republic of Ireland and in Northern Ireland. The directory covers over 14,000 collections and sources, and contains over 100,000 pieces of information from 262 repositories.

Women in Twentieth-Century Ireland: Sources from the Department of the Taoiseach, 1922–1966, is the result of a survey that involved examining the files of the Department of the Taoiseach between the years 1922 and 1966. Approximately 2,000 boxes of files were examined. Every page within each file was perused to ascertain whether it contained any reference to women. This database contains approximately 20,000 entries. Go to: www.nationalarchives.ie/wh/w20/

The Irish Queer Archive contains an impressive collection of press cuttings and periodicals from 1976 on relating to LGBT rights internationally, as well as a library of over 150 LGBT titles. Go to www.outhouse.ie for further information. Contact the Irish Queer Archive at 35a Patrick Street, Dún Laoghaire, Co. Dublin or e-mail irishqueerarchive@ireland.com

Northern Ireland Women's Movement Lynda Walker holds a collection of uncatalogued photographs dating from 1970 to 1990, and a video interview between Walker and Betty Sinclair about women's rights in Northern Ireland. Contact Lynda Walker, Co-Ordinator Diploma in Women's Studies, Belfast Institute of Further   and   Higher   Education,   Belfast   BT1   6DJ;   email: lwalker@belfastinstitute.ac.uk. Tel: 028–90265042.

Women's Education Research and Resource Centre (WERRC), University College Dublin, has developed and produced extensive materials and resources documenting Irish feminist research. Go to: www.ucd.ie/werrc/ for full details.

The *Women's News* Magazine archive contains documentary material and photographs relating to the publication of *Women's News* itself over the past 20 years, giving an overall perspective of political activism, particularly feminist activism, in Northern Ireland during that period. An impressive collection of feminist periodicals from Ireland and the UK, and some international titles, are also held. This material is uncatalogued, and is accessible to researchers in a fairly limited way. *Women's News* can be contacted at Cathedral Quarter Managed Workspace, 109–113 Royal Avenue, Belfast BT11FF. Tel: 028–903222823.

RTÉ Sound Archives hold a selection of news, sports, arts, traditional music, documentaries and drama recordings that relate to Irish women. Historical recordings are available on reel-to-reel ¼" tape from 1926. More comprehensive holdings date from circa 1947. From 1996 on, live daytime RTÉ Radio 1 programmes, 2FM and flagship news programmes transmitted on a daily or weekly basis have been recorded. Due to funding limitations, the RTÉ Sound Archive is not open to the public. However, researchers and academics may be able to gain access in order to consult materials unavailable elsewhere, following prior agreement with the Librarian. Contact: Malachy Moran, Manager, Audio Services and Archives via e-mail at: malachy.moran@rte.ie

Papers and Materials held by Individuals/Groups

Access to an extensive range of photographs taken by Clodagh Boyd, an activist in the women's movement, and Derek Speirs, *Irish Times* photographer, were invaluable to the Irish Women's Movement Project and the production of this book. These photographs provide a graphic account of the movement in action over the last three decades. Currently, however, there is no dedicated photographic archive of the women's movement in Ireland despite the existence of these sources.

The Irish Women's Movement Project and the Women's History Project both came across individual activists and organisations in Ireland who personally hold significant papers and collections of material, which are not widely known about or publicly available. Examples include: the papers of Hilda Tweedy (founding member of the Irish Housewives Association); the archives of the Irish Countrywomen's Association (see Ferriter, 1994); archives in Women's Aid, Dublin; a series of documents and letters sent by women from all over the country in crisis pregnancy situations to the Well Woman Centre that were retrieved by the Women's History Project, which will be held in the Library at University College Dublin but closed for several years due to the sensitivity of the material; and documents held by the Rape Crisis Centres. Limited public access to archives from the Council for the Status of Women/the National Women's Council represents a major gap in Irish repositories and in feminist research, given the importance of this organisation in the history of the women's movement.

In the course of this research, individual activists gave us material, which we will add to the existing corpus in the Boole Library at University College Cork. However, more significant resources will be necessary from the Irish State to add this kind of informally held material to existing collections in Irish libraries and to create new significant repositories in other settings.

International Sources

The Canadian Women's Movement Archives, Morriset Library, University of Ottawa, have been in existence in different forms since 1982, when the Canadian government gave the Women's Information Centre in Toronto a grant for a project – Canadian Women's Archives: A History Project. The project aimed to document the achievements of Canadian women's organisations and individual women, and to make this material has accessible to researchers and members of the local community. The project operated for ten years as an independent, non-profit, community-based, and collectively run archive. Subsequently, the CWMA became part of the Archives/Special Collections Department of the Morriset Library at the University of Ottawa. It is openly accessible to researchers by contacting the Library Archivist, Lucie Desjardins. Go to: www.biblio.uottawa.ca/archives/cwma-acmf-e for full details and to peruse the catalogue for this collection.

The National Women's Library based in the London Guildhall University is a new library, formerly known as the Fawcett Library. The library holds extensive collections documenting women's lives and collects new material relating to the changing role of women in society. Go to: www.thewomenslibrary.ac.uk for further details.

International Information Centre and Archives for the Women's Movement (**IIAV**) is a women's library, which holds the archives of the Dutch women's movement and is based in Amsterdam. Go to: www.iiav.nl/ for details.

Using Archives in Feminist Research

In the completion of this study, a number of questions both about the public role of movement archives and, more specifically, feminist archives in Ireland materialised. Moreover, the basic question – *what is* "an archive"? – arose at several stages. Several examples of what is not available out there were apparent, in terms of gaps in accessible collections, the selectivity of what is catalogued in library archives, and how accessible documents really are to researchers and the wider community. For example, the geographical bias of existing sources documenting Irish feminist politics is clear – hence the tendency to connect "Irish feminism" mainly with Dublin-based/urban activism.

During the next wave of feminist research and activism, a range of methodologies which can focus on the differences that in reality have determined Irish feminist politics can only be properly addressed by more sustained analysis of feminism in terms of social and economic class and circumstance, geographical location, urban and rural context, age and marital status, sexuality, race, ethnicity and religion. In the Irish Women's Movement Project, we endeavoured to examine both publicly available archives and informal sources, including smaller repositories held by individuals and community projects. Consequently, we hope that the material documented and reproduced in this volume will make a contribution to the advancement of a more complex and diverse agenda in the analysis and study of Irish feminist politics. However, there are limited sources in key areas, as each chapter will demonstrate.

What is distinct about a feminist archive? Feminist archives tend to maintain other "documents" not generally available in conventional archives (such as badges, t-shirts and banners) as well as ephemera (such as flyers, ticket stubs, and programmes). Many archives consider it beyond their scope to collect three-dimensional objects, often suggesting that these objects are appropriate to museums only. A good example of this is one of the items that the Canadian Women's Movement Archive maintained – the original brass Morgenthaler Clinic sign, which belonged to one of the first abortion clinics in Canada, and had been dam-

Reproduced with permission of the Canadian Women's Movement Archive

aged beyond use by red paint graffiti scrawled on it by pro-life demonstrators. This raises questions for the researcher about the kinds of documents available for study. Is a brass sign a document? Is graffiti, for example, a source? On the basis that archaeologists and ethnographers read etchings and engravings on stone and other materials, the answer has to be *yes*. Slogans on t-shirts, messages on badges, banners, the text of protest chants and protest songs also form part of the available histories of feminist activism in Ireland, contributing to the overall development of a movement in action. Historians generally focus on paper documents as archives. However, as each chapter in this book demonstrates, the diversity of archives we encountered broadened this study of Irish feminisms and the women's movement into the realm of the symbolic order and cultural production/representation in social movement activism.

A number of questions as to where archives or repositories of activist information are or could be located were raised in the Irish Women's Movement Project. In the international context, study visits to the Fawcett National Women's Library in London and the Archive of the Canadian Women's Movement at the University of Ottawa were revealing. The way in which the Archive of the Canadian Women's

Movement was set up demonstrated to us how a feminist archive can be used as a resource both within the academy and the community. The dissolution of the Canadian Women's Movement as an activist group and subsequent difficulties in attracting funding to maintain the archive meant that it was rendered homeless in the early 1990s. In 1992, it was relocated at the Library Network at the University of Ottawa. As is evident from their own reflections on this transition, this change meant that many of the commitments the group had made to a base in the community, and to accessibility issues, had to be given up in favour of a long-term and secure future for the material.[13]

Similarly, the Attic Press/Róisín Conroy Collection has found a home within a university library in Cork, while Irish community groups such as Women's Aid and the Cork Rape Crisis Centre are beginning to look at the ways in which they can archive their material and make it accessible to researchers and policy-makers. In some situations, keeping archives may also be seen as something of a luxury, a question of space and resources – for example, when the Dublin LGBT resource centre Outhouse moved premises in 2001, it was decided that they could no longer afford the space necessary to house the Irish Queer Archive, which remained in storage for several years and has only recently become accessible again.[14] How archives are maintained will affect the way in which Irish history is and will be constructed in the future.

Documentary research raises important issues relating to the way in which material is preserved – what is preserved, by whom is it preserved, and for what reason. The absence of material in an archive relating to a particular group or groups can tell us a lot about how a group as well as the archive was set up and constituted. Furthermore, what is included in archival material can reveal as much about Irish society as well as the politics of Irish feminism. For example, the lack of primary documentary material relating to the Irish Traveller movement, other ethnic minorities and black feminism, suggests an invisibility of ethnic and racial politics in the Irish women's movement. Writing from the perspective of the early twenty-first century, when in-migration has *finally* placed questions of multi-racial and multi-ethnic identities on the agenda of Irish feminist debate, this now represents a significant absence. Similarly, limited sources documenting working class women's activism are available.

Another significant gap in available Irish documentary sources relates to the area of migration. Scholars working in the field of migration have demonstrated the motivation for thousands of Irish women to emigrate during the 1980s (Kelly & Nic Giolla Choille, 1990: 9; O'Carroll, 1990; Maguire, 1995; Gray, 2000: 68; Lúibhéid, 1997: 58). The political atmosphere of the 1980s is reflected in the migration of many feminist activists throughout the period studied, coupled with the ongoing migration of single mothers, Travellers, members of other ethnic minorities, and members of the LGBT communities, as well as those migrating to Britain for HIV treatment or for abortions. The experience of these emigrants is largely recorded via letters, oral accounts and the "alternative" press. However, until quite recently Irish studies relating to women, feminism and emigration have been rare (see Gray, 2004).[15] Materials relating to the Irish Women's Conferences run by the London Irish Women's Centre (LIWC) in the mid-1980s are among the very few documents in the Attic Press/Róisín Conroy Collection that address Irish women's experience of migration during the period. For example, a report from the second Irish Women's Conference held on 21 September 1985 identifies links between activists in Ireland and Britain. This document suggests that activists who emigrated from Ireland because of hostile social attitudes also encountered hostility among the Irish in Britain.[16] Because the LIWC maintained contacts between individual activists and women's groups in Britain and Ireland during the period of this study, their materials were archived.

Mainstream historians tend to approach a body of documents as a cohesive whole which one can "read" in order to form an account of a particular individual, group or event in a given period. However, the disparate material that constitutes the archives studied for this project consisted of both catalogued archives and bodies of disjointed documents produced by different individuals and groups, in a variety of contexts.

There are obvious pitfalls in relying solely on preserved documents as a research tool. Feminist groups, indeed community groups of all kinds, are often too busy getting on with their activism to keep extensive records. The documents they do keep may be accidental or they may be partial, telling only some of the story. This presented practical methodological difficulties, as there may be a conference programme in the archive but no other information relating to it, such as a report on the proceedings, or an account of its recommendations. The disparate nature of Irish women's labour history archives is a case in point.

Another important consideration for both archivists and researchers of this kind of material is the rate at which women's groups formed and disbanded in the 1970s and 1980s during which, no doubt, many of their records disappeared forever. Thus, we cannot hope, nor do we attempt, to form a whole picture of the entire movement, or even of the history of one group, by focusing on the extant documentation. For this reason, interviews, first-hand accounts and other published research were used to supplement the documentary evidence gathered for this book.

As is evident from the issues addressed here, in our approach to documentary sources we did not adopt a realist position, which ignores the ideological implications of the material. The primary material that is a key focus in the study, the documents themselves, is not neutral. For example, reports carried in feminist presses of the same campaign or event may give the impression that it had a bigger impact than it did, or the reporter may highlight a particular group or individual's participation. The material that has formed the basis of a growing corpus of feminist archives in Ireland clearly originates in a very particular milieu – political activism. Furthermore, the cataloguing, maintenance and organisation of documents within a particular location, such as a university archive or a community centre, provides an additional layer of meaning, while the approach taken in any study interprets or constructs evidence in a particular way. Neither is the material detached from wider social, political, cultural or historical conditions and constraints. For example, the anti-establishment nature of many activities and groups is often reflected in concerns about confidentiality in some of the minutes of meetings and on restricted membership lists. This is particularly evident when it comes to pro-choice campaigns, domestic violence organisations and lesbian groups, in which women did not want to be named.

Documents are undoubtedly critical tools for feminist and social movement research. They are, however, socially and politically constructed repositories of activism, with their own limitations which should be combined with other sources of data in order to develop a comprehensive analysis of second-wave feminisms in Ireland.

Theoretical Framework

The women's movement in Ireland has frequently been characterised, or stereotyped, as a unified entity. However, as the archives of the movement demonstrate, feminist groups have constantly worked to confront, debate and overcome real *differences* among Irish women – as well as differences about the kind of society envisaged. In the process, a multifaceted movement was created. Both in the title of this book and in our approach to the research, we have used the term "Irish feminisms." For instance, the fact that Irish emigrants have participated in the women's movement internationally, sometimes by forming "Irish" women's groups in other countries, is an important consideration in how we locate and define "Irish" feminism.[17] Likewise the contested political status of Northern Ireland complicates any simplistic correlation between the categories "Irish" and "feminism" (see Chapter 5). Furthermore, the "Irish" movement has not existed in isolation from feminist movements in other countries and cross-cultural influences and links are apparent in several campaigns and groups.

Recent feminist theoretical approaches that emphasise difference, as well as new studies of the history of the movement itself, have established the complexity of the Irish women's movement. On the other hand, where differences have been acknowledged there has been a tendency to perceive these only in terms of strife, conflict, or through the stereotype of "women fighting with each other". However, as each chapter in this study demonstrates, the very diversity of the women's movement – including its interrogation of "Irishness" and what that *is* – is in many ways its lifeblood, and reflects the movement's engagement with a range of social, cultural and political perspectives, as well its own ability to change and continue as societal and historical circumstances demand.

The study period is one in which feminist theories were hotly contested both within the Irish women's movement and in the wider society. Futhermore, widespread opposition to feminist ideas emerged, as well as the mobilisation of organisations on the Catholic right. Theoretical perspectives evolving within Anglo-American feminist activist groups were published and became core reading for feminists in Ireland as in other countries from the 1960s on. The work of prominent theorists such as Betty Friedan and Germaine Greer, to name just two, were read and discussed openly in reading groups, consciousness-raising sessions, political meetings, classrooms, public debates and conferences in Ireland. More recently, the writings of Lynne Segal, Naomi Wolf and others have been widely debated and read.

It is necessary to outline in brief the main groupings, or kinds of feminist stances, within the women's movement in order to address how these were expressed within an Irish context.

Liberal feminists tend to lobby for equal rights for women within the existing structures of society. In general, liberals consider the *status quo* to be established. Although this position tends to be criticised by other feminist activists, this kind of feminist work is crucial to the mainstreaming of feminist values and rights within the wider structures of society, especially the political and legal system, and has accomplished many important rights for women in Ireland over the past 30 years or more.

This investment in the *status quo* differentiates liberals from socialist feminists, those committed to a left-wing agenda. Unlike Marxist feminists who worked for women's rights within wider leftist groupings, socialist feminists formed groups within the women's movement. Socialists campaigned against class inequality alongside gender inequality, and established a sense of solidarity with women workers and trade unionists in the international arena. A number of socialist feminists were involved in different Irish feminist groups and organisations over time.

Initially (particularly in North America) radical feminism was associated with those who prioritised sexual oppression. As a consequence, early radical feminists and lesbian feminists tended to be grouped together. However, over time, radicalism became associated with feminists who were more involved in grassroots activism and for whom social and cultural revolution was/is intrinsic to their politics. In the Irish context, groups such as the Irish Women's Liberation Movement and Irishwomen United, among others, could be characterised as being radical feminist groups. Direct action is more associated with radical than liberal feminism – and events such as the Contraception Train which was organised by the IWLM in 1971, can be read very clearly as radical feminist actions.

Separatist feminists in North America, for instance, attempted to create self-sustaining female communities and to withdraw as much as possible from patriarchal society. Separatism was not really a dominant feature of feminism in Ireland, although there were elements of separatist values in the establishment of women-only spaces during the period.

However, as this study demonstrates, feminist theory is something which changed and evolved throughout the second wave, and terms referring to different feminist approaches – radical feminism, liberal feminism, etc. – changed over time and were not as fixed as we tend to view them today. A sense of clarity or of distinct lines drawn between particular groups and theoretical perspectives is not really evident in the documents relating to Irish feminist activism. It may have been possible in the larger urban centres of North America to form groups espousing a particular theoretical stance but, given the scale of the Irish movement, there tended to be a lot of fluidity between groups, individuals, and particular political stances. For example, the same names often crop up both in feminist campaigns considered "liberal" or "radical". Activists involved in mainstream politics, socialist politics, Republicanism, civil rights and housing rights at times cooperated in campaigns, and solidarity between dissimilar groups and theoretical perspectives was not uncommon. Furthermore, activists who concentrated their activism primarily within feminist groups often held different and, at times, oppositional political stances – such as those within the core group of the Irish Women's Liberation Movement who differed over the stated aims of the group and whether or not direct action tactics (such as the Contraception Train) would alienate the public to the demands of the women's movement (see Connolly, 2003b).

In terms of a history of ideas within Irish feminist activism, there is room for much further investigation in this area in Irish studies. Many of those involved in the movement during the 1970s and 1980s were not fully aware of the history of feminist activism in Ireland – such as the late nineteenth century campaign against the Contagious Diseases Acts (1864), the suffrage movement and the involvement of feminists in the national struggle during the first wave of Irish feminism. However, they were well versed in Anglo-American feminist campaigns, books and theories during the period. Nonetheless, feminist theories developed "elsewhere" were not simply directly absorbed in Irish feminist debates and publications. Numerous movement documents (such as position papers produced in IWU, held in the Attic Press/Róisín Conroy Collection) demonstrate that second-wave thought and theory was significantly adapted to the particularity of Irish culture and society. In fact, innovative theoretical approaches were conceptualised by Irish activists throughout the period covered in this study. Although the distinct project of mapping in detail the development of feminist theories in the documents of the Irish women's movement was beyond the scope of this text, several perspectives are revealed.

Recently, women's studies has embraced the compelling critique of the ethnic and class bias of second-wave feminism in its initial stages. These developments have appeared slowly in Irish feminist debate. The successes of the women's movement in Ireland over the last three decades have been in large part due to the way in which feminists managed to create common causes among Irish women. At the same time, we now know that the call for universal rights for "all (Irish) women" has had an uneven effect. As the chapters on class, education and community activism will demonstrate, the original goals and priorities of second-wave feminism in Ireland have been subject to a profound revision and critique by women who feel they were excluded from the main agenda or "left behind" by the women's movement. New collective voices are beginning to transform the women's movement as we have recently known it – the outcome of which remains to be seen.

Outline of the Book

While some chapters in this volume require a broader historical context, the study by and large focuses on introducing readers to the development of second-wave feminism in Ireland. Most commentators date second-wave Irish feminism from 1968 – when the IHA and Association of Business and Professional Women established an ad hoc committee (see Chapter 1) to call on the Government to establish a National Commission on the Status of Women – until the 1990s. The scope of this study and the documents and images reproduced broadly correspond with this timeframe. The resurgence of a distinctive, second wave of feminist activism was especially evident in Irish society by 1970, when the Report of the First National Commission on the Status of Women was published and the defiant and pioneering radical group, the Irish Women's Liberation Movement (IWLM), emerged in the public arena. Nonetheless, recent research points out that ongoing feminist work sustained in the aftermath of the Civil War until the end of the 1960s directly links second-wave feminism organisationally with activism originating in the early decades of the century. It is now widely acknowledged that the second wave of feminism has far more continuity with previous phases of activism (such as campaigns conducted in the middle decades of the twentieth century) than originally thought (Connolly, 2003b).

However, in comparison with previous decades, the women's movement grew significantly in impact and size throughout the 1970s and the second wave is clearly a distinct period of activism that merits in-depth analysis. A period of advancement, incorporating the growth of both national women's organisations and networks and a parallel expansion of grassroots radical activism on a national scale occurred in this decade. Central mobilising issues included contraception and equality in employment.

By the 1980s, while the women's movement scaled down significantly in comparison with the previous decade, many feminist groups were beginning to mainstream their activities more intensely. Several organisations acquired government funding and established premises, for example. At the same time, new movement centres and campaigns were emerging in this period. Pro-choice campaigns were particularly prominent in light of the pro-life amendment to the Constitution in 1983. By the end of the 1980s, women's groups had also begun to form in local communities in significant numbers. In the field of education, women's studies was developing while in Irish cultural life the work of feminist artists, intellectuals and writers progressively flourished.

In the 1990s, the professionalism of a now "established" women's movement was evident and longstanding feminist activists focused much of their energies in mainstream contexts and institutions. The election of Mary Robinson, a prominent feminist activist and lawyer, as President of Ireland epitomised this trend. For many commentators, the 1990s signalled the onset of a post-feminist era or, at best, a third wave of feminism more characterised by political fragmentation and identity politics than feminist solidarity. Young women are considered to have rejected feminism and the women's movement. And yet, as this volume will demonstrate, new campaigns and concerns did emerge with vigour in the 1990s – for example, the reaction of the public to the *X* case and the associated campaign was notable (see Chapter 2).

Chapter 1 documents the emergence of pioneering groups and organisations in the 1970s, including the Council for the Status of Women, the Irish Women's Liberation Movement and Irishwomen United. Chapter 2 examines the centrality of contraception, abortion and reproductive rights in Irish feminist discourses and campaigns throughout the study period. Chapter 3 provides an analysis of the intersection of feminist activism in Ireland with the state, the legal system, family law and social policy. Chapter 4 examines the development of cultural projects in Irish feminism and the way in which feminism established a counter culture in the study period. Chapter 5 examines feminism in Northern Ireland and examines how "the North" was addressed by feminists in the South. Chapter 6 addresses the role of lesbian feminists in the Irish women's movement and the wider question of sexualities in Ireland. Chapter 7 discusses socialist feminism, the marginalisation of working class and rural women in Irish feminist debate, and charts the emergence of locally based women's community groups in rural and urban Ireland since the 1980s. And Chapter 8 reveals the growth and impact of feminism in Irish education in recent decades, focusing in particular on the development of women's studies.

Several chapters include case studies, most of which are the personal stories of women (including Marie McMahon, Joanne Hayes and Anne Lovett) whose lives and actions stirred the consciousness of the women's movement, and indeed Irish society, at important stages. Numerous documents, images and photographs are interweaved with the narrative in each chapter. Finally, an extensive range of archival sources and documents are referred to in the endnotes of each chapter and a detailed chronology and a bibliography is provided.

Notes

1 The full catalogue for this collection is available for consultation in the Library Archives of the Boole Library, University College Cork. Go to www.ucc.ie to access the library's database.

2 Connolly (2003b: 43) develops the following definition of a social movement: "A social movement is a conscious, collective activity to promote social change, representing a protest against the established power structure and against the dominant norms and values. The commitment and active participation of its members or activists constitute the main resource of any social movement" (cited from Dahlerup, 1986: 2). For a review of the various definitions of a social movement, see Crossley (2003: 1–7).

3 See: Connolly (1996) and Connolly and Hourigan (2005).

4 Material reproduced from this collection is sourced as Attic Press Archive, with reference to the catalogue code (BL/F/AP) and file number, throughout this text.

5 The issues of sexual abuse and rape are a good example of this. Mary McLoughlin, principal officer with the Department of Health and Children, recently reported to the Government-appointed Commission on Child Abuse that until the 1960s, the Department of Health's only awareness of child abuse in Ireland concerned neglect and, to a lesser extent, physical abuse. She said the first official policy document produced by the department on physical abuse was the 1977 "Memorandum on Non-Accidental Injury to Children". The memorandum made no mention of sexual or institutional abuse. Today, the number of former residents of industrial schools and other Church-run institutions who have made allegations to the Commission on Child Abuse is in the thousands (see report by David Quinn, *Irish Independent*, 28 June 2004).

6 Connolly's, *The Irish Women's Movement: From Revolution to Devolution* (2003) was based on over 50 intensive interviews with Irish feminist activists. See also: Beale, 1986; Fennell and Arnold, 1987; Levine, 1982; Tweedy, 1992; Coulter, 1993; Mahon, 1995; Smyth, 1993; Galligan, 1998; Connolly, 1996; Connolly, 1997; Connolly, 1999a; O'Connor, 1998.

7 Volumes IV and V of the *Field Day Anthology of Irish Writing* published in 2002 by Cork University Press, is the result of a major interdisciplinary project covering literature, journalism, history and criticism, as well as legal, medical, theological, and scientific writings, and includes sections on oral traditions, sexuality, religion and theology, and contemporary writing. The volumes contain the work of over 900 Irish women writers. See Kelleher (2004) for a discussion.

8 This directory of information sources relating to the history of women in Ireland contains information and descriptions of over 14,000 collections and sources in 262 repositories in the Republic of Ireland and in Northern Ireland. See www.nationalarchives.ie/wh/ for further information.

9 This project, based at the Department of English, UCC, has produced a hard-cover dictionary and online searchable database of over 560 writers, working both in the English and Irish languages, in the Munster region (that is, Clare, Cork, Kerry, Limerick, Tipperary and Waterford) between the years 1800 and 2000. The dictionary will be published by Cork University Press early next year, at which point the online database will also go live.

10 The Irish Women's Movement Project was instrumental in encouraging the Boole Library to catalogue the Attic Press/Róisín Conroy Collection expeditiously for public use. Through its work, the project has also generated important additions to the impressive collection of feminist material now held in the Boole Library and will continue to explore ways of advancing the further expansion

of this corpus of archives in the university with new sources. The project has also displayed this material to the public. On 1 February 2003, a public seminar and exhibition of materials from the Attic Press/Róisín Conroy Collection, which also included a multimedia presentation incorporating photographs and other images, was held.

11 The Attic Press/Róisín Conroy Collection catalogue, held in the Boole Library at UCC, contains a full discussion of the history and background of the archive.

12 A complete set of Attic Press publications also lies alongside books published by Arlen House and Women's Community Press at the Women's Studies Centre in NUI Galway.

13 This is reflected in articles related to this move, such as *Centre/Fold: The Newsletter of the Toronto Centre for Lesbian and Gay Studies* 4 (Spring 1993)

14 Efforts are currently underway to re-establish the archive as an accessible community resource.

15 A 2002 issue of the *LINC* magazine (Cork), for example, published contemporary lesbian migration narratives. The magazine can be downloaded from the L.Inc group website at www.linc.ie/magazine/linc5.pdf

16 "Single mothers have found their own Irish community very unsupportive. Lesbians feel more accepted here [...] The last thing you want to do when you come over here is find the Irish community." (File BL/F/AP/1475, Attic Press Archive)

17 Ruth Fletcher is currently pioneering comparative research at the University of Keele on the links developed between pro-choice services in a number of centres in Ireland and the UK, which also involves documenting the experience of Irish women who have to travel and use these services in both jurisdictions while seeking terminations.

Chapter 1
The Emergence of Second-wave Feminism in Ireland

Colette O'Neill making IWLM statement after disembarking from the Contraceptive Train at Amiens Street Station, May 1971 (BL/F/AP/1140, Attic Press Archive)

The emergence of a range of women's organisations in Ireland throughout the course of the twentieth century can tell us a great deal about the development of the women's movement and feminist politics. Women's historians in Ireland have demonstrated how, from at least the second half of the nineteenth century, numerous feminist organisations and individuals have maintained an active women's movement in the Irish context – even in periods when it was assumed feminism had "disappeared".[1] A growing corpus of archives in Ireland and publications in women's history now provide excellent insights into the politics of Irish feminist organisations both in the late nineteenth century and throughout the course of the twentieth century.[2]

The emergence of a second wave of feminism in Ireland is generally connected to the emergence of several new women's organisations and networks, throughout the 1970s in particular. It is important to acknowledge, however, that the campaigns of several long-standing feminist groups both up to and after the 1970s provided a necessary organisational base for a second peak wave, in a number of respects. Feminist historians have charted the development of a number of Irish feminist organisations, coalitions and campaigns both in pre and post-independence Ireland, suggesting that the women's movement in Ireland has always been much more than a sporadic or invisible entity.[3] The recent recovery of one organisation in Irish history, in particular, demonstrates this. The Irish Housewives Association, founded in the 1940s, became a direct catalyst for setting up an *ad hoc* committee on women's rights in 1968[4]. Mainly by lobbying the government, the *ad hoc* committee achieved the establishment of the first National Commission on the Status of Women in 1970, which subsequently led to the formation of the Council for the Status of Women (csw) in 1972, which became the largest interest group representing women in Ireland[5]. The continuity of organisations and networks, over extensive historical periods, has only recently been recognised in mainstream Irish studies, which have tended to portray feminism as a disconnected and intermittent movement in modern Irish society.

During the second peak wave, the csw, now the National Women's Council, became the chief liberal feminist organisation in Ireland, adopting a role similar to the National Organisation for Women in the US, for example. However, two other Dublin-based organisations also became particularly prominent in the public arena of Irish feminist politics in the 1970s, providing a forum for the development of a radical feminist perspective in Ireland: the Irish Women's Liberation Movement (iwlm), which was formed in 1970 primarily by a small group of journalists and left-wing and professional women, and had dispersed by 1972; and the more radical Irishwomen United (iwu), which emerged in 1975 for a period of about 18 months. Alongside these prominent groups, several organisations, frequently in the form of small consciousness-raising groups, single-issue campaigns or groups with the function of providing services for women also emerged. Many of these groups were formed by women who left the prominent radical organisations in the 1970s, while others emerged autonomously. iwu, for example, was the main catalyst for the formation of the Contraceptive Action Campaign (cap) in 1976, the first Rape Crisis Centre in 1977 and the first Women's Right to Choose group in 1979.

The Council for the Status of Women

As the only Irish women's organisation affiliated to the International Alliance of Women (iaw), the iha delegates at the 1967 iaw Congress in London were told that the un Commission on the Status of Women had issued a directive to women's international non-governmental organisations to ask their affiliates to examine the status of women in their respective countries and encourage their governments to set up national commissions on the status of women. The

SECOND PROGRESS REPORT
on the implementation of the
Recommendations in the
Report of the Commission
on the Status of Women

FINAL REPORT OF THE
WOMEN'S REPRESENTATIVE
COMMITTEE   DECEMBER 1978

Second Progress Report on the Implementation of the Recommendations in the Report of the Commission on the Status of Women, **prepared by the Women's Representative Committee, December 1976 (BL/F/AP/1165, Attic Press Archive)**

Association of Business and Professional Women had received the same directive at their international congress that same year. As a result, the two organisations called for a National Commission on the Status of Women in Ireland. In 1968, an *ad hoc* committee on women's rights was formed by the IHA, the Association of Business and Professional Women, Altrusa Club, the Irish Countrywomen's Association (ICA), Irish Nursing Organisation (INO), Dublin University Women Graduates Association, The National Association of Widows, The Soroptimists' Clubs of Ireland, Women's International Zionist Organisation, Irish Council of Women, Association of Women Citizens and the Association of Secondary Teachers of Ireland (ASTI).

Following intense lobbying by the *ad hoc* committee, the Taoiseach, Jack Lynch, established the First Commission on the Status of Women on 31 March 1970 to:

> … examine and report on the status of women in Irish society, to make recommendations on the steps necessary to ensure the participation of women on equal terms and conditions with men in the political, social, cultural and economic life of the country and to indicate the implications generally – including the estimated cost – of such recommendations.

The Commission supported the implementation of a series of social and political reforms. In the interim period, the Minister for Finance requested a report dealing with the question of equal pay, particularly in relation to the public sector. The Commission sought submissions from trade unions, employers and women's organisations. The significance of the First Commission is that the report directly challenged the main thrust of discriminatory legislation that had been progressively institutionalised since 1922. The interim report, published in August 1971, recommended the implementation of equal pay and the removal of the marriage bar.[6]

The Commission on the Status of Women presented its findings to the Government in 1972, having received submissions from 41 groups (which included a women's liberation group and a number of non-aligned individuals). Some 17 of the 49 recommendations related to equal pay and women in employment. The report included detailed recommendations in the areas of equal pay, promotion and equal opportunity. The *ad hoc* committee, having met again to consider the interim report of the Commission, tactically decided it would be necessary to form a permanent Council for the Status of Women to monitor the implementation of the report's recommendations. Accordingly, it wrote to the press inviting interested women's organisations to join with the *ad hoc* committee and form a national women's organisation.

The initial aims of the CSW were:

1. to provide liaison between government departments, the Commission of the European Communities, Women's Organisations and the Council;
2. to press for the implementation of the Report of the Commission on the Status of Women (the Beere Report);
3. to provide educational and developmental programmes for women aimed at giving them the opportunity of participating fully in the social, economic and political life of this country and to highlight areas of discrimination;
4. to examine cases of discrimination against women and, where necessary, to take appropriate action;
5. to consider any other legislative proposals of concern to women; and
6. to be non-party political.

Membership of the CSW in October 1972 included:

AIM, Altrusa, Association of Women Citizens of Ireland, Business and Professional Women's Clubs, Chartered Society of Physiotherapists, Cork Federation of Women's Organisations, Dublin University Women Graduates Association, the ICA, Irish Association of Dieticians, the IHA, National Association of Widows, National University Women Graduates Association, Soroptimists Clubs of Ireland, Women's International Zionist Organisation, Women's Liberation Movement, Women's Progressive Association (later Women's Political Association), ZONTA.

In general, the CSW relied on the politics of persuasion and non-confrontational tactics (although some organisations, such as the National Association of Widows, aligned to the CSW, engaged in direct-action tactics). Its strategy was clearly consistent with the backgrounds and experience of leaders in this sector, and the political environment in which the CSW mobilised initially. Although internationally radical social movements were emerging, this expanding women's-rights sector was more attuned to the established political structures of Irish society and incorporated a number of groups that were active since the first half of the twentieth century. The careful approach of these activists generated much criticism from newly emerging confrontational direct-action groups. However, mainstream activism seemed necessary and useful to the leaders of the CSW. Activists felt they had to build on rather than reject whatever sources of support were in evidence[7].

The CSW, now called the National Women's Council of Ireland, was clearly influential in many of the political/legal gains for women in Ireland throughout the 1970s. As a state-funded organisation it was unique in the context of the European women's movement. Over the last three decades, it has sustained its role as a major organisation representing women in Ireland.

The Irish Women's Liberation Movement

In 1970, the Irish Women's Liberation Movement (IWLM) mobilised in the public arena. This branch of feminism took the form of more expressive and spontaneous action. An array of informal radical feminist groups, some in the universities and the new suburban housing estates in Ireland, mobilised throughout the country in the early 1970s. The original group of activists who formed the IWLM were considered extremely radical and aroused widespread interest. In particular, their methods of protest were highly controversial.

The distinctive character of the IWLM was related to the particular social composition of the founding group and the kind of strategies and ideologies employed. The IWLM was clearly more influenced by the radical style of activism, already mobilising internationally in the new social movements of the 1960s (including the student, peace, and civil rights movements). Radical feminist organising in America had an influence on some of the founding members, who were there as journalists when second-wave feminism emerged.

The IWLM encompassed different groups of activists and ideas – for instance, political women (including left-wing and Republican activists), women in the media (newspaper journalists), and professional/university-educated women. Some of the group encouraged a distinctive confrontational style of organisation and direct action. The mobilisation of the civil rights movement in Northern Ireland in 1968 and the emergence of Republican, student and left-wing organisations encouraged a new social movement sector across Irish society in this period. The women from the left in the IWLM tended to be involved in other movements and politics (such as the occupation of the Hume Street Houses in 1969–1970, the

```
                    CHAINS - OR CHANGE?

         THE CIVIL WRONGS OF IRISHWOMEN



   1.      THE LEGAL INEQUITIES AND HOW THEY BETRAY
           THE CONSTITUTION

   11.     THE SAD PROFILE OF IRISHWOMEN IN EMPLOYMENT

   111.    THE EDUCATION - OR MISEDUCATION - OF GIRLS

   1V.     DISCRIMINATION AT WORK AND JOB BARS TO WOMEN

   V.      WOMEN IN DISTRESS:

              (i)      The Widow
              (ii)     The Deserted Wife
              (iii)    The Unmarried Mother
              (iv)     The Single Woman

   V1.     INCIDENTAL FACTS:

              The laws against Family Planning;
              The lack of baby-minding regulations;
              Lack of playgrounds, nursery schools
               and creches;
              Lack of re-training facilities for
              women.

   V11.    TAXATION AND WOMEN - DESIGNED TO PENALISE

   V111.   FIVE REASONS TO LIVE IN SIN

Published by the Irish Women's Liberation Movement:    Dublin
Founding Group.

Enquiries to - 18, Fairbrook Lawn, Dublin 14.
```

Contents of *Chains – or Change? The Civil Wrongs of Irishwomen,* published by IWLM, Dublin Founding Group, 1971 (BL/F/AP/1139, Attic Press Archive)

anti-Vietnam war demonstration of 1971, People's Democracy organisation and the civil rights movement), and knew how to organise radically and strategically.

The IWLM's repertoire of strategies included meeting weekly with a view to producing a set of demands (which resulted in the IWLM manifesto, *Chains – or Change?*). Other inter-organisational activities included regular consciousness-raising and the planning of confrontational direct-action tactics (which resulted in a protest at the Pro-Cathedral in Dublin and the staging of a "Contraceptive Train" to Belfast).[8] In the process, a close relationship with the media in particular was fostered.

The methods and ideas of Anglo-American feminism were being adapted to the particular circumstances of Irish women's lives in the early 1970s. In particular, consciousness-raising brought about collective knowledge of the reality of women's lived experience, still "invisible" and unexplored in Irish public discourse at this time. Consequently, subjects such as reproduction and sexuality entered the political arena. Consciousness raising was introduced by activists in the IWLM who had experienced the American women's movement in particular. It became a popular activity in radical women's groups nationally (including in small local groups that formed in suburban/urban areas and in the universities). So far, we know little about the activities and impact of consciousness-raising groups in Ireland outside of the prominent Dublin-based organisations like the IWLM. In the US, for example, there was a consciousness-raising group in almost every area and it was extremely fashionable (Ryan, 1992). It was out of these groups that many of the major English-speaking writings on radical feminism emerged. Consciousness raising tended to provide both political insight and collective support in the face of a hostile community/society to feminist demands.

A number of events propelled the IWLM into the public arena in a dramatic manner. The IWLM was invited to manage an entire programme of *The Late Late Show* in 1971. The appearance was intended to mark the official launch of the movement. The event generated widespread public reaction and the group's demands (outlined in *Chains – or Change*) were fully reviewed in the media as a result. The core mobilising issues of the IWLM included "one family one house", removal of the marriage bar, equal pay, equal access to education, legal rights and availability of contraception. A number of independent speakers outlined the groups manifesto on *The Late Late Show*. Mary Robinson agreed to appear on the panel to point out the legal inequities in Irish law; Mary Cullen, a historian at Maynooth College, made the case for working mothers; Lelia Doolin, one of Ireland's few female television producers, spoke on education and social conditioning, with particular reference to the effects of the media; Máirín Johnson, a journalist, talked about discrimination in the workplace; and Nell McCafferty made the case for deserted wives, single mothers and widows.

The IWLM staged a mass meeting in response to the widespread coverage received and subsequent media attention. A public meeting was held in the Mansion House, Dublin, in April 1971. This event became another major turning point. Over 1,000 women attended, which was far in excess of the numbers expected. The demands of the movement were outlined and discussed. On the surface, there was overall consensus between the large audience of women that night. Following the Mansion House meeting, a plethora of women's liberation groups formed. Women's liberation was mobilising the energy of young educated women; creating a forum for consciousness raising; influencing the mass media; and developing a new radical politics in Ireland.

A consensus was reached in the IWLM that contraception was a fundamental issue for Irish women's liberation. The "Contraceptive Train" was subsequently staged in May 1971. IWLM members, and many other women on the day, travelled to Belfast and brought contraceptives (of which the sale, import and advertisement was banned in the Irish Republic since the 1935 Censorship of Publications Act)

Poster advertising the Mansion House meeting (BL/F/AP/1110/6, Attic Press Archive)

into the state illegally and in a confrontational manner marched through customs at Connolly Station, Dublin. After half an hour of chaos, the women were let through customs without being stopped, chanting and waving banners. The protest created huge international media attention and publicity. The protest was criticised, however for "going too far", which reflected the conservative nature of irish society at that time. Negative reactions emerged within the IWLM, in other women's organisations and across the whole social spectrum of Irish society as a whole.

The direct-action tactics of the movement had both a positive and negative effect within the organisation. More moderate activists within the original group

<u>Choice Action.</u>

1. Declare nothing and risk being searched.

2. " contraceptives and refuse.

3. "   "   "   " to hand over.

4. "   "   and hand over with protest of infringement
          of your cons. rights.

5. "   " and throw over barrier to sisters waiting beyond.

6. "   " and sit down in anticipation of Custon Action.

7. " Internal cont. Allow search from Female Officer only and
        shout "April Fool" before entry.

   In the event of being searched between Belfast and Dublin, you
may take any of the above actions but you risk being detained while
train passed on. In event of taking action on points 2,3,& 5. You
are liable to prosecution & appear in court.
   Free Legal aid is guaranteed or you may defend yourself.
.ny of the above actions may be taken individually; in the presence
of another sister or collectively.
   Please read carefully and decide.
Your Cons.Rights are;

Art. 44. Sub Sect.2. Par.1.
 " 42. "   "   1.
 " 41. "   "   1. parl 1 & 2.
 " 41.   "   2. par. 2.

   This means that if you have more children than you can afford
you will be forced to work for a living.

Art. 40. Sect. 6. par. 1.
Ref. to bit on Birth Control.

8. You will be supplied with a pill. Declare it and swallow it.

The leaflet providing instructions to those who went on the contraceptive train, May 1971
(BL/F/AP/1140, Attic Press Archive)

felt alienated. Some women subsequently diverted their energies away from the
IWLM and became involved in the provision of new services for women. Others
maintained their radical commitments through involvement in specific campaigns (especially the ongoing campaign for contraception and in legal reform,
such as the repeal of the Juries Act 1927). These strategies animated a broader
women's liberation constituency in a range of areas throughout the 1970s and the
radical movement expanded beyond the original IWLM group. While a number of
women's organisations had highlighted similar issues from the 1920s to the 1960s,
it is significant that the reaction created by the IWLM alerted Irish women in a new
way to international feminist demands and illuminated through publications and
activism, in some depth, their significant grievances. The cultural effect of radical
feminism in Ireland, in this period, has yet to be fully realized.

   Activists oriented towards achieving women's rights on a gradual basis recognised the merits of political lobbying and some distanced themselves from what

VOL 1 NO 6 NOVEMBER 1972

FOWNES STREET JOURNAL

WOMEN'S LIBERATION MOVEMENT

7 Fownes Street
DUBLIN 2
Telephone: 770679

PRICE EASON
5½p

Fownes Street Journal, Women's Liberation Movement, November 1972 (BL/F/AP/1492, Attic Press Archive)

were extremely radical tactics in the context of Irish society in the 1970s. The "undignified" nature of events like the Contraceptive Train led a broader constituency of activists to call for the IWLM to moderate its tone. The pragmatism of women with experience of the left also clashed with the sense of personal liberation and urgency articulated by influential radical feminists. The impending fragmentation of the IWLM after the Mansion House meeting became more pronounced because of internal divisions over preferred tactics and strategies. These divisions were exacerbated by disagreement about feminist ideologies, diverging views on the Northern Irish question, and the development of a "hierarchy of per-

Some of the founding members of the IWLM: (from left) Máire Woods, Nell McCafferty, Máirín de Burca, Nuala Fennell and Mary Maher (BL/F/AP/113/12, Attic Press Archive)

sonalities" within the initial founding group. Gradually, activists left the IWLM or else diffused into a range of new groups that were more congruent with their ideological and tactical preferences.

The prominence of the iwlm coincided with the consolidation of the CSW in the early 1970s and provided the necessary organisational base for the formation or progression of several organisations. New groups that formed between 1970 and 1975 included: AIM (1972), Adapt (1973), Women's Aid (1974), the Women's Progressive Association (subsequently the Women's Political Association, 1970), Ally (1971), Family Planning Services (1972), the Cork Federation of Women's Organisations (1972, representing 17 local associations, and responsible for opening the first Citizen's Advice Bureau) and Cherish (1972). Feminist organisations which developed into effective political lobby groups, and provided practical women's services, were in increasing demand by Irish women throughout this period. After the breakup of the IWLM, the related Fownes Street group succeeded in producing two issues of the *Fownes Street Journal*. However, it was not until 1975 that a women's liberation group comparable in scale to the IWLM emerged – Irishwomen United (IWU).

Irishwomen United

IWU was formed by activists with a background in radical and socialist politics. IWU's membership encompassed a diverse grouping of left-wing philosophies, including for instance the Movement for a Socialist Republic, the Communist Party of Ireland, the Socialist Workers Movement and the Irish Republican Socialist Party. The Working Women's Charter drawn up by the ITGWU provided an organisational focus. In addition to the key demands of the IWLM, IWU added free contraception, self-determined sexuality, equal pay based on a national minimum wage, and the establishment of women's centres. Although some activists in IWU were former members of the IWLM, IWU was in many respects a different type of organisation and recruited a new constituency of feminist activists to the radical Irish women's movement.[9] In addition to the key demands of the IWLM, IWU added free contraception, self-determined sexuality, equal pay based on a national minimum wage, and the establishment of women's centres. Although some activists in the IWU were former members of the IWLM, IWU was in many respects a different type of organisation and recruited a new constituency of feminist activists to the radical Irish women's movement.

IWU held its first public conference in Liberty Hall on 8 June 1975. At that meeting, the principles of internal democracy and a communal approach to the administrative work of the group were explicitly adopted. *Banshee*, the group's magazine, had a rotating editorial committee[10]. The advertisement stated (see p. 38):

IRISH WOMEN UNITED CHARTER

PREAMBLE:

At this time, the women of Ireland are beginning to see the need for, and are fighting for liberation. This is an inevitable step in the course of full human liberation. Although within the movement, we form diverse groups with variant ways of approaching the problem, we have joined together around these basic issues. We pledge ourselves to challenge and fight sexism in all forms and oppose all forms of exploitation of women which keep them oppressed. These demands are all part of the essential right of women to self-determination of our own lives — equality in education and work; control of our own bodies; an adequate standard of living and freedom from sexist conditioning. We present these demands as the following women's charter.

1 THE REMOVAL OF ALL LEGAL AND BUREAUCRATIC OBSTACLES TO EQUALITY:

1 i.e. with regard to tenancies, mortgages, pension schemes, taxation, jury service, equal responsibility for children, social welfare benefits and hire purchase agreements.

2 The right to divorce.

The Constitution should be reviewed with a view to examining the role of women and updated to eliminate discrimination against women.

2 FREE LEGAL CONTRACEPTION:

1 State financed birth-control clinics.

2 The right to a free, legal and safe abortion.

3 THE RECOGNITION OF MOTHERHOOD AND PARENTHOOD AS A SOCIAL FUNCTION WITH SPECIAL PROVISION FOR:

1 State support for programmes implementing the socialisation of housework, i.e. community laundries, kitchens, eating places etc.

2 State provision of an adequate place to live, irrespective of sex, age, number of children and marital status.

3 The provision of local authority, free of charge, twenty-four-hour nurseries, giving every satisfaction in respect of hygiene and education; to be staffed by trained personnel and under the control of the communities in which they are located.

4 EQUALITY IN EDUCATION— STATE-FINANCED, SECULAR, CO-EDUCATIONAL SCHOOLS WITH FULL COMMUNITY CONTROL AT ALL LEVELS, SPECIFICALLY:

1 An end to enforced conditioning of sex roles through curriculum, teaching methods and materials (i.e. textbooks, games etc.)

2 The provision of local pre-school centres for all desiring to use them

3 An end to segmentation of education, to be replaced by fully comprehensive second and third level schools, incorporating both technical and academic learning.

4 Ending of discriminatory barring from particular courses traditionally relegated to men; encouragement for women to enter these courses through programmes of reserved places, etc.

5 Funding and encouragement of a Women's Studies Programme at second and third level.

6 Provision of free creches on campuses

7 Provision of a women's centre on campuses

8 Equal access to further education for all women, regardless of age or marital status.

5 THE MALE RATE FOR THE JOB WHERE MEN AND WOMEN ARE WORKING TOGETHER:

Where the labour force is wholly female, the jobs done by these women should be upgraded and a national minimum wage implemented, linked to the cost of living increase. We reject the use of job evaluation techniques for the purpose of negotiating pay claims.

The right of women to have access to all types of employment, including all types of skilled, and promotion regardless of marital status, pregnancy or maternity.

The right to training and re-training for all occupations including apprenticeships, and the present system of apprenticeships to be restructured. That it be compulsory for all employers to make readily available day release courses, with pay, for all employees.

Working conditions to be, without deterioration of present conditions, the same for women as for men. In addition, the institution of worker-determined flexible hours. The removal of protective legislation should not be a condition to gaining equal pay, and should be extended to include men.

The right to statutory maternity leave of twenty weeks with full net pay; additional leave with pay in cases of illness connected therewith, the right to attend pre-natal and post-natal clinics as required.

Prohibition of dismissal from employment on the grounds of pregnancy or maternity.

Employers to ensure that every effort is made to facilitate employees who are pregnant insofar as the latter's duties are concerned, the guarantee of reintegration into employment without loss of status or service, the right to further training or re-training after statutory or prolonged maternity leave, and the option for equivalent forms of paternity leave.

6 State provision of funds and premises for the establishment of women's centres in major population areas to be controlled by the women themselves.

7 The right of all women to a self-determined sexuality

The vertical margin text reads: SISTERHOOD IS POWERFUL

"Irishwomen United Charter", published in each edition of *Banshee*, the journal of IWU (c. 1976) (BL/F/AP/1515, Attic Press Archive)

Photograph of IWU picket on contraception at Dáil Éireann in *Banshee* (c. 1976)
(BL/F/AP/1515, Attic Press Archive)

Anne Speed, Activist IWU, Trade Unionist, Republican (photo: Derek Speirs)

Cover of *Banshee,* **the journal of IWU (c. 1976) (BL/F/AP/1515, Attic Press Archive)**

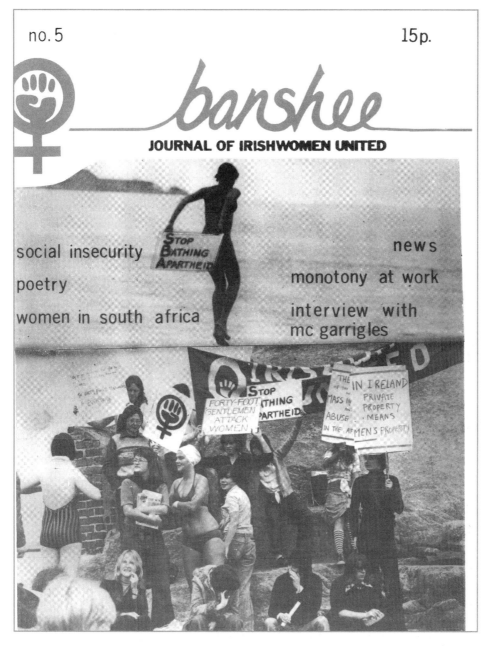

no. 5   **15p.**

banshee

JOURNAL OF IRISHWOMEN UNITED

social insecurity   news

poetry   monotony at work

women in south africa   interview with
                                          mc garrigles

Cover of *Banshee* documenting the IWU invasion of the Forty Foot all-male bathing area, Sandycove 1976 (BL/F/AP/15151, Attic Press Archive)

IWU invasion of the Forty Foot (BL/F/AP/1139/9, Attic Press Archive)

BOYCOTT THESE PUBS!

Irish Women United intend to continue their campaign of protest against places who discriminate against women socially.

In future issues of *Banshee* we will highlight and expose places of entertainment, sport etc. where women are banned or discriminated against.

This issue we will begin by naming a few of the places who either refuse to serve women at all or who refuse to let them drink from pint glasses:

Either boycott these pubs or else go in with a few friends and demand to be served the same way as men are:

NEARY'S
1 Chatham Street, Dublin 2.

BRIAN BORO
Cross Guns Bridge,
Glasnevin, Dublin

LOWES,
Dolphins Barn, Dublin 8

SEARSONS,
42 Upr. Baggot Street
Dublin 4

SCOTCH HOUSE
6/7 Burgh Quay, Dublin 2.

More next issue and all future issues!

IWU boycotted pubs in Dublin that either refused to serve women drink at all or refused to serve them pints 1976 (BL/F/AP/1551/1, Attic Press Archive)

IWU confront directors of the Federated Union of Employers during their occupation of the Federation's headquarters 1976 (BL/F/AP/1211, Attic Press Archive)

> Irishwomen United works on the basis of general meetings (discussions and action planning), joint actions (e.g. pickets, public meetings, workshops; at present on women in trade unions, contraception, social welfare and political theory) and consciousness-raising groups. (also in Fennell and Arnold, 1987: 12)

IWU's stated aims were focused on the need for an autonomous women's movement. While IWU used a similar repertoire of tactics and group-centred activities to the IWLM, this group was highly politicised. Inter-organisational documents now available, including discussion/position papers, workshop proceedings, letters and minutes of meetings, provide evidence of vibrant ideological debate within the organisation[11]. The group's agenda was a mixture of participatory democracy, direct action, consciousness raising and political campaigns. Organisational publications show that the far-reaching demands of the group included state-financed community-run birth-control clinics throughout the country, staffed by those trained to advise on all aspects of birth control. The group advocated that contraceptives of all types and attendant services should be provided free with full, free sex-education programmes in these clinics, in maternity hospitals and in schools. More fundamentally, the legal right to advocate contraception through literature, meetings and discussion was demanded.[12] Between 1975 and 1977 the organisation's mobilising agenda was intense. The Contraceptive Action Programme (CAP) was initiated by members of IWU in 1976 and became a focal mobilising issue. Members of IWU were later involved with the setting up of the group that preceded the abortion referral/information organisation, Open Line Counselling, in 1979, and also in setting up the first Rape Crisis Centre in 1977.

Case Study

The Marie McMahon Case

Spare Rib magazine 1977
(BL/F/AP/1515, Attic Press Archive)

Banshee, journal of IWU (BL/F/AP/1515,
Attic Press Archive)

In June 1977, Irishwomen United were organising a demonstration against censorship – *Spare Rib* had been banned under the Censorship of Publications Act 1946 because it carried information on contraception. Marie McMahon was one of the organisers of this demo, and on 27 July 1977 she was out postering for the event. While engaged in this, she was arrested by gardaí and initially held under the Emergency Powers Act 1976. In custody, McMahon was interrogated about the politics and activities surrounding the women's movement. She was finally charged with loitering and prostitution under section 14(11) of the Dublin Police Act 1843:

> For that you said defendant being a common prostitute or nightwalker were found loitering at Lower Baggot Street/Herbert Place a public place in the Dublin Metropolitan District between 12.35 a.m. and 12.55 a.m. on the 27th Day of July for the purpose of prostitution to the annoyance of inhabitants and passers-by.

Róisín Conroy at picket on Mountjoy prison in support of Marie McMahon, 11 March 1980 (photo: Derek Speirs)

Posters to protest the censorship of *Spare Rib* in 1977 (BL/F/AP/1340/3, Attic Press Archive)

McMahon was also charged with using obscene language and breach of the peace when placed under arrest. Bail of £1,000 was demanded for the charges against her, which carried a maximum fine of £2. After the final court hearing in August 1978, McMahon refused to be bound to the peace, and was given a suspended sentence. According to Irishwomen United, which started a campaign for her release on the first night she was imprisoned, both she and members of her family were harassed by the police during the three years of her suspended sentence: "Special Branch detectives have continued to question Marie's friends and associates, causing some trouble and repercussions" (*In Dublin: Women's Issue*, November 1978). Three years later, the charge was brought up against her, and she was jailed. By the time McMahon was imprisoned in 1980 *Spare Rib* was legal, and censorship relating to prostitution relaxed.

Born and reared in the centre of Dublin, Marie McMahon was 31 at the time of her arrest. A typesetter by profession, she ran her own typesetting and printing firm in Baggot Street and she was a trade union member. Her involvement in civil rights and feminist issues was well known, beginning in 1968 when she joined the Labour Party. She was part of the Hume Street occupation in 1969–1970, as well as participating in demonstrations in support of political prisoners. Thus, the events of 27 July were not her first

Marie McMahon pictured after her release in 1980 (BL/F/AP/1340/1, Attic Press Archive)

encounter with the gardaí, and she had been arrested and jailed for three months for civil disobedience following a protest against the Vietnam war in 1969. From 1973 to 1975 she was an executive member and PRO of the Irish Civil Rights Association, and she was a member of the group People's Democracy and joint editor of its weekly newspaper *Unfree Citizens* during the same period. Her involvement in rights for political prisoners led her to join and become secretary of the Campaign against Capital Punishment, 1976–1977.

Thus, garda claims that they had no information relating to McMahon to suggest that she was anything other than a prostitute, seem groundless: "[Ms McMahon] said that the gardaí would have had no difficulty finding out all about her as there was a file on her in Dublin Castle arising out of her political activity" (*Irish Times,* 15 September 1978). One (unnamed) feminist spokesperson said at the time: "Marie was charged despite the fact that the police were well aware of her identity, and [in the full knowledge that] she is not or never was a prostitute".

McMahon was a well-known figure in the Irish feminist movement during the same period. She was a founder member of the Irish Women's Liberation Movement in 1970, and later a prominent member of Irishwomen United.

IWU **women protest the banning of** *Spare Rib* **by organising another train to Belfast (c. 1977) (AP/1515/7, Attic Press Archive)**

From 1976 to 1977 she was a member of the Editorial Board of *Banshee*. Thus, when researchers for the *Day by Day* series (presented by Pat Kenny at RTÉ) were looking for assistance in gathering information on items relating to feminism in the late 1970s, they contacted her. During the campaign to secure her release, her friends claimed that her involvement in a programme, which focused on prostitution in Dublin, was the direct cause of her arrest. The programme in question had become the subject of a legal controversy between the police and RTÉ, as allegations were made of garda corruption and involvement in the exploitation of prostitutes in Dublin at that time: "During the live broadcast a prostitute had alleged that certain gardaí had assaulted girls and she went on to name one member of the Garda Siochána. Ms. McMahon said yesterday that she understood that this matter might be the subject of court proeceedings by the Gardaí against RTÉ" (*Irish Times* 15 September 1978). McMahon's involvement with the programme, and her solidarity with some of the women who had participated in it, including Lynn Gray, was viewed with disapproval. On the day of her arrest McMahon met Lynn Gray, and they had a short conversation on the street. It was while this conversation was going on – and not while McMahon was actually putting up the posters – that the gardaí arrived on the scene and arrested her.

The campaign for the release and vindication of Marie McMahon was a key instance of the mobilisation of the women's movement. Materials in the Róisín Conroy/Attic Press archive relating to this campaign show all the signs of an effective lobby group in action.[13] Drafts of the press releases illustrate a familiarity with the workings of media, and also the style in which feminist public statements of this period were made. Interestingly, these demands also reach beyond the specifics of the case in hand to a more general perspective on the judicial system:

> An *Ad Hoc* Committee organised in response to the prisoning of Marie McMahon demanding:[14]
> 1. The immediate release of Marie McMahon
> 2. A review of the legal procedures whereby a warrant for any person can be enforced two years after the final court hearing was held
> 3. A commitment by the Government to stop all plans relating to the building of a women's prison. As most women presently in prison are convicted of petty crimes, no need exists for such a building.

Beyond a circle of feminist activists, those in the wider community who signed letters to the *Irish Times* and the gardaí demanding McMahon's vindication are an impressive rollcall of the great and the good in Ireland in the late 1970s. Feminist demonstrations were held in support of McMahon both during the court case and three years later, when all-night vigils were held outside Mountjoy Prison, where McMahon was held. One of these was the occasion of a poem by Mary Dorcey, "Night Protest",[15] printed in *Banshee* at the time. As a result of mounting public pressure, McMahon was released after serving only seven days of her sentence. However, the questions raised by the case continued to be asked, and as an editorial in the *Irish Times* concludes: "That leaves Miss McMahon's name totally clear, but it also leaves the very disturbing question as to why such damaging charges were ever brought against a woman who, it appears, was already known to the gardaí in a completely different and *wholly respectable context*" [our italics].

The implications of the Marie McMahon case were far-reaching. In the material relating to this case, there is a statement dated 13 September 1978 and written by Anne Connolly, calling on feminists to come together to set up the organisation Women Against Violence Against Women. Violence against women became one of the key issues of the late 1970s. Key issues in this case were censorship, contraception, prostitution, women's freedom of movement in the public sphere on city streets, activism and the freedom to protest.

Conclusion: Into the 1980s

It is evident that by the end of the 1970s the Irish women's movement had, in terms of its structure and organisation, evolved into a broad-based social movement with activists involved in a wide range of activities. While the collective action of pioneering organisations like the IWLM and IWU had scaled down by the 1980s, feminism had not disappeared – it had, however, diffused more widely as a political discourse and as a network of mainstreaming organisations across Irish society.

While radical feminist organising became less controversial, at the same time the original radical concepts (such as on domestic violence and rape) had entered the public sphere and policy arena by the 1980s. The women's movement maintained activism in several areas despite the general retreat of social movements in this period and, in some sectors, grew in strength and impact by developing professional organisational structures and formal leadership. The CSW expanded significantly in this period and the work of mainstreaming organisations, such as the Women's Political Association, was realised in an increase in the number of women elected to the Dáil.

By the 1980s, greater convergence between liberal and radical feminists became necessary in the face of organised conservative opposition – notably in the aftermath of the 1983 abortion referendum. However, it is clear that professional developments in the wider movement did not completely hinder the development of grassroots initiatives in new sectors, some of which provided strong criticism of the focus of 1970s activism. A number of new grassroots initiatives were apparent by the end of the 1980s in education, in publishing and in local communities especially. In addition, new debates about difference and class and ethnicity emerged internationally, initially in the writings of black feminists.

The critique of early second-wave feminism that occurred from within new feminisms internationally marked a new phase of activism and thinking which is increasingly being realised in the Irish case. For some, this indicates a fragmentation of the unity which characterised Irish feminist activism in the 1970s. For others, it marks a healthy critique of the dominant biases and universalising assumptions of early second-wave theorising. By the 1990s, individual women concentrated their social movement commitments in new areas and institutions, particularly in the consolidation of women's studies programmes in Irish universities; in the publication of Irish feminist texts; in the formation of community-based women's groups; and as individuals in professional careers. The distinctive women's liberation and women's rights sectors which conceptualised the resurging women's movement in the early 1970s had transformed. The following chapters will attempt to reflect the transitions that have occurred in Irish feminisms throughout this period.

Service Organisations Established in the 1970s

1970   Women's Progressive Association

Became the Women's Political Association in 1973, to encourage the participation of women in public and political life. First President was Mary Robinson.

1971   Ally

Primarily a family placement service for pregnant single women or single mothers. The work carried out by Fergal O'Connor O.P. culminated in the founding of Ally.

1972   Family Planning Services (became the Irish Family Planning Association)

A company set up to provide non-medical and non-pharmaceutical contraceptive devices.

1972   Cherish

Founded by Maura O'Dea (now Richards) and four other single mothers to give advice and support to single parents. First President was Mary Robinson. Now subsidised by the Eastern Health Board. Campaigned vigorously for the Status of Children Act 1987, providing legal status for non-marital children (previously regarded in the law as "filius nullius" – the child of nobody).

Council for the Status of Women was established.

1972   The Cork Federation of Women's Organisations

Representing 17 local associations, was responsible for opening the first Citizens Advice Bureau.

1972   AIM (Action, Information, Motivation)

A pressure group concerned mainly with family, maintenance, and justice, founded by Nuala Fennell following her resignation from IWLM.[16] Its primary function was to provide information and legal advice for women. It became one of the most successful and effective women's organisations, campaigning for the rights of wives and children to protection and maintenance and lobbying for a revision of the law regarding marriage and the family.

1973 Adapt

The Association for Deserted and Alone Parents (Adapt) was primarily a support group.

1974 Women's Aid

Provides refuge and support for victims of domestic violence. It was responsible for highlighting the scale of this problem in Irish society.

1977 Rape Crisis Centre

Emerged from Irishwomen United. It has succeeded in creating awareness of rape as a crime of violence and provide a comprehensive counselling service for victims and has campaigned successfully for anti-rape legislation. In a recent article in the *Guardian* (June 1994) it was stated that the Irish Rape Crisis Centre organisation is one of the most radical in Europe. The Sexual Assault Unit in Rotunda Hospital was established in 1985.

Employment Equality Agency was established by the government.

1979 The first Women's Right to Choose group met and established the Irish Pregnancy Counselling Centre.

AWARENESS

Arlen House Feminist Publishing house. For entry forms and information about Maxwell House Short Story Competition, 2 Strand Road, Baldoyle, Co. Dublin

Bookstall, Feminist Literature, Dandelion Market, Dublin 2 weekends

Contraception Action Programme PO Box 997, D1

Consciousness Raising Group Dublin Resources Centre, 168 Rathgar Rd, D6. Fridays 8pm

Council for the Status of Women 27 Merrion Sq, D2, 763448. 9.30-1pm (see box).

Wicca Magazine c/o Roisin Boyd, 16 Sydney Ave, Blackrock 889819. Meetings, Tues, 7.00, Resources Centre, 168 Rathgar Rd, D6

Women's Centre (see box) The Steering Collective for a Women's Centre c/o 48, Elmwood Ave, Ranelagh D6

Woman's Disco, Parliment Inn, Every Fri 9-11pm.

Women's Liberation Movement basement 38 Parnell Sq. D1. Every Tues 8.40pm

---

Council For The Status of Women
*represents 30 major national organisations, with a membership of 250,000
its objectives are:
*to provide liaison between Government Departments and Women's Organisations.
*to press for implementation of the Report of the Commission on the Status of Women
*to consider any other legislative proposals of concern to women
*to examine and combat cases of discrimination against women.

CHILDREN

Adapt Advice centre for deserted and alone parents. 50 Aungier St.

Cherish 2 Lwr Pembroke St, D2, 682744 Meetings fortnightly every Wednesday (see box).

Civics Institute of Ireland Ltd, Mountjoy Sq. Park North. D1, 744340 9-12.30pm

Day Nurseries: St Brigids, Mountjoy Sq Park; St Josephs, Morning Star Rd, Maryland D8, 757891

Dept. of Social Welfare, Phibsboro Towers, D7, 300922 (Children's Allowance)

Eastern Health Board (Child Health Service, Free Milk) Carnegie Clinic, Lord Edward St D2, 776811

Federation of Services for unmarried parents and their children, 11 Clonskeagh Rd. D6, 961944 10am-1pm

Irish Pre-School Playgroups Assoc. for information concerning members in your area contact Mrs Margaret Clark, 881213

Liberty Creche 92 Meath St. D8,

Women's Aid
*Women's Aid is a voluntary organisation which provides advice and accommodation for women and their children who have been forced to leave their homes because of violence. The accommodation is available 24 hours a day. Over 200 women and their children use it every year. Over 200 seek advice and assistance.

To provide a service that is adequate to meet the demand, Women's Aid relies heavily on the services of volunteers to help with the work, and because it is a voluntary organisation money has to be raised all year, every year.

There is a meeting of the fund-raising group on Friday, 20th November at 7.30pm, at 7, Harcourt Terrace Fund-raising events coming up are a Pub Crawl on 24th Nov. (Volunteers are needed to collect, or provide transport, or help organise the event.), and a Book Auction where signed copies of books by well-known authors will be auctioned.

Any woman needing help or anyone wanting to help please contact Women's Aid at phone number in listings.

Women's Centre
A group of women have come together with the specific aim of establishing the first all Ireland Women's Centre.

The centre would be a place where individual women can come together, socialise, exchange information and advice, share skills and experience etc., in an informal relaxed atmosphere.

It would provide an alternative for many women who need support as individuals in their personal lives and in their work situations. Women's groups and organisations also suffer from this unnecessary isolation which could be overcome by direct and frequent contact with each other. It is only by listening and learning that an understanding of each other's aims and objectives can be developed.

The idea has been received enthusiastically by both groups, organisations, and individual women all over the country. It is hoped to launch a nationwide fund-raising campaign shortly.

The next meeting will be held on Saturday, 3rd December, in the ATGWU Hall, Marlboro St., D1.

Address of Steering Committee Collective under Women's Centre in listings.

HEALTH

Family Planning Clinics:
10 Mountjoy Sq. D1, 767552
15, Mountjoy Sq. D1, 744133
59 Synge St. D8, 682420
67 Pembroke Rd D4, 681108
Well Woman Centre 63 Lwr Leeson St D2, 789366/789504 Mon-Fri 10am-6pm
Bray Family Planning Centre 6 Eglinton Rd Bray. 860410. Open 9-5, 5 days a week.

CONTA

a pull-out gu
women's gr

Special issue of *In Dublin* magazine, November 1978, Women's Editorial Collective (BL/F/AP/1492/21, Attic Press Archive)

Self-help Health for information on workshops being formed contact Nicola Quinn 680008.
City of Dublin Skin & Cancer Hospital Hume St D2,766935 Clinic for screening for breast and cervical cancer. Every Fri morning from 9am. By appointment with doctor's letter only.
Emmet House 138 Thomas St D8, 719222 for applications for Medical Cards and Maternity Services

Cherish
is a voluntary organisation which gives emotional and practical support to single parent families. It can provide information and advice concerning the Social Welfare system, legal advice and help and also second-hand baby clothes, cots, prams etc.

Cherish needs sponsors for its children's Christmas party and also donations of anything which children might need.

Cherish is also involved in a campaign to abolish the status of illegitimacy (see page four).

Contact Cherish to give or receive help at the address in the listings.

Employment Equality Agency
*The Employment Equality Agency is an independent body, set up under the Employment Equality Act, 1977, to ensure the effective enforcement of the Employment Equality Act and the Anti-Discrimination (Pay) Act and to promote equal opportunities between the sexes generally.
*It is comprised of a Chairperson, Sylvia Meehan, and ten ordinary members appointed by the Minster for Labour. The members include two nominees each of the Irish Congress of Trade Unions and the Federation of Employers, three representatives of women's organisations and three members appointed by the Minister. Its functions are:
*To promote equality of oportunity in employment between men and women generally.
*To work towards the elimination of discrimination in relation to employment.
*To keep under review the working of the Employment Equality Act, 1977 and the Anti-Discrimination (Pay) Act, 1974.
*The Agency has the power to hold formal investigations, and if it finds evidence of practices contravening the Equal Play legislation can issue non-discrimination notices requiring that they cease. It also has the power to seek a High Court injunction in respect of persistent discrimination; and, only the Agency can bring proceedings in matters to do with discriminatory advertisements, pressure on persons to discriminate and general policy of discriminatory practices.
*If you feel unsure of your rights or have a complaint to make or need more information contact the Agency at the address in the listings.

WORK

woman's allowance) Phibsboro Tower, D7, 717111
Employment Equality Agency Dept of Labour, Mespil Rd D4,765861 (see box)
Employment Exchanges 23 Nth Cumberland St D1,742883. Victoria St, D8,752128
Trade Union Women's Forum 35 Windmill Rd, D12. A group of women from a wide range of unions, formed to promote the idea of women's rights in the Trade Unions. Their booklet, "Make Sure You Get Equal Pay" is available from above address.

HELP
AIM group Women's Centre, 14 Upr Leeson St, 763589. Tues, Wed, Thurs. 10-12pm
Ally c/o Dominican Priory, Upr Dorset St D1,740300
Assoc of Widows in Ireland 3 Nth Earl St D1, 748679
Dept of Social Welfare Phibsboro Tower D7,300922 (Deserted Wives Allowance & Benefits; Prisoner's Wives Allowance; Unmarried Mother's Allowance, Widows and Orphans' Pensions)
Fembrook Befriending for gay women, Box J4049 "In Dublin" 14 Bachelor's Walk, D1
FLAC (Free Legal Aid Centres) Central Office for information on 2nd floor, 3, Nth. Earl St, D1.
FLAC Offices:
Ozanam House 53 Mountjoy Sq D1,747171 Wed.
I.S.P.C.C. Office 20 Molesworth St D2. 760452 Tues
Rialto Parish Centre 19 St Anthony's Rd D8,754517 Wed
The Dispensary Ballyfermot 364000 Wed
Crumlin Social Service Centre Convent Grounds, Armagh Rd D12, 504733 Fri
Finglas Community Service Centre Wellmount Rd D11,342843 Tues
Padraig Pearse Tower Ballymun Thurs
St. Mary's Youth and Community Centre Monkstown Wed
Open 7.30-9.30pm on day specified
Coolock Community Law Centre Northside Shopping Centre D5 313174 Open Mon-Fri 9.30am-1pm Thurs 7.30-9pm, Sat 10-12pm
LIL Campaigning to remove discrimination against lesbians. Meetings Thursday evening 168 Rathgar Rd. D6.
Rape Crisis Centre (See page 4).
Women's Aid P.O. Box 791, Dublin 1. Phone 681583 (see box)
Tallaght area: Call to or phone Community Service Centre, Tues morning before 11am
Ballymun call to or phone Health

Wicca magazine documents the movement in action (c. 1977) (BL/F/AP/1498, Attic Press Archive)

Notes

1 Coulter, 1993; Tweedy, 1992; Beaumont, 1997; and Connolly, 2003b deal with this period of feminist activism in some depth.

2 See, for example, several contributions in O'Dowd and Valiulis (eds), 1997; Luddy and Murphy (eds), 1990; O'Dowd and Wichert, 1995; MacCurtain and O Corrain (eds), 1978; and Cullen and Luddy, 1995). See also: Ward, 1989; Cullen, 1986; Murphy, 1989; and Cullen-Owens, 1984.

3 See Connolly, 2003b: 56–88 for a discussion.

4 Tweedy (1992) provides a detailed account of the history of the Irish Housewives Association, which was founded in 1942. File BL/F/AP/1495, Attic Press Archive, contains copies of "Housewives Voice: Official Publication of the Irish Housewives Association" (c.1975–1976). See also Connolly (2003b: 56–88).

5 Files BL/F/AP/1155–1164, Attic Press Archive, contain items relating to the activities of the Council for the Status of Women from 1975–1994.

6 The Civil Service (Employment and Married Women) Act 1973 removed the ban that existed on married women working in the civil service, local authorities and health boards.

7 File BL/F/AP/1165, Attic Press Archive: contains "Progress Report on the Implementation of the Recommendations on the Report of the Commission on the Status of Women", prepared by the Women's Representative Committee (Dec 1976).

8 File BL/F/AP/1140, Attic Press Archive: contains 42 items (Feb 1974–81), including notes by Patricia Kelleher on the IWLM and programme of action; notes in relation to the Contraceptive Train (May 1971); photograph of Colette O'Neill making her statement after disembarking from train at Amiens Street Station; and the programme of the IWLM conference (Feb 1972). File BL/F/AP/1139: contains IWLM's manifesto and publication *Chains – or Change?: The Civil Wrongs of Irishwomen* (IWLM: Dublin Founding group) and an article "Women's Lib" (1971) written by Mary Maher.

9 File BL/F/AP/1139, Attic Press Archive: contains 35 items in relation to the activities of radical women's groups (from 1971 to 1979), including: list of demands of Irishwomen United; papers delivered at the debate on abortion at UCD (1975) by Anne Connolly and Anne Speed; material relating to the Contraceptive Action Programme; and article entitled "Women in Revolt" by Pat Brennan (April 1979).

10 File BL/F/AP/1515, Attic Press Archive, contains eight editions of *Banshee: Journal of Irishwomen United* (nos.1–8).

11 File BL/F/AP/1175, Attic Press Archive (20 items): includes minutes of meetings of IWU (1975). The minutes are concerned mainly with the organisation of campaigns, rallies and workshops relating to women's issues.

12 File BL/F/AP/1173, Attic Press Archive: relates to IWU's Welfare Rights Committee (1975) and includes minutes of meetings and copies of letters circulated. Activities of the committee include a campaign to secure equal treatment for women in respect of unemployment assistance. File BL/F/AP/1180, Attic Press Archive: relates to the IWU campaign for equal pay (1975–1976).

13 File BL/F/AP/1339, Attic Press Archive, relates to the campaign by the *ad hoc* committee against the jailing of Marie McMahon for failing to sign a bond to keep the peace after being charged with a postering offence in 1977 and a soliciting offence in 1988. Copy of press release (11 Mar 1980) details reasons for the arrest of McMahon and profiles her involvement with civil rights and feminist issues. File BL/F/AP/1340 relates to the arrest and subsequent acquittal of Marie McMahon and

includes an article by Mairin de Burca in *Hibernia*, "A Woman's Place" (21 September 1978). File BL/F/AP/1142 contains a leaflet from IWU relating to Marie McMahon and her arrest.

14 See File BL/F/AP/1339, Attic Press Archive.

15 This was later published in her collection, *Kindling* (1982: 44).

16 File BL/F/AP/1494, Attic Press Archive, contains editions of *The AIM Group Newsletter*, nos. 10–17 (1975–1977). File BL/F/AP/1504 contains *Women's AIM*, nos. 1–3, 5–9, 11, 12, 14 (1979–1984).

Chapter 2
The Politics of the Body:
Fertility Control and Reproduction

Defend "the Clinics" march and rally, Dublin, 7 February 1987 (photo: Clodagh Boyd)

In the 1970s, the women's movement profoundly questioned the long held assumption that women's bodies should be taken for granted and regulated. Reproductive rights, pregnancy, sexuality, violence, rape, pornography, new reproductive technologies, and several aspects of women's health have all been the subject of feminist campaigns, debate and writing in Ireland over the last three decades. Recent studies have built upon the themes of earlier feminist campaigns and reveal a multitude of other ways in which we live in our bodies and through them. A feminist politics of the body now deals extensively with how sexuality, disability, health and illness, fashion, food and childbirth are all heavily influenced by the social and cultural world we live in today.

Many of these debates can be traced to the politics of reproductive choice and control that first emerged in Ireland, in the 1960s. For much of the twentieth century, Ireland had the highest marital fertility rate in Europe. For social activists, the social and economic condition of very large families in Ireland was a longstanding concern. Patricia Kennedy (2002) describes how women suffering from ill health, malnutrition and anaemia were expected to bear children frequently and then to rear them in often squalid conditions, provided they were married. Pregnancy outside of marriage carried a huge social stigma and large numbers of illegitimate children were adopted at birth.[1] The widespread practice of institutionalising "fallen" women in Magdalen asylums has, in particular, been a subject of recent debate in Ireland. A high incidence of infanticide and evidence of backstreet abortions in Ireland was also notable throughout the last century.

By the 1960s, artificial contraceptive methods were being discussed in response to the distinctive familial structure of Irish society. In this chapter, the centrality of campaigns to provide contraception and abortion, during the second-wave of Irish feminist politics, are discussed.

Fertility Control: Contraception

During the 1970s, feminist activists and groups focused in particular on fertility control and reproductive choice as key to Irish women's liberation. As attitudes among Irish citizens changed in relation to Catholic social teaching, intimate relations, marriage, fertility obligations and sexual freedom, family-planning services in Ireland have developed since the 1960s and facilitated women in exercising the right to control and plan their fertility. In recent decades, the marital fertility rate in Ireland has significantly declined[2] (although the birth rate has increased in recent years, this is partly due to an increase in the total number of women who have entered the mean childbearing phase since the mid-1990s). Campaigns for the provision of contraception in Ireland, therefore, can be said to have had some effect on the changing demographic and familial structure of Irish society. Securing the legal right to use contraception to plan a family, combined with other factors, has contributed to the quite dramatic reduction in the average size of families that occurred in late twentieth century Ireland. In addition, more women have entered the labour force. In the process, the relationship of Irish women to their bodies, sexuality and reproductive health has changed.

In short, Irish women today are, on average, having fewer children and are entering the workforce in significantly larger numbers than in previous decades. It is notable that among Irish women, it is no longer the case that *all* heterosexual acts are categorically viewed as a potential conception, as the Catholic Church traditionally advocated. The pursuit of sex and obligatory reproduction can now, in principle, be treated as two separable matters, both institutionally and intimately, in contemporary Ireland.

The provision of contraception in Ireland has not been a straightforward product of EU membership, however, as some commentators have suggested. The activism of feminist organisations has been especially important in generating social change. Mahon *et al* (1997: 77) demonstrate how access to contraception in Ireland was prohibited by the dominant attitude of the Catholic Church for much of the twentieth century. In 1951 Pope Pius XII reiterated the use of the "safe period" as the only acceptable form of fertility control. Activism by a secular group

Women attending a CAP public meeting in Ballyfermot Neighbourhood Centre (c. 1976) (BL/F/AP/1291, Attic Press Archive)

ICA Family Planning Survey (c. 1972) (BL/F/AP/1592, Attic Press Archive)

Wicca

C. A. P.

CLODAGH BOYD

Over the last few months the whole issue of availablity of contraception and the threat to the continuing existence of the Family Planning Clinics has gathered interest in all quarters. There are properably more Irish people interested on and talking about contraception than ever before. Up to recently it was still a taboo subject to discuss openly. When the Contraception Action Programme began its campaign for free legal and safe contraception, three years ago, they organised the collection of a petition. The response in the streets and at doors was generally positive but all too often one of embarrassment and ignorance. Unfortunately there is still a lot of embarrassment and ignorance around but the general attitude toward contraception particularly among young people has become more open, informed and liberal. People are realising that it must be a personal choice and that it is particularly important for a woman to have full access to all methods of contraception.

If women are ever to obtain control of there own lives, control over their own fertility is one of the first and most basic demands particularly in Ireland, where the Church and State are hand in hand in their determination to keep women idealogically and materially in their control. Their continued position and very existence depends on the women remaining without real choices.

radicalization

A slowly growing awareness of women's position in society and a broad radicalization of women and workers in general on issues like pay and conditions of work etc., has affected the improving attitude towards the right to contraception. Things like the R.T.E. programme "Women Today" with its open and informative discussions has helped and Gay Byrne who is listened to by so many women, even though he insults us constantly, came out earlier this year as being in favour of contraception. This general radicalization which may not look very radical in terms as the rest of Europe but is , when one thinks of traditional Catholic Ireland, frightened the Knights of Columbanus and the Catholic hierarchy into persuading the Pope to visit Ireland. It was pointed out by Anne Speed of CAP at the Feminist Federation meeting

around the Popes visit that yes, thousands of people would go, pray, enjoy the festivities in the Park and elsewhere but lots of them would come home and continue to use contraceptives afterwards.

church

Thousands of people in Ireland have already made the decision to use contraceptives whether or not the Church agrees. The numbers of people using the clinics and CAP service in the Dandelion Market have not declined since the visit, they increase all the time. as

people are looking for information and methods to run their own lives. But of course the thing that brought on the discussion the most was the actual introduction and passing of legislation that gives the Minister power to put total responsibility for the Family Planning service in the hands of doctors, a lot of whom have no training, and pharmacists. This will make a service more expensive and for some people harder to obtain. The law gives the Minister the power to close the clinics and fine or jail people for a year, who sell contraceptives illegally, as CAP does in the Dandeline.

shop opens

And alongside the legislation the fight-back by the clinics and CAP. CAP fight has included things like the opening of the shop in Harcourt Road last year, which later moved to the Dandelion Market, the Festival to celebrate 10 years of contraception in Ireland, the Womens Health and Sexuality Conference, and several meetings and demonstrations, the 'pregnant poster' and the mobile clinic.

CAP attempts and hopes to bring together any groups or individuals interested in fighting for free legal and safe contraception. Recent CAP Activities: CAP over the last month or so organised a mobile clinic which sold non-medical contraceptives, gave out information and most importantly talked with people in suburban areas where there is no local service.

mobile clinic

CAP has groups in Cork, Limerick and Galway as well as Dublin and the Mobile went to the different cities setting up 'shop' in highly populated areas around the cities. There was a very positive response everywhere and it was particularly interesting in Cork and Limerick who had had contraceptives siezed from them by the Gardai when they sold last year. This time the Gardai only watched closely. Mainly, because in effect they could not arrest us as the old law is obsolete since the new law was passed yet the new one is not enforcible until the regulations and details of its workings are written and included.

14

The aims of the CAP 1975–1979, *Wicca* magazine (BL/F/AP/1498, Attic Press Archive)

PROPOSAL FOR AN AMENDMENT
by IRISH WOMEN UNITED

Because we believe that women in Ireland should have the full right to control their own fertility:
We demand FREE LEGAL CONTRACEPTION

1. We demand state financed birth control clinics. These be administered and staffed by those trained in all methods of birth control, and the education of men and women of childbearing age, in the use and the possibilities of birth control.

It should be mandatory for every regional health area to set up or finance existing clinics, for the provision of contraception and attendant services. These clinics should be based in, but independent from health clinics throughout the country. In areas where there are no health clinics, the provision of birth control clinics would be connected to the domicilliary service in the area.

2. We demand that contraceptives of all types and attendent services be provided free and where necessary importation of contraceptives (of all types) be done through the birth control clinics. Wider distribution of contraceptives would be provided through dispensaries.

3. We demand that a full sex education programme be provided in the birth control clinics, maternity hospitals, V.D. clinics etc. by those trained in such education. This programme should incorporate birth control education to schools (primary and secondary), teachers (at all levels), social workers, doctors, nurses etc. The objective would be to make birth control free and available in the broadest sense of the word.

4. We demand that there be the right to discuss, publish literature, distribute literature, publicly display, hold meetings etc. advocating contraception.

5. We demand that women in Ireland would at all times receive the best and safest forms of contraceptives, of all types, available.

6. We demand that all literature concerning contraception which is banned under the censorship act be immediately removed from the banned list.

The IWU campaign for free legalised contraception (c. 1975–6) (BL/F/AP/1515/1, Attic Press Archive)

CONTRACEPTION ACTION PROGRAMME

Public Meeting: TCD R.1408 Monday 29th January 1978 to Discuss Bill
                  FREE,LEGAL CONTRACEPTION NOW
                  EVERY CHILD A WANTED CHILD.

Ten years since the first Family Planning Clinic was established by voluntary groups the State & successive Governments have failed to introduce a comprehensive service. Instead, we have a situation where only certain sections of population can use the clinics, and Haughey's proposals will legitimise, what is implicity a discrimination against a large number of people, particularly in the rural and working areas. If the proposed Bill becomes law, it will have disasterous consequences for present services and militate against the development of any new services listed below are only some of the implications:

(1)   It removes from family planning clinics the power to provide the comprehensive service which has been available for the last few years. They will not be able to provide supplies as they have been doing, clinic visitors will have to go to a chemist for contraceptive supplies.

(2)   It will make contraception very expensive since doctors' fees and chemists prescribing charges will be addedto the full retail price. This will hit the poorer sections of the population hardest.

(3)   The 13,000 women getting contraceptives under the GMS on medical card will no longer be able to do so. Haughey has said no artifical contraceptives will be supplied.

(4)   Grants for research and exemptions from licences will be made to clinics providing information/service on"Natural" family planning only.

(5)   It is an infringement of personal privacy since a person has to discuss their private affairs with the doctor even if no medical aspect is involved. Also the prescription must state it is a family planning prescription - thus revealing the persons private affairs to the chemist also (where is the right of marital privacy now?)

(6)   It gives the Minister many arbitary powers since he may change the regulations and conditions of licences at any time. Why are these draconian powers necessary

If this Bill is passed it will be, a reversal of the trends towards separation of Church and State as the power of the Catholic Church is clearly evident in the present Bill's emphasis on "natural" methods. It will mean the handing over of what should be a state funded service to private enterprise (which will mean no service at all) and lastly it will be a blow against the fight for womens equality, by denying to women the democratic right to choose how to control their own fertility.

Students, Tradeunionists, housewives, feminists, concerned individuals have a responsibility to ensure the greatest pressure is mounted against the Bill. It seems likely that it will be passed, we in C.A.P. believe that the clinics should ignore the restrictions and continue to provide their services. We believe they can take a lead in this and can draw on support from their clients.

Trade Unions, Political organisations and parties, the womrens movement have a responsibility to defend and extend the right to choose.

SEND A REPRESENTATIVE TO THE NATIONAL PLANNING MEETING OF CONTRACEPTION CAMPAIGN ON·
SAT. FEBRUARY 17th in TCD. 2 - 6pm   Sponsored by CAP

Press statement from CAP detailing aims of the group/campaign (c. 1975–6) (BL/F/AP/1291, Attic Press Archive)

in opposition to the position of both the Church and the state first brought the issue of contraception into the political arena in the 1960s. In April 1963, the first family-planning clinic was opened in Holles Street Hospital in Dublin to give advice on the safe period. By then, doctors had begun to prescribe the pill as a cycle regulator despite church opposition. Access to family planning was further facilitated in 1969, when a Fertility Guidance Clinic, supported by the International Planned Parenthood Association, opened in Dublin and a Family Planning Rights group was formed. According to Mahon *et al* (1997: 77): "While it was, at that time, illegal to *sell* contraceptives, the clinic subverted this by dispensing contraceptives free of charge, while at the same time requesting 'donations' from its clients."

Legalisation and provision of contraception became a core demand of a range of feminist individuals and organizations by the early 1970s, including the IWLM, IWU, individual politicians (Mary Robinson moved a Bill in 1971 in the Senate), women's health groups, the Contraceptive Action Programme (CAP), and legal campaigns/test cases (such as the *McGee* case).[3] Despite being illegal, contraception was practically provided by feminist organisations (such as the CAP and Well Woman Centre) as well as individual doctors by the 1970s.[4] The launch of the CAP in 1976 by members of IWU formed a coalition of various women's groups, the Labour Women's National Council and family-planning organisations.[5] The campaign received support from different constituencies – Trade Unions, students unions, Community and Tenants Associations, the CSW, the Bray Women's Group, the Limerick Women's Action Group, the Young Socialists of the Labour Party, the Women's Group of the Socialist Labour Party, and individual activists. Direct-action tactics, which included opening an illegal contraception shop and stall at the Dandelion Market, had a considerable effect.

The aims of the CAP included (see *Wicca*, 1977: 16, BL/F/AP/1498, Attic Press Archive):

1. Legislation of contraception and the end of restrictive legislation;
2. Availability of all methods to all who wish to use them;
3. Provision of contraception advice and counselling in all maternity and child welfare clinics;
4. Introduction of education programmes on sex, birth, contraception and personal relationships in schools and colleges;
5. Inclusion of methods of birth control in the training of doctors, nurses, health visitors, social workers and lay counsellors;
6. Distribution of contraceptives free through Health Service Clinics and at a controlled minimum cost through general practitioners, pharmacies and specialised voluntary clinics.

The CAP's agenda included the opening of a shop in Harcourt Road, which later moved to the Dandelion Market, a festival to celebrate ten years of contraception in Ireland, a Women's Health and Sexuality Conference, regular meetings and demonstrations, poster campaigns, and a mobile clinic, which sold non-medical

CAP stall selling condoms, Coal Quay, Cork, 10 November 1979 (photo: Clodagh Boyd)

Dublin Well Woman Centre advertisement 1980 (BL/F/AP/1220, Attic Press Archive)

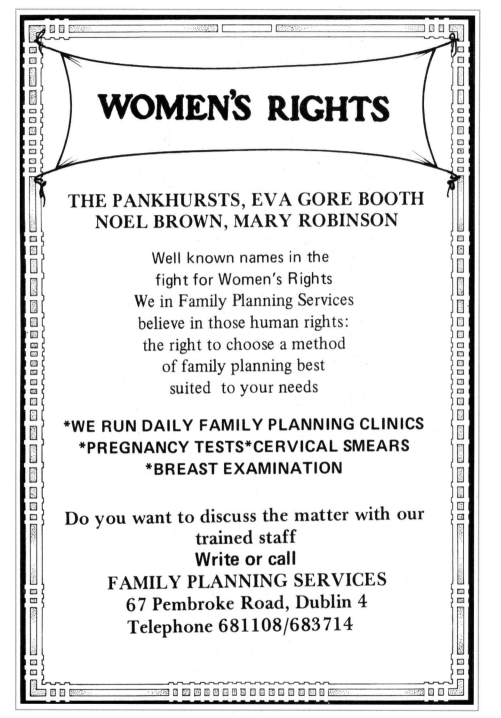

Family-planning services advertisement (n.d.) (BL/F/AP/1492/4, Attic Press Archive)

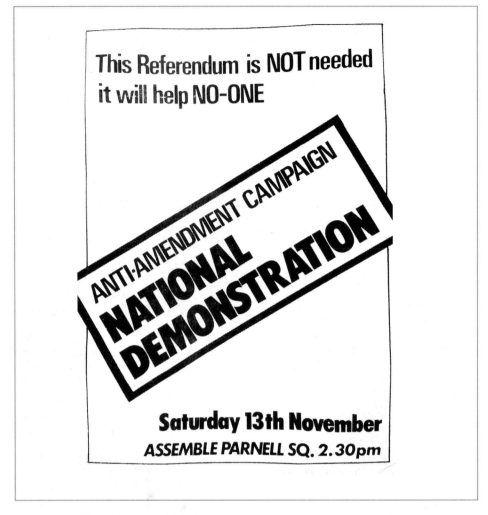

Anti-amendment poster, 1983(BL/F/AP/1591/4, Attic Press Archive)

contraceptives, gave out information and, most importantly, talked with people in suburban areas where there was *no* local service.

The cross-movement campaign for contraceptive rights and services demonstrates how feminism continuously nurtured new organizations and coalitions in the sphere of reproductive rights. The legality of contraception was challenged in a landmark Supreme Court case in 1973, *McGee v. Attorney General*. The court ruled that the constitutional right to marital privacy included the right to obtain contraceptives for personal use, rendering section 17 of the Criminal Law (Amendment) Act 1935, which prohibited the importation of contraceptives unconstitutional. In 1979, the Health (Family Planning) Act was passed, legalising contraception by prescription (including condoms) for married couples only. The 1979 Act did not nearly meet feminist demands for free, public family-planning

Defend "the Clinics" march and rally, Dublin, 7 February 1987 (BL/F/AP/1591/3, Attic Press Archive)

services, and further significant legislation was not introduced until 1985, when legislation to permit the sale of condoms without prescription to those over 18 was introduced in response to the AIDS virus.

A range of groups organised around the contraception question throughout the 1970s, which involved campaigning at the level of political and legal reform; direct action and dramatic movement events (such as the Contraceptive Train and breaking into the Senate during the hearing of Mary Robinson's Bill chanting "we shall not conceive"); and the practical provision of services (through the Well Woman Centres, the nation-wide activities of the CAP and the Irish Family Planning Association).

The Irish Family Planning Association (IFPA) is a national voluntary organisation and registered charity that has been pioneering reproductive health and rights in Ireland since 1969. In 1969 the appalling health and social circumstances in which many families in Ireland lived and, in particular, the health consequences for mothers and their children of repeated pregnancies, were major concerns for the IFPA founders, who were both men and women. The IFPA today is committed to promoting and protecting individual basic human rights in relation to reproductive and sexual health, relationships and sexuality. The IFPA continues to be an important advocate of reproductive rights both within Ireland and worldwide. The association regularly makes submissions to government as well as providing reproductive health care in a network of centres to women and men, and non-directive counselling for women with crisis pregnancies.

The Dublin Well Woman Centres were founded in 1978, with the aim of helping Irish women access family-planning information and services – at a time when contraception was illegal. Throughout the 1980s, Well Woman campaigned for the right to provide information to women facing crisis pregnancy, and it is outlined in the next section how in the 1990s it won a landmark case at the European Court of Human Rights with other groups. Over the years, Well Woman has extended its range of services and, like the IFPA, it now provides broader-based primary health-care services to both women and men, including cervical screening and sexual health. In Dublin alone, Well Woman provides employment to over 60 doctors, nurses, counsellors, and reception/administration staff, and remains the leading provider of women's health services.

Case Study

Ann Lovett

Ann Lovett was found lying beside the body of her newborn child, under the shadow of a statue of the Virgin Mary, in a churchyard in Granard, Co. Longford, in February 1984. The town of Granard became headline news when Ann, a 15-year-old schoolgirl, was found bleeding to death, having given birth in the open air in the grounds of a grotto in the town. Although she had carried a child to full term, in a small village where little went unnoticed, no-one would admit to having known she was pregnant when she died. When Ann was found, her newborn baby was already dead. She was treated at the scene by a local doctor, and then taken to hospital in Meath, where she too died.

Less than four months previously, the Eighth Amendment to the Constitution of the Irish Republic was approved in a referendum by two-thirds of the voters. Article 40.3.3 of the Constitution reads: "The State acknowledges the right to life of the unborn and, with due regard to the equal right to life of the mother, guarantees in its laws to respect, and as far as practicable, by its laws to defend and vindicate that right."

The death of Ann Lovett stands as a testimony to the many thousands of Irish women who experienced and concealed "crisis" pregnancies in twentieth century Ireland.

The Statue of the Virgin at Granard Speaks

by Paula Meehan

It can be bitter here at times like this,
November wind sweeping across the border.
Its seeds of ice would cut you to the quick.
The whole town tucked up safe and dreaming,
even wild things gone to earth, and I
stuck up here in this grotto, without as much as
star or planet to ease my vigil.

The howling won't let up. Trees
cavort in agony as if they would be free

and take off – ghost voyagers
on the wind that carries intimations
of garrison towns, walled cities, ghetto lanes
where men hunt each other and invoke
the various names of God as blessing
on their death tactics, their night manoeuvres.
Closer to home the wind sails over
dying lakes. I hear fish drowning.
I taste the stagnant water mingled
with turf smoke from outlying farms.

They call me Mary – Blessed, Holy, Virgin.
They fit me to a myth of a man crucified:
the scourging and the falling, and the falling again,
the thorny crown, the hammer blow of iron
into wrist and ankle, the sacred bleeding heart.

They name me Mother of all this grief
though mated to no mortal man.
They kneel before me and their prayers
fly up like sparks from a bonfire
that blaze a moment, then wink out.

It can be lovely here at times. Springtime,
early summer. Girls in Communion frocks
pale rivals to the riot in the hedgerows
of cow parsley and haw blossom, the perfume
from every rushy acre that's left for hay
when the light swings longer with the sun's push north.

Or the grace of a midsummer wedding
when the earth herself calls out for coupling
and I would break loose of my stony robes,
pure blue, pure white, as if they had robbed
a child's sky for their colour. My being
cries out to be incarnate, incarnate,
maculate and tousled in a honeyed bed.

Even an autumn burial can work its own pageantry.
The hedges heavy with the burden of fruiting
crab, sloe, berry, hip; clouds scud east
pear scented, windfalls secret in long

orchard grasses, and some old soul is lowered
to his kin. Death is just another harvest
scripted to the season's play.

But on this All Souls' Night there is
no respite from the keening of the wind.
I would not be amazed if every corpse came risen
from the graveyard to join in exaltation with the gale,
a cacophony of bone imploring sky for judgement
and release from being the conscience of the town.

On a night like this I remember the child
who came with fifteen summers to her name,
and she lay down alone at my feet
without midwife or doctor or friend to hold her hand
and she pushed her secret out into the night,
far from the town tucked up in little scandals,
bargains struck, words broken, prayers, promises,
and though she cried out to me in extremis
I did not move,
I didn't lift a finger to help her,
I didn't intercede with heaven,
nor whisper the charmed word in God's ear.

On a night like this I number the days to the solstice
and the turn back to the light.
O sun,

centre of our foolish dance,
burning heart of stone,
molten mother of us all,
hear me and have pity.

Reproduced by permission of the author, Paula Meehan (see also Meehan, 1991: 40–42)

Anti-abortion march, Dublin, 12 May 1979 (photo: Clodagh Boyd)

Abortion

By the 1980s, the changing economic and political climate in Ireland became a tangible constraint for all feminist groups (particularly service organisations such as the Well Woman Centres, Women's Aid and the Rape Crisis Centre, which were vastly under-resourced and overwhelmed with demand for their services). In this period, reproductive rights campaigns began to expand beyond the question of fertility control and prevention to looking at the question of termination.[6]

As already demonstrated, contraception was partially legalised in 1979, but was already being provided illegally by the Well Woman Centre, the CAP and family-planning clinics for some time. Abortion has a related history in Ireland. Induced abortion was in fact commonplace in Ireland for centuries, and it continued to occur in an underground manner until the introduction of legal abortion in Britain in 1967, when Irish women began to travel for safer terminations.

The first legal prohibition in Ireland was introduced under the 1861 Offences Against the State Act, which made performing, attempting or assisting in an abortion punishable up to penal life sentence. Traditional doctrine adhered to by the Catholic Church suggested that the foetus did not become "ensouled" until quickening. In 1869, Pope Pius IX dropped the reference to "ensouled foetus" and in 1917 excommunication from the church was introduced for the act of abortion. Prior to 1981, when a Pro-Life Amendment Campaign (PLAC) was established to lobby for a referendum to insert a pro-life clause into the Irish Constitution, there had never been a comprehensive debate about abortion in the political arena in Ireland. Yet, the existence of abortion (and infanticide) has been central to the social history of Irish women's lives (Jackson, 1986; 1987).

Irish women have mainly gone to the UK for abortions since it was legalised there in 1967. Today, it is estimated that over 7,000 women travel each year to England for abortions (Mahon, Conlon and Dillon, 1998) and the Irish abortion rate remains one of the highest in the European Union. Backstreet abortions in Ireland were more numerous in periods when travel to England was restricted, for example during World War II. The 1954 Commission on Emigration reported a sharp rise in prosecutions for backstreet abortion, cases of infanticide and rates of illegitimacy in this period (Jackson, 1987).

Legislation pertaining to the right of Irish women to access abortion services in Ireland has a complicated history both within the women's movement and in Irish society, in general. Few women's organisations confronted the Irish abortion rate as a critical feminist issue in the 1970s (some degree of discussion in IWU was an exception) until a Women's Right to Choose Group emerged at the end of the decade.

Abortion was debated in IWU but tactically the group decided not to engage in public direct-action as it was considered too risky. A radical feminist organisation with a pro-choice focus is considered to have emerged comparatively late in the *public* arena in Irish society.[7] Abortion was already legalised in Britain in 1967, when the British women's liberation movement mobilised and with the landmark *Roe v. Wade* ruling in the US in 1973. A pro-choice sector from within the women's movement was forced to organise in response to the development of the Pro-Life Amendment Campaign in 1981, however. The Anti-Amendment Campaign consolidated alongside abortion information and referral services in this period.

The first IPCC (Irish Pregnancy Counselling Centre) was formed by a group of IWU activists in 1979 and it was later replaced by Open Door Counselling (which subsequently became Open Line Counselling, when banned by the High Court from operating a service in a premises). The principal strategies of the first Women's Right to Choose group were the decriminalisation of abortion and the establishment of a feminist pregnancy counselling service. The first Irish Pregnancy Counselling Centre was set up in June 1980. Early in 1981 a conference on "Abortion, Contraception and Sterilisation" was organised by activists at Trinity College Dublin. In March of that year, a public meeting was held at Liberty Hall to publicise the demands of the group and recruit members. Counter pickets were mounted on the Liberty Hall meeting and the audience was antagonistic to the pro-choice platform.

The emergence of an organised right in Ireland, however, dates from before the formation of the Women's Right to Choose group. By the 1980s, the anti-abortion movement escalated and hardened its tactics internationally. In the US, anti-abortion activists attacked and picketed clinics, and confrontationally dissuaded women from having abortions. According to Ruth Riddick, in Ireland abortion became widely perceived as *the* single issue around which to "halt the permissive tide in other areas" (John O'Reilly,[8] *Need for a Human Life Amendment*, January 1981 in Riddick, 1994: 142). The Pro-life Amendment Campaign (PLAC) in 1981 in reality had its foundations in the 1970s and was generally opposed to changes in the status of women that occurred in a number of areas in the previous decade. Around the single issue of abortion, the campaign was launched on a rather quiet note in April 1981, and few political activists at the time could have realised the impact it would subsequently generate. Pro-choice activists began to realise the implications of the campaign after the Fianna Fáil wording of the proposed amendment was disputed and the campaign intensified. Gradually various sections of Irish society became embroiled in a complex political debate, which culminated in a constitutional referendum in September 1983.

The pro-life movement thought it could successfully block pro-choice organisations from providing information and abortion referral services by winning a constitutional referendum. A pro-life clause in the Constitution was considered the most successful way to guarantee the "right to life of the unborn". The political campaign was long, bitter and divisive. A complex debate culminated in the issuing of a proposed amendment to the Constitution by the Government:

> The State acknowledges the right to life of the unborn and, with due regard to the equal right to life of the mother, guarantees in its laws to respect and as far as practicable by its laws to defend and vindicate that right.

Right-to-choose groups, prominent journalists/media personalities, family-planning clinic workers, students' unions and other feminist activists tentatively formed an anti-amendment campaign. Opposing the referendum was an extremely difficult task for a disparate group of this scale, with a limited constituency and resources to fight a national referendum campaign.[9]

As the campaign progressed, the issue of a women's right to choose became increasingly side-lined in the Anti-Amendment Campaign's strategy and in the general political debate. Opponents of the amendment produced leaflets and canvassed the electorate giving several *other* reasons why the amendment should be opposed. Principally they argued that an amendment to the Constitution was unnecessary and would do nothing to help those Irish women who had sought, and were continuing to seek, abortions in Britain. Strategically, the principle of an Irish women's right to choose abortion was not among the arguments. The politics of the campaign essentially silenced women's reproductive control as a subject of debate. Thus, the practical concerns of those feminist activists engaged in the direct provision of abortion information and non-directive pregnancy counselling were basically hidden and the abortion rate/number of Irish women travelling to Britain continued to rise.

The PLAC was supported by the main opposition party, Fianna Fáil; the majority of senior maternity hospital consultant obstetricians; and the bishops of the Catholic Church. The Irish Nurses Organisation and Catholic lay organisations (such as Opus Dei and the Knights of Columbanus) actively campaigned *for* the amendment (see O'Reilly, 1988; Hesketh, 1990). Pamphlets and leaflets were issued to Catholic churchgoers on Sundays. Church-run hospitals and schools were used as organising centres in favour of the amendment. Anti-feminist women who regarded changes in contraception and abortion laws as threats to the traditional status of motherhood as well as a group of pro-life feminists also emerged in this period.

Political opposition to the proposed amendment to the Constitution intensified at only a very late stage of the campaign. The final three weeks of the campaign started with the Minister for Finance, Alan Dukes, stating his opposition to the amendment, and he was followed by ministerial colleagues Gemma Hussey and Nuala Fennell (activist in the Women's Political Association, Women's Aid and AIM). In medical organisations, seven professors of paediatrics came out against the amendment, while a new group of several hundred pro-amendment doctors was formed. In September 1983, the Tánaiste and Leader of the Labour Party, Dick Spring, said that a concerted campaign was being waged with the support of the hierarchy to "roll back the tide on social issues." He issued a statement strongly criticising the amendment and urged people to vote "no". The same month, the Taoiseach Dr Garret Fitzgerald acknowledged that he shared equal responsibility for accepting without adequate legal advice wording which he described as both doubtful and dangerous. A letter from the Archbishop of Dublin, Dr Ryan, was read out at all Catholic masses in Dublin on the Sunday preceding the referendum, stating that a rejection of the amendment would leave open the possibility of abortion becoming legal sooner or later in Ireland. The letter concluded by advising the electorate to vote "yes". On 7 September 1983, some 53 per cent of the electorate went to the polls – 66 per cent voted in favour of the amendment, with the majority more pronounced in rural areas. Only one constituency voted against the amendment (Dún Laoghaire). Article 40.3.3 of the Constitution was intended to guarantee the "right to life of the unborn" and to keep abortion out of Ireland, permanently.

After the referendum, both the Women's Right to Choose group and the break-away Right to Choose campaign eventually disbanded. However, the campaigning focus of a small group of pro-choice activists within the women's movement shifted and subsequently became focused on the right to access information about legal abortion services *in another jurisdiction*. Alliances with sympathetic organisations and individuals were gradually built in the aftermath of the referendum (with students unions, individual doctors, lawyers, politicians and media personalities). However, a subsequent series of legal cases taken through the courts against pro-choice services in Ireland drove abortion referral and information services *underground*. Individual doctors, family-planning practitioners and students' union officials continued to either provide written information on abortion services in other jurisdictions or to directly refer women to Irish feminist information/referral services.

Gradually, abortion information, in particular, became recognised as an integral feminist mobilising issue in the other sectors of the mainstream women's move-

Women's Right to Choose meeting, Dublin, 5 December 1981 (photo: Clodagh Boyd)

ment. The campaign became diverted into the right to procure information about abortion in another jurisdiction – a more acceptable demand to the wider mainstream constituency in the women's movement and to the general public. The legal constraints imposed through court cases taken throughout the 1980s acted as a catalyst for reappraisal within the marginalised pro-choice sector and, in the process, new intra-movement alliances and tensions gradually developed. This mobilising issue recruited a number of radical activists to the women's movement who were "not there" in the 1970s – some whom had had illegal abortions themselves, discovered the extent of the problem as family-planning practitioners or doctors, and/or were drawn into referral work by previous involvement in other related organisations (such as rape crisis work and women's health services).

The Women's Information Network (WIN) was the successor to the Women's Right to Choose group and operated independently of the (former) pregnancy counselling services. WIN was established in November 1987 as an underground, voluntary emergency non-directive helpline service for women with crisis pregnancies. The helpline was founded by a group of women appalled by the 1986 Hamilton ruling, which banned the dissemination of abortion information.[10] It was launched with the support and assistance of the then Defend the Clinics campaign. Contact with British abortion clinics was particularly important, and the helpline volunteer group undertook continuous training in counselling skills and visited and monitored abortion clinics in Britain. WIN included 20 women working in a variety of professions (including psychologists, film makers, teachers, administrators and students) (WIN *Information Pamphlet*, 1993).

Women's Right to Choose meeting, Dublin, 5 December 1981 – pro-life activist in disguise unmasked (photo: Clodagh Boyd)

By 1992, change in public opinion opinion was influenced by rulings in favour of abortion information and the right to travel by the European Court of Human Rights and the European Court of Justice. Following the Hamilton ruling (1986), Open Door Counselling appealed to the European Court of Human Rights, to which Ireland is a signatory under the European Convention on Human Rights. In October 1992, the Court found that the order of the Irish courts was in breach of the Convention's information rights clause, Article 10:

> Everyone has the right to freedom of expression. This right shall include freedom to hold opinions and to receive and impart information and ideas without interference by public authority and without frontiers.

This judgment was regarded as a moral victory by feminist activists and the successful outcome of "eight years of legal wrangling and five years curtailment of much needed services for women" (Riddick, 1993). Open Door Counselling subsequently initiated proceedings to have the restraining order of the Supreme Court lifted in order to restore services.

One of the most important turning points in the campaign occurred in 1992, when the Attorney General successfully sought a High Court injunction against "Miss X", which prevented a 14-year-old girl, who had been raped, from travelling to England for a termination (see several chapters in Smyth, 1992).[11] A subsequent appeal to the Supreme Court lifted this injunction, and in its judgment found that Article 40.3.3 could actually *permit abortion* in certain circumstances.

The Supreme Court interpreted this to mean that an abortion could be performed in Ireland if the woman's health was endangered by her threatened suicide. In addition, the Court decided that there could be restrictions on the right to travel, independent of the *X* case, if there was a conflict between the right to life of the foetus and that of the mother. The implications of this judgment was that a woman could be prevented from travelling to Britain on the grounds that the life of her foetus rather than her own life was threatened.[12] In response, a referendum was held in November 1992 and the majority of the electorate supported the right to obtain abortion information and the right to travel. However, the electorate rejected a third clause permitting limited abortion in Ireland. The CSW directly negotiated with the Government on the wording of the referenda in 1992, indicating a growing consensus on abortion in liberal feminist politics. The focus of the politics of reproductive rights – abortion on demand – remains unresolved and contentious within the Irish women's movement, however.

A government-funded study of abortion was published in 1998 (Mahon, Conlon and Dillon, 1998) and the Green Paper on Abortion was published in 1999. The Regulation of Information Act, which stipulates that information on abortion services can be given only within the context of counselling, was introduced in 1995.[13] And a public tribunal was followed by another referendum on abortion in 2002, which rejected an attempt to curtail the Supreme Court's ruling on the *X* case. The substantive issue of the circumstances in which legal abortion can occur in Ireland remains unlegislated for. A recent press release issued by the Cork Women's Right to Choose Group captures the current state of the debate:

The Cork Women's Right to Choose Group Press Release 2003

Thursday 6 March will be the first anniversary of the defeat of the government's attempt to roll back the *X* case judgement and impose penalties of up to twelve years imprisonment on women who had abortions and those who assisted them.

During the debate important issues were exposed including cases such as Deirdre de Barra's and the fact that an average of 19 women a day travelled to Britain for abortions.

On the issue of Choice
- We welcome the new leaflet produced by the Crisis Pregnancy Agency which provides information on where women can access non-directive counselling. Having access to this information is an important step in recognising women's right to choose.
- We call for funding to be provided to provide adequate non-denominational, non-directive counselling services in Cork City and County.

On non-viable pregnancies
- During their press conference on the referendum, the masters of the maternity hospitals admitted that they believed that abortion should be available in Ireland in such cases.
- It still does not appear to be legal to abort such pregnancies here.

- We call on the government to recognise that Irish women in this painful situation need to access abortion services in their own country.
- We call on them to find a more compassionate and just response than directing them to other jurisdictions for their abortions.

On the issue of rape
- The message of two referenda has been clear. The people do not want to roll back the X case judgement, which provided for abortion in Ireland in certain circumstances.
- The way is clear for the government to legislate on this issue. It should clarify the issue by doing so as a matter of urgency.

Article 40.3.3
- Article 40.3.3 of our Constitution has resulted in many thousands of women being treated cruelly and unjustly and in successive governments failing and abandoning them.

In this the twentieth anniversary year of the referendum that inserted Article 40.3.3 in our Constitution, we call on the State to face up to the reality of many real women's lives and choices and initiate a campaign to repeal it.

The short-term gains of the Catholic right through the courts in the 1980s were in reality reversed quickly in the 1990s and there was a change of public attitude in relation to abortion information and referral, particularly following the X case. Setbacks for the Catholic right in Ireland (including, the 1992 referendum in favour of abortion information and the right to travel) provoked open confrontation and hostility in the 1995 divorce referendum campaign, which paved the way for the legalisation of divorce in Ireland.

The setting up of the Crisis Pregnancy Agency by the Government suggests abortion is finally being addressed in the Irish context. However, the legalisation of abortion in Ireland remains an elusive prospect.

Technology and Reproduction

Focusing on the politics of contraception and abortion reveals the institutional norms and values that determined Irish women's lives for much of the twentieth century. The question of fertility control has been politically controversial in Ireland since the 1970s. The natural association between marriage and fertility was fundamentally questioned by second-wave feminists, who provided contraception and abortion information services. However, according to Patricia Kennedy (2002: 67), the tremendous energy spent on fertility control in those years was to the neglect of the rights of women who chose to give birth or proceed with pregnancy in Ireland each year. Maternity and care in Ireland have provoked new debates in feminism about social policy for mothers and maternity-related services in recent years. Concern about infertility and controversy over reproductive technologies have also emerged.[14]

After many years of experimentation in several countries world-wide, the birth in Britain in 1978 of the world's first baby conceived in laboratory conditions occurred by means of in vitro fertilisation (IVF). The technique of IVF has formed the basis for further developments – the use of donor sperm, donor eggs, donor embryo, contract surrogacy, the freezing of sperm and embryos, (the latter meaning that twin, or other multiple embryo developments, can now be born years apart). More recently, sex pre-selection and post-menopausal pregnancy by means of embryo transfer have been introduced and recently under consideration (and rejected in Britain) is the taking of eggs from ovarian tissue from a deceased female or from an aborted female foetus for the purposes of biological mothering. New reproductive technology is now established in Ireland as in many other countries throughout the world. Reproductive technologies can involve invasive medical probing, drug programmes and surgical interventions into women's bodies. IVF has a low success rate and incurs high financial costs: it generally involves creating and implanting several embryos before pregnancy is achieved. The practice of continual medical intervention, in the determined effort to bear a child by laboratory means, has been received both positively and negatively therefore.

Many thousands of children have been born world-wide as a result of the IVF technique, with hundreds of clinics established throughout the Western world advancing and applying the technology. With an approximate 30 per cent increase in infertility over the past two decades, more women and couples are turning to new reproductive technology as the answer to the problem of infertility. Furthermore, a growing number of women who postpone childbirth until later in life are encountering problems with conception and turning to medical intervention. Up until recently the technology has been highly regarded; but some apprehensions about its effects are now evident, particularly in the critical writings of biologists and scientists initially involved in the IVF research. Public anxiety has also been evident about the ethics of IVF and there has been intense debate in many countries. The most vehement criticism has most often come from feminist organisations and from religious groups.

The technique of IVF was first introduced into Ireland at Clane General Hospital, Co. Kildare, in 1987 and other units offering the IVF technology were subsequently established. The whole nature of human reproduction has been dramatically altered within a few short years with the development of new reproductive technologies – yet feminist debate and campaigns in Ireland typically focused on the prevention of fertility and other issues which concern family life. Positive presentation of the technology by the medical profession and the media informs us about the "miracle baby" the new cure for infertility, and the wonders of scientific development. Apart from occasional media attention to individual results of the technology and sensationalised stories (for example, the age at which a post-menopausal woman might give birth to an IVF baby), the meanings and values that lie behind the technology itself have not been publicly questioned.

IVF is sometimes portrayed as a development in favour of women, an extension of women's freedom with regard to her reproductive control (Ryan-Sheridan,

1994). While there is no denying the anguish of infertility, the concern which women and men often have about their involuntary childlessness is often described in the literature about infertility as being overwhelming and obsessional – provoking a more critical debate about the social values and expectations about motherhood that are connected to this kind of technological intervention in women's bodies.

Conclusion

Whether a woman's bodily experience is positive or negative in matters concerning fertility and reproduction is highly dependant on the social and medical support available. In the 1970s, feminist groups took it upon themselves to provide woman-centred services primarily in the area of fertility *control*.[15] In the 1980s, pro-choice pregnancy counselling services were provided. Contemporary feminism also asks questions about the adequacy of health, welfare and labour market policies for women in Ireland and elsewhere, as they experience pregnancy and motherhood (Kennedy, 2002).

While the issue of terminating pregnancies provoked government response in the 1990s, childbirth is a central experience in many women's lives. Public debate now tends to focus on the crisis in the healthcare system and maternity services in Ireland as opposed to more entrenched questions about gender and power in maternity-related services, which feminist writers have recently focused on (Murphy Lawless, 1998). Childbirth in Ireland has become increasingly medicalised since the 1970s, which has led a growing number of women to opt for home births and community midwives – the conventional mode of childbirth in Ireland until the 1950s.

Furthermore, recognition that women in Ireland are not a homogenous group now compels us to consider the rights of very young mothers, disabled mothers, Travellers, asylum-seeking mothers, lesbian mothers and mothers with a history of drug abuse in any debate about fertility, reproduction and the experience of childbirth in Ireland.[16]

Notes

1 Finola Kennedy's (2001) *From Cottage to Creche* discusses the issue of adoption in Ireland, in the twentieth century.

2 Ireland had the highest fertility rate in Europe and the number of first births in 2000 was the highest on record, a new report from the Economic and Social Research Institute (ESRI) has found. The report, *Family Formation in Ireland,* found that the number of births to unmarried mothers rose from 5% in 1980 to 32% in 2000. Patterns and limited evidence suggest that 'large proportions are in cohabiting unions and many enter marriage after the birth of the child', according to the ESRI. Around 12% of children under the age of 15 are in lone-parent families. This represents almost a doubling of the extent of lone parents since the early 1980s. Marital breakdown and births outside of marriage are the two most common routes into lone parenthood. However, the ESRI emphasises that a lack of data means it is not possible to be precise on this issue. There is also little information available on the role of the 'absent' parent in lone-parent families, it added. The report found that the vast majority of lone parents are women and they tend to have lower levels of education than married mothers in the same age group.

3 In 1974, the Supreme Court ruled in favour of Mary McGee, finding the ban on the importation of contraceptives for private use unconstitutional. The existence of a constitutional right to marital privacy was recognised by the court.

4 File BL/F/AP/1177, Attic Press Archive (44 items): relates to the IWU contraception group as well as the Contraception Action Programme (CAP). Includes minutes of meetings, circulars and documentation relating to the working of the committee. Files BLF/AP/1290–1297, Attic Press Archive, contain various documents relating to the contraception issue in Ireland (1974–1982).

5 File BL/F/AP/1291, Attic Press Archive: relates to the CAP and the Irishwomen United (IWU) campaign for legalised contraception. Includes press statement from CAP detailing the launch of the group with a list of their aims; minutes of a CAP meeting detailing the organisation of the contraception campaign, those who attended and the organisations they represented; circular letter requesting support for the Family Planning Bill introduced in the Senate by Mary Robinson.

6 File BL/F/AP/1281, Attic Press Archive: file of papers (13 items) relating to the abortion debate in Ireland (1975–84), including "The deadly solution to an Irish Problem – Backstreet Abortion" written by Pauline Jackson and published by the Women's Right to Choose Campaign, and draft material for a paper entitled "Guidelines for Abortion" by Róisín Conroy.

7 File BL/F/AP/1172, Attic Press Archive: relates to a conference held on abortion at UCD (11 December 1975). The file (containing 7 items) includes papers delivered by Monica Adams, Anne Connolly and Anne Speed.

8 John O'Reilly is named as a central figure in a number of campaigns by the Catholic right in Emily O'Reilly's book *Masterminds of the Right* (1992).

9 File BL/F/AP/1284, Attic Press Archive: pamphlets and circular material (17 items) relating to pro-choice activism and services (1977–1984). Includes material from the Anti-Amendment Campaign, the Women's Right to Choose Campaign, the National Abortion Campaign London and Publishers against the Amendment. File BL/F/1285 contains material relating to the work of the steering committee of the Anti-Amendment Campaign, including: a list of committee members, press releases, minutes of meetings, press cuttings.

10 File BL/F/AP/1286, Attic Press Archive, relates to the Right to Know Campaign (1985–1987), which was formed after the 1986 High Court judgement prohibiting the Well Woman Centre and

Open Line Counselling from providing information about the availability of abortion in Britain. The judgement was a result of an action taken by the Society for the Protection of the Unborn Child (SPUC).

11 File BL/F/AP/1287, Attic Press Archive: file of material (28 items) relating to the High Court decision to prevent a 14-year-old rape victim from leaving the country to have an abortion (the *X* case) and the subsequent campaign (1991–1992) to the have repealed the 8th Amendment to the Constitution, which outlawed the provision of abortion in Ireland. The file includes letters of protest and press releases from various organisations, a submission made by the Irish Council for Civil Liberties o the Right of Women to Reproductive Choice and Reproductive Health Services, and the referendum on the Right to Travel and Right to Information (September 1992).

12 This issue remains contentious and unresolved in Irish law. See the Green Paper on Abortion (1999).

13 Aine McCarthy in the *Irish Times* (5 July 2000: 15) points out that only three Irish pregnancy counselling agencies currently provide non-directive counselling: the Irish Family Planning Association (IFPA), Well Woman and Marie Stopes. Other agencies, such as Life and CURA, counsel their clients in relation to adoption or lone parenting only. These organisations tend to receive more funding from government than non-directive agencies. For example, CURA received a grant of £375,000 in 1999 for pregnancy counselling services, while the IFPA received £100,000 and Well Woman £87,000.

14 File BL/F/AP/1261, Attic Press Archive, contains documents in relation to reproductive technologies, including information on international conferences and a workshop held at UCD.

15 However, there is evidence of activism in Irish feminism concerning maternity issues and motherhood. For example, file BL/F/AP/1258, Attic Press Archive, contains an information leaflet issued by the Dublin Women's Maternity Action Group (1976) stating its opposition to induced labour in maternity hospitals.

16 In 1995 22.2% of births in Ireland were outside marriage, and the figure was 31.1% in 2002. In Ireland, the 2002 Census of Population has recorded that 8.4 per cent of family units involved partners who are cohabiting. Census data published in 2004 shows that one in three births is now outside marriage in Ireland compared to one in five in 1995.

Chapter 3
Feminism, Politics and Society

Reclaim the Night March Dublin, 29 September 1982 (photo: Clodagh Boyd)

This chapter focuses on the question of how second-wave feminism in the Republic of Ireland has engaged with the state, the political establishment and its major institutions. Chapter 5 will address the political context specific to Northern Ireland.

Since the emergence of the second wave, feminism and feminists have impressively permeated and transformed the Irish Republic's political mainstream, notably through the greater participation of some activists in mainstream political parties; challenges to the law through the courts (domestic and European); concerted campaigns to tackle discrimination in the workplace; the provision of rape crisis and domestic violence services; and family law and social policy reform. For some commentators, political mainstreaming is the main outcome of second-wave feminism in Ireland and is its dominant feature (Galligan, 1999). Several groups adopted an explicit mainstreaming strategy. For instance, the Women's Political Association (originally called the Women's Progressive Association in 1970 until it was re-named in 1973) was deliberately set up to promote the participation of women in the political mainstream. In several professions today, the growing contribution of women who have directly benefited from the earlier and ongoing feminist challenge to sexism and gender inequality in the workplace in particular is palpable. Although gender equality has not nearly been fully realised, the number of female professionals in sectors such as medicine, teaching, law, the universities and politics has evidently increased since the 1980s especially (see O'Connor, 1999).

Nonetheless, while this chapter focuses on mainstream political activism as an integral dynamic in the development, success and current professionalism of Irish feminism, feminist activism beyond the state and outside the institutional realm is not negated. Subsequent chapters will go on to demonstrate specifically how autonomous activism (in domains such as culture, literature, sexuality, socialist and other radical politics, and community development) are as important as the liberal mainstream is to the history of Irish feminism.[1]

Furthermore, we will also go on to consider how the international successes of the liberal feminist agenda are now being reviewed in a more critical light in Irish feminist studies – notably in academic theories which challenge its prioritising of the autonomous, self-contained individual over deconstruction of the differences which, in reality, underpin the category "woman" (such as class, race and ethnicity) and from activists who question the assumption of "shared" female interests that guide its political agenda (Gray, 1995).

Women's Rights and the Establishment of the Irish State

In comparative terms, the development of feminism in modern Ireland has been marked by the institutional development of the independent Irish nation-state, established in 1922. In the period before independence, the achievements of the first-wave of feminism in Ireland have been documented extensively in the field of women's history. However, the first evidence of individual feminist activism (Cullen and Luddy et al, 1995) and/or organisations and campaigns led by women dates to the 1830s, when women were involved in anti-slavery and other social and political campaigns in Ireland (see Luddy, 1997). Mary Cullen highlighted the impressive achievements of nineteenth century feminism in a pioneering article published in 1985 (Cullen, 1985). Significant advances were made in the areas of married women's control of their own property, education, employment, prostitution and participation in local government in that period.

Women's history has established the multifaceted and complex nature of first wave feminism in Ireland (for example, Cullen and Luddy, 1995; Luddy and Murphy, 1990; Cullen, 1985; O'Dowd and Valiulus, 1997). In relation to the first decades of the twentieth century, analysis has tended to focus on the vibrant relationship between feminism, nationalism and other social and political movements (including the labour movement and socialism, cultural nationalism, and unionism).

In the early decades of the twentieth century, the expanding women's movement was visibly divided over whether to campaign for the right to vote for a British parliament (suffrage) or to put the cause of Irish independence from Britain first (nationalist feminism) (see Ryan, 1996). Irish women were first granted the right to vote in 1918 prior to the establishment of the "Irish Free State" and the partitioning of "the six counties" of Northern Ireland in 1922.

A great deal of historical debate has also focused on how the state defined and circumscribed women's role in the new Irish Republic, in the aftermath of independence (see Clancy, 1990 and Valiulis, 1997). While women were extremely dynamic in nationalist and other political causes prior to independence, as political leaders they and the feminist cause were essentially marginalised by the elites that took over the new political establishment in the 1920s. The subsequent regulation of women's lives in this period of nation-building in the Republic of Ireland was reinforced by the dominant position of the Catholic Church via the state and society. For these reasons, feminists in Ireland have for the most part concentrated on maintaining opposition to church-state authority and control in the Irish political mainstream since independence.

The Cumann na nGaedhael government, the first government of the Irish Free State, introduced direct legislation that served to restrict and even undo some existing rights of women. It introduced legislation regarding women's access to employment and equal treatment; contraception; bar from jury service; illegitimacy; and marital separation and divorce. The social and political climate in this period discouraged women's involvement in public life in general, and institutional discrimination persisted for some decades. In 1935, for example, the government introduced restrictions on women's employment in certain industries. A new Constitution, written in close consultation with the Catholic hierarchy, was introduced by Eamon de Valera in 1937. Article 41 of the 1937 Constitution included a clause concerning women's life (as opposed to work) in the home:

> In particular the State recognises that by her life within the home, woman gives to the State a support without which the common good cannot be achieved. (Article 41.2.1)

> The State shall, therefore, endeavour to ensure that mothers shall not be obliged by economic necessity to engage in labour to the neglect of their duties in the home. (Article 41.2.2)

At all stages, women's groups objected to the battery of inequitable legislation introduced by successive Irish governments from the period of the foundation of the state up to the period when a second wave of feminism emerged. Contrary to the assumption that feminism retreated in the aftermath of independence, numerous campaigns were organised in the period from the foundation of the State until the 1970s. A considerably repressed but innovative women's movement survived in the 1920s and managed to sustain a network that incorporated various organisations in the post-independence decades, including: the IWWU, Cumann na mBan (until the 1930s), the Women's Prisoners Dependants League, the Women's Social and Progressive League, the Suffrage and Local Government Association, the Joint Committee of Women's Societies and Social Workers (formed in 1931) and the IHA, which was founded in the 1940s (see Tweedy, 1992; Beaumont, 1997; Lagerkvist, 1997).

The Women's Citizens (the continuation of the original Dublin Women's Suffrage Association founded in 1876) and the two women graduate associations of Trinity and the National University were continually active after independence (see Valiulis, 1997; Beaumont, 1997). During the 1920s and 1930s, especially, they campaigned on issues such as jury service for women, sex and marriage barriers in the civil service, and imposed limitations on women's employment. The National University Women's Graduates Association played a leading role in the campaign against the first draft of the 1937 Constitution and its treatment of women. The Joint Committee of Women's Societies also opposed various articles of the Constitution, along with the IWWU, the Women's Social and Progressive League and the Standing Committee on Legislation Affecting Women (Clancy, 1990: 231).

By the 1970s feminist activists concentrated much of their energy on reforming the series of discriminatory laws that had been progressively introduced since the 1920s. However, political mainstreaming had already been a key strategy of Irish feminist activists for several decades. The antecedents of liberal feminism are therefore evident in groups that were in existence some decades before the second wave became apparent. Most of the groups that established the *ad hoc* committee on women's rights in 1968, which successfully led to the First National Commission on the Status of Women and to the setting up of the Council for the Status of Women, were long established and not newly formed radical feminist groups. Some groups were even the offspring of groups that had mobilised suffrage campaigns during the first wave, such as the IHA (see Connolly, 2003b).

Any analysis of the mainstreaming of feminism that occurred in Ireland in the last three decades of the twentieth century must therefore take into account the preceding activities and campaigns of these pioneering women's organisations and the liberal feminist legacy they established in the early decades of that century.

The Equality Agenda

The 1950s in Ireland was a decade dominated by economic stagnation, poverty and large-scale emigration. However, by the 1960s economic modernisation became the focus of successive governments, which generated social unrest and new opportunities for change. Moreover, as a consequence of this target, the dominant position of the Catholic Church vis-à-vis the Irish State was visibly beginning to wane, to at least some degree. The women's movement emerged in this period with the key aims of encouraging Irish women to both reduce the number of children they were having and enter the workforce in increasing numbers.

The rapid emergence of a second wave of feminism was facilitated by the more open and liberal climate developing in Irish society at that time. As demonstrated in Chapter 1, in 1970 the First Commission on the Status of Women was established by the Government.

EQUALITY OF OPPORTUNITY IN THE PUBLIC SECTOR

REPORT OF A SEMINAR
DUBLIN NOVEMBER 1981

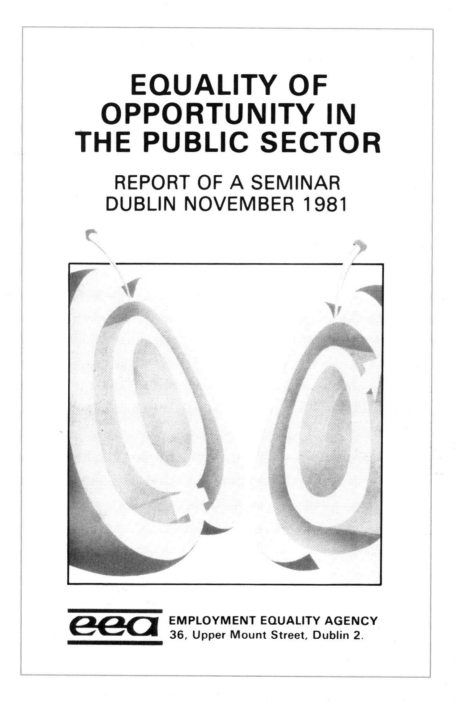

eea **EMPLOYMENT EQUALITY AGENCY**
36, Upper Mount Street, Dublin 2.

Employment Equality Agency publication, "Equality of Opportunity in the Public Sector, Report of a Seminar in Dublin", November 1981

Employment Equality Agency publications

The issue of access to employment and equal pay dominated the report.[2] The Commission, chaired by Thekla Beere, published an interim report on equal pay in 1971 and presented its extensive findings and full report to the Government in May 1972.[3] The Commission's final report formed an invaluable basis for discussion and policy formation. The *ad hoc* committee on women's rights decided to set up the Council for the Status of Women (which later changed its name to the National Women's Council) in 1973 to monitor the implementation of the recommendations of the Report of the First Commission on the Status of Women. The Commission's report provided the institutional framework for a series of legal changes regarding the status of women in Ireland (see Chapter 1).

In stark contrast to the limited success of feminist campaigns since independence, significant and rapid progress was made in this arena throughout the 1970s. In 1973, the ban on married women working in the civil service, local authorities and health boards was removed. The provision of allowances for deserted wives, unmarried mothers and prisoners wives were implemented in the Social Welfare Act 1974, a significant development in the treatment of women with children living in non-marital circumstances in Irish social policy. In addition, the courts became a focus of specific feminist campaigns. In 1974, Máirín de Burca and Mary Anderson (both were members of the Irish Women's Liberation Movement) took a case to the Supreme Court, which deemed unconstitutional the Juries Act 1927, which had effectively banned women from sitting on juries.

Ireland's entry into the EEC in 1973 facilitated other campaigns opposing the treatment of women by the Irish State. An EEC Directive, signed on 10 February 1975, required member states to eliminate all discrimination on grounds of sex with regard to all aspects and conditions of remuneration. In accordance with this, Ireland's Anti-Discrimination (Pay) Act came into operation in December 1975. The Act established the right of men and women to equal pay if they are employed in like work by the same (or an associated) employer. Women active in the trade unions, however, highlighted several problems in implementing the Act along with Irishwomen United, which had adopted the ICTU "Working Women's Charter".

Working Women's Charter

PREPARED BY ITGWU IN 1975 AND ADOPTED BY THE IRISH CONGRESS OF TRADE UNIONS IN 1976

"The Irish Congress of Trade Unions recognises and demands the right of everyone, irrespective of race, ethnic origin, creed, political opinion, age, sex or marital status to have the means to pursue their economic independence and to full participation in the social, cultural and political life of the community, in conditions of freedom, dignity and equal opportunity.

The ICTU will therefore campaign for the following Charter of Rights for women and appeals to all trade unions to do their utmost to further the principles set out in this Charter—

Complete Equality of Opportunity and Access to all levels right through the Educational System.

Complete Equality of Access to Employment. All efforts should be made to eliminate any discrimination based on sex or marital status regarding access to employment.

Equality of Basic Pay, Bonuses and Fringe Benefits. There should be a national minimum income to alleviate the real problem of low pay.

Access to all Apprenticeships and all Vocational Training and Guidance and a programme of positive encouragement for the involvement of women in training should be introduced.

Special measures to give Refresher and Retraining Courses for all women who wish to re-enter the labour force.

Equal Promotional Opportunities for both men and women in all fields and under the same conditions.

Working Conditions to be, without deterioration of previous conditions, the same for all workers. Special protective legislation for pregnant women where necessary.

Feminist campaigners active in politics: (from left) Mary Robinson, Monica Barnes, Gemma Hussey and Sylvia Meehan (c. 1975) (BL/F/AP/1139, Attic Press Archive)

Postcard illustrating International Women's Year, 1975 (BL/F/AP/1590, Attic Press Archive)

Protest during Taoiseach Charles Haughey's speech, opening the Women's Forum in the RDS, 1975 (BL/F/AP/113/18, Attic Press Archive)

Equality of Treatment with regard to Sick Pay and the same Pension Conditions for every worker, irrespective of sex.

26 Weeks paid Maternity Leave on Full Pay. No dismissal during pregnancy or maternity leave. The working woman should be allowed to prolong her maternity leave for up to one year, and the rights linked to her employment should not be forfeited, particularly as far as employment security, promotional prospects, pensions and other rights are concerned.

Provision for State controlled Creches, Day Nurseries and Nursery Schools with adequately trained personnel. Provision of after-school and holiday care facilities and school meals.

Comprehensive Family-Planning Services should be freely available and easily accessible to all. All necessary measures should be adopted to ensure that all persons have access to the necessary information, education, and means to exercise their basic right to decide freely and responsibly on the number and spacing of their children.

The Elimination of all Discrimination against women in the field of Social Security.

All appropriate measures should be taken to ensure to women Equal Rights with men in the field of Civil and Criminal Law."

[Source: Equality for Women, ITGWU Discussion Paper presented to the Annual Delegate Conference (1980: 57–58).[4]]

The fact that working women were segregated in the lowest-paid industries and employment sectors was also central to several campaigns, in addition to the issues of maternity leave, childcare provision and access to contraception. The vast majority of women in Ireland dropped out of the workforce either upon marriage or after having children in the 1970s. In general, housework, maternity, childcare and the caring of other dependants (such as the elderly and disabled) were considered the full-time, unpaid occupation of women and the dominant ideology was that regardless of personal choice, married women were not expected or encouraged to participate in the labour force. Feminists right across the radical and liberal ideological spectrum of the women's movement united on this question and challenged these traditional stereotypes. Those on the left and in the trade unions, in particular, aimed to develop the conditions in which a majority of women in Ireland could at least choose to combine motherhood and employment, regardless of their social class and marital status.[5]

In the mid-1970s, Ireland's first employment equality legislation was passed. The Anti-Discrimination (Pay) Act 1974 was followed by the Employment Equality Act in July 1977. In October 1977, the Employment Equality Agency was established. These acts and initiatives were intended to eliminate sex discrimination in employment and, despite their limitations in practice, they marked significant change in attitude to women and work in Ireland. When 1975 was designated International Women's Year, political attention was given to the principle of equality in Ireland. However, the following year the government tried to renege its commitment to introduce equal pay in the public service and a vigorous campaign was mounted by trade unions and women's organisations. A petition was organised and 10,000 signatures were collected. Ultimately, the government was obliged to back down and honour its commitment. The naive assertion that the Irish state, as a matter of course, improved the status of women in Ireland in the 1970s is therefore rather simplistic. Strategic campaigns to compel the state to honour the conditions of EEC membership were essential to ensure key legislative and political changes were introduced.

Along with the removal of the "marriage bar" from the public service, other progress included the elimination of discrimination against single women in relation to social welfare payments and important changes were introduced in the arena of family law (such as the establishment of the state's duty to provide free legal aid in family law cases and changes in the tax treatment of married couples).[6] In the 1980s, developments in relation to marital separation and reproductive rights also materialised.[7] The changing nature of Irish family life in the latter decades of the twentieth century is now widely documented (Fahey 1995; Kennedy, 1986; Kennedy, 2001). In tandem with the wider project of economic modernisation, concerted feminist campaigns encouraged women to reduce their childbearing by using contraception, to participate in the professions in greater numbers and to assert their economic independence in marriage. The transformation that has occurred in family life in Irish society has been to a large extent stimulated by the fundamental changes that have occurred in Irish women's lives.

Ireland's entry into the EEC on 1 January 1973 provided the women's movement with political currency in areas that complemented the state's modernisation project. EEC Directives were a key resource in numerous campaigns for equality legislation in Ireland. However, it is important to recognise that the Irish state did not merely implement substantive change as an inevitable consequence of EU membership. In most cases, feminist and other liberal campaigns had to push the State to act on EU directives. Recourse to the European Courts has been a necessary strategy in some instances.

In 1993, the Government appointed a Second Commission on the Status of Women. The Commission's Final Report acknowledged both the achievements and the limitations of the equality agenda in Ireland:

> The principle of equal treatment to date in the European Community has been directed to the "working population." Equality for women in spheres other than work does not have any underpinning in the Constitution, the basic law of our country. The struggle to implement equality between women and men even in the context of work required constant recourse to the European Court of Justice and the issuing of directives from the Council. (Report of the Second Commission on the Status of Women, 1993: 26)

An ESRI report, based on 1997 data, indicated that women in Ireland earned approximately 15 per cent less than men (Gilvarry, 2002). The comparison was against 1987 data, when the differential was 20 per cent. Ireland's admission to the European Economic Community in 1972 meant it was obligated to pay men and women equally. This requirement was given legislative effect by the provisions of the Anti-Discrimination (Pay) Act of 1974, which along with the Employment Equality Act 1977 has now been replaced by the Employment Equality Act 1998. If men and women are doing similar work but are being paid differently, the burden is on the employer to demonstrate some reason other than their sex as to why they are not receiving the same pay. In order to succeed in an equal pay claim, however, the complainant must show that he or she is earning less than a comparable man or woman.

Recent cases in this area also demonstrate the absolute requirement to treat all applicants for a job equally, and that each step in the recruitment process is transparent. Of the 202 cases taken under the Employment Equality Legislation in the year 2000, 120 were initiated on grounds of gender discrimination with particular reference to pregnancy discrimination, equal pay and sexual harassment. The prominent issues in those cases related to working conditions and access to promotion. Cases such as *Grady v. ICC* and *Allen v. the Sunday Independent* also highlighted the need for companies to have in place clear guidelines and policies in regard to bullying and sexual harassment. The Health and Safety Authority and the Equality Authority have both recently issued guidelines for the preparation of procedures to include a complaints procedure to deal with bullying and harassment in the workplace.

After over three decades of activism in the arena of employment equality, the civil procedures now open to employees who feel they have been bullied or harassed are vast. In the first instance an employee might consider constructive dismissal and make an application to the Employment Appeals Tribunal. The employee could also choose to stay employed and pursue a claim within the equality legislation. Finally, if the employee is so traumatised as to be suffering from a mental injury, the employee can maintain a civil claim to the High Court for damages. None of these legal avenues are mutually exclusive. In fact, where an employee claims constructive dismissal, it is usual that he/she would also initiate proceedings in the High Court for damages for personal injury. An employee can also take a criminal prosecution against his/her employer.

The creation and implementation of bullying and harassment policies are important first steps towards creating a structure in a workplace that stamps out discrimination. Gilvarry (2002) writes: "Employers also need to be open to implementing family friendly policies, endorsing diversity, and showing a real commitment to values which leave no room for discrimination. Such values are not just driven by legal risk management but should have the improvement of culture and ethos at their core."

Family Law

By the early 1980s, change was also manifest in the arena of family law reform.[8] Key pieces of legislation include:

The Married Women Status Act 1957 gave a woman separate rights to property and allowed her formal contractual capacity.

The Guardianship of Infants Act 1964 gave a woman legal rights to her own children by giving parents the right to joint guardianship of their children, and allowed courts to make decisions on custody and access.

The Succession Act 1965 reformed the law relating to the estates of people who had died, especially the administration and distribution of property where there is no will. It specified the shares of spouses and children on intestacy.

The Marriages Act 1972 raised the minimum marriage age to 16 for boys and girls.

The Maintenance Orders Act 1974 allowed the reciprocal enforcement of maintenance orders between the Republic of Ireland, Northern Ireland, England and Wales, and Scotland.

The Family Law (Maintenance of Spouses and Children) Act 1976 provided for periodical payments by one spouse to another in cases of failure to provide reasonable maintenance, with deductions of earnings at source and barring orders. The Act placed a legal obligation on a husband to provide financially for this wife and family and also contained a provision which enabled a woman to take out an order barring a violent husband from the family home.

The Family Home Protection Act 1976 protected the family home and required prior written consent of both spouses for sale of family home or chattels. The Act meant that the sale of a family home, its furniture and fittings, could no longer be made without a wife's consent.

Women could claim children's allowance in their own name, they could apply to be taxed separately, and working wives received the same personal tax allowance as their husbands.

Separated, deserted and single mothers qualified for a social welfare allowance in 1974.

Separated wives and mothers were recognised as local authority tenants in their own right.

Campaigns to legalise divorce first surfaced in Ireland in the 1980s.[9] Divorce remained banned in Irish law until it was passed in a consitutional referendum held in 1995, with the legislation following in 1997.

A national pressure group, the Divorce Action Group (DAG), was launched on 15 April 1980 (Duncan, 1982). DAG was formed following a public meeting in Liberty Hall on 23 January 1980. This meeting was sponsored jointly by a group, mostly of women, from the Coolock area of Dublin and by the Irish Council of Civil Liberties. The objectives of DAG were the abolition of the constitutional ban on divorce and the introduction of legislation allowing for divorce. By 1982, DAG had branches in several parts of the country, including Cork, Dundalk and Drogheda, and it had a number of affiliated organisations, including AIM (the group that was formed originally by feminist activists), the Irish Association of Social Workers and Gingerbread. Duncan wrote (1982: 86):

> DAG's campaign has proceeded on a number of fronts. It has lobbied public representatives. It has organised and participated in public meetings around the country. The largest was one held in the Mansion House, Dublin, on 4 February 1981, attended by an estimated 800 persons.

The organisation was particularly critical of the lack of reliable data on the scale of marital breakdown in Irish society. For instance, the Central Statistics Office listed within the category "married" those persons who in the 1979 census returned themselves as other. DAG unsuccessfully campaigned to have the additional category "separated" included in the 1981 census, but the category was included in the 1986 census for the first time.

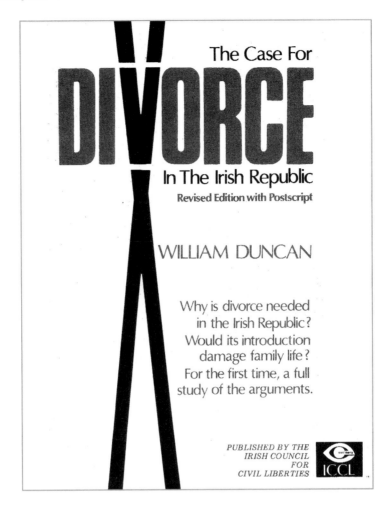

ICCL Publication, *The Case For Divorce in the Irish Republic* (Duncan, 1982)

Introduction of divorce was rejected by the Irish electorate in a referendum held in 1986, following a protracted campaign that involved the direct intervention of the Catholic Church in the campaign. The reasons why the electorate rejected divorce have been widely debated. Obviously the direct intervention of the Church in the campaign combined with political uncertainty about issues concerning property rights and inheritance were critical factors in the final outcome.

Important legislation was subsequently introduced in the aftermath of the referendum, however, which liberalised the laws dealing with marital breakdown and separation in Ireland. In 1989 the Judicial Separation Act was introduced, which dealt with division of property, maintenance and issues related to child custody. While it was now possible to obtain a legal separation, this Act did not grant Irish citizens the right to divorce or remarry. In 1987, the Status of Children Act removed the differential treatment of "illegitimate children" in Irish law and protection for the rights for children born outside marriage was introduced.

Divorce was later introduced in Ireland following the referendum of 1995, and it is clear that both the referendum of 1986 and the Judicial Separation Act had created the necessary basis for later change in the law and helped transform the public perception of marital breakdown.

Irish Family Law since the 1980s

Courts Act 1981: widened the jurisdiction in family law matters.

Family Law Act 1981: abolished actions for enticement of spouse and breach of promise to marry. Allowed the courts to decide disputes over gifts after broken engagements.

Family Law (Protection of Spouses and Children) Act 1981: gave the Circuit and District Courts power to grant barring and protection orders. (Repealed by Domestic Violence Act 1996.)

Domicile and Recognition of Foreign Divorces Act 1986: confirmed independent domiciles of wives, recognised divorces granted where either spouse was domiciled.

Status of Children Act 1987: abolished status of illegitimacy and amended law on maintenance and succession for non-marital children. Allowed unmarried fathers to apply for guardianship of their children. Provided for blood tests to establish paternity.

Family Law Act 1988: abolished actions for the restitution of conjugal rights.

Children Act 1989: gave health boards powers to care for children.

Judicial Separation and Family Law Reform Act 1989: amended the grounds for judicial separation, assisted reconciliation between estranged spouses and provided for ancillary orders, such as maintenance, property adjustment and custody of children.

Childcare Act 1991: gave powers to health boards to care for children who were ill-treated, neglected or sexually abused.

Child Abduction and Enforcement of Custody Orders Act 1991: dealt with wrongful retention of children. Implemented the Hague Convention 1980 and the Luxembourg Convention 1980.

Maintenance Act 1994: simplified procedures for recovering maintenance debts from other countries.

Family Law Act 1995: raised the minimum age for marriage to 18 and required three months' written notice to local registrar; abolished petitions for jactitation of marriage (falsely claiming to be married to someone); provided for declarations of marital status and for ancillary orders after judicial separation or foreign divorce.

Domestic Violence Act 1996: extended safety, barring and protection orders to non-spouses; gave health boards powers to apply for orders; allowed arrest without warrant for breach.

Family Law (Divorce) Act 1996: allowed divorce and remarriage, with all ancillary orders.

Children Act 1997: recognised natural fathers as guardians; allowed children's views to be considered in guardianship, access and custody matters; allowed parents to have joint custody.

Family Law (Miscellaneous Provisions) Act 1997: amended the law in relation to notification of intention to marry, barring orders, powers of attorney and distribution of disclaimed estates.

European Council Regulation 1347/2000 allowed – subject to certain conditions – the mutual recognition in all EU Member States (except Denmark) of court orders relating to divorce, legal separation, nullity or child custody.

Children Act 2001: authorised courts to order health boards to convene a family welfare conference where a child requires special care or protection. The health board can apply for a care order or supervision order if necessary.

Domestic Violence (Amendment) Act 2002: amended the Domestic Violence Act to provide eight-day limit for *ex parte* interim barring orders, changed grounds on which *ex parte* orders could be granted.

The changing situation of women in family life has created a social and political controversy in contemporary debate that has mobilised the Catholic right in Ireland. A key myth promoted by organised advocates of traditional values is that "feminists" in Ireland prioritised the promotion of women in the workforce to the complete neglect of women's rights in the home. However, greater economic recognition of the work women carry out in the home (in the case of both stay-at-home and working mothers) has in fact been the subject of several campaigns, such as Wages for Housework in the 1970s and in the 1990s, the National Women's Council childcare campaign (which incorporated childcare services for stay at home mothers). While women's right to participate in the workforce is key to second-wave feminism, countless sources reveal vibrant debates concerning the protection of women who choose to stay in the home.

In general, there is now widespread agreement that there is a significant shift away from the traditional division of labour in the household, in which authority and decision-making rested primarily with the father/male head of household and emotional support and nurturance with the mother. Yet, while a significant degree of change has occurred in how personal relationships are negotiated between men and women in the household, several studies suggest that in the case of domestic labour women still have primary responsibility. For the ever-increasing number of women with children who work both in and outside the home in Ireland today, this "double burden" is especially apparent.

Legal developments regarding child custody and single parenting have also created controversy in public debate, not least from some organised groups of single and separated fathers. One third of all births now take place outside of marriage in Ireland and the incidence of marital breakdown and single-parenthood has increased substantially in recent decades. Feminists have become the enemy of some men's rights campaigners, some of whom believe that it is feminism that caused their partners to (have both the right and inclination to) separate from them. In this hypothesis, it is sometimes also assumed that the law has been infiltrated by feminists who are trying to separate men from their children. The fact that women are generally granted more custody than men in the family law courts is considered symptomatic of this "conspiracy."

In a society that has experienced such recent and radical change in both family life and in the institutional framework governing women's lives, such controversy is not surprising. Neither is it surprising that the now established challenge to traditional male authority and power in family life is perceived as a threat by some sections of society. Yet, several other men's rights campaigns have also emerged in Ireland that are associating with the existing equality agenda in family law reform. Many groups are using the achievements of feminism so far as a basis to create more egalitarian family structures in general. Academic feminism and social policy practitioners have been studying, for some decades now, ways of developing more egalitarian approaches to childcare and parenting among men and women in the case of single parenthood and marital separation. Father's-rights activists are therefore faced with a paradox. While many men do want more access to their children after separation or relationship breakdown than the courts grant, why some men disengage from their children and fail to provide financial assistance following a separation must also be understood. This is therefore a debate that requires a more complex interpretation in Irish public discourse.

The Final Report of the National Commission on the Family (1998: 79) recommended that Article 41.2.3 of the Constitution be amended, to read:

> The State recognises that home and family life gives a support to society without which the common good cannot be achieved. The State shall endeavour to support persons caring for others within the home.

It is the Commission's stated view that the revised wording proposed is more in tune with developments in family life today and provides for recognition of the contribution within the home of both men and women in caring for children and other family members. The original Article 41.2.2 of the 1937 Constitution remains intact, however. Social values and changing attitudes in Irish society recognise at least in principle, the right of women to participate in all aspects of life outside the home even if the Constitution has not yet adapted.

Violence and Sexual Assault

The fact that it was Irish feminism that ultimately shattered the traditional view of the idyllic Irish family, by exposing the reality that the family can also be a dangerous place to be, has also produced inevitable controversy. Feminism has worked relentlessly on this question to protect women in the home and in family life. Since the 1970s, feminist theory has been extremely influential in highlighting the scale of both physical and sexual violence. Until the recent past, both the law in Ireland and the Catholic Church tended to regard domestic violence as a private matter to be dealt with within the private sphere of the family, and this invisibility was mirrored in academic writing and research and in other areas such as the law and policing. In this area in particular, Irish feminists have struggled for decades to achieve social and political recognition for the nature and extent of physical, psychological and sexual violence against women and children in society. In the process, important services were established.[10]

Research on domestic violence has grown at a very rapid rate in the last three decades. McWilliam's and McKiernan's (1993) study of domestic violence in Northern Ireland provides a useful framework and review of data. In Britain and Ireland the key source of data has been police statistics and court records. In the UK, research has suggested that violence against women in the home occurs somewhere between every one in four and one in ten relationships. Homicide figures are frequently used to highlight the seriousness of domestic violence in contemporary societies. In Britain, on average 40% of all female murders are committed by husbands and in the US approximately half of women murdered are killed by a current or former male partner. In Sweden, where it is generally believed that equality between men and women has advanced further than most other Western industrialised countries, police statistics (the only source of "official" data) for 1989 showed that 39 women were battered daily. Research in the US shows that women have been killed because they left a violent relationship and demonstrates that often women remain in a violent relationship because of the husbands' or partners' threats of murder if they leave.

McWilliams and McKiernan (1993) illustrate how the literature on the causes of domestic violence revolves around key schools of thought. Within the individual pathology approach – sometimes called the "blame the victims" (perpetrator and receiver of violence) approach – either or both partners are described as neu-

Women Against Violence Against Women, a march by thousands of women through the centre of Dublin, 13 October 1978 (BL/F/AP/1330, Attic Press Archive) (photo: Derek Speirs)[11]

Women Against Violence Against Women march Dublin, 13 October 1978 (photo: Derek Speirs)

rotic or mentally ill. Gayford (1975), for example, suggested in his study that women can provoke the use of violent behaviour towards them and applied derogatory stereotypes to female victims. This approach also took the view that there are certain weaknesses characteristic of men who assault their wives, one of which is susceptibility to alcohol or drug abuse.

Alcohol apart, another popular theory within this approach is that violence is transmitted from one generation to the next, establishing a cycle of violence. According to this theory, people who witness violence or were abused themselves become socialised into seeing violence as a way of life. Others have argued that witnessing violence as a child produces and condones aggressive forms of behaviour in men while producing a passive response in women or causing women to accept violent partners. Research has shown, however, that the process by which violence is transferred from one generation to the next is more complex than simple modelling of behaviour. The explanatory power of the cycle-of-violence thesis must be seen as only partial and should be treated in the same way as the explanation regarding excessive use of alcohol – as a frequent contributing factor but not as a sole or primary cause.

Social structural explanations emphasise domestic violence as a response to social factors. Typically this perspective argues that stress in the family results from lack of resources, such as low income and bad housing, and can precipitate violence. For example, some commentators have suggested that violence can enable working-class men to compensate for their low-status jobs. Middle-class

Women Against Violence Against Women picket Rainbow's End, Dublin, 3 April 1982 (photo: Derek Speirs)

men who perceive a threat to their status of the "successful breadwinner" due to increasing participation of women in the workplace may also respond by using violence.

Social structural theories are also used to explain why women generally return to an abusive relationship. An abused woman with few resources or access to employment may perceive her alternatives inside the marriage as being more rewarding and less costly than alternatives outside (e.g. she has no other home or income for her and her children to live on if she is not engaged in the workforce).[12] In such cases the woman's pressing economic needs take precedence over her physical and emotional needs to be free from abuse and she returns to the abusive situation. Rather than the individual's pathology being analysed, this approach shows that the woman's decision-making process about leaving or returning is a complex one involving economic and social factors. Moreover, it shifts the problem from just being a personal and psychological one to being a social one.

All of these theories have, of course, inherent problems and limitations. The reasons why violence in the home occurs are always complex. Feminist theory and activism challenged the dominant explanations for the high incidence of violence in the home in the 1970s and created an additional perspective based on an understanding of gender inequality.

Women protesting outside the Dáil against the Bill on rape (BL/F/AP/1498, Attic Press Archive)

Women's Aid Dublin was founded in May 1974 by a voluntary group of women and men as a community response to the problem of violence against women in the home. Chiswick Women's Aid had opened in London in 1971. Contact with Chiswick showed that substantial numbers of Irish women and children were making their way there in the absence of a refuge service in Ireland. In July 1974, the first Irish refuge opened in Harcourt Street, Dublin. The house was loaned by a Dublin businessman and was staffed by voluntary labour. On July 24 the first family moved in.

Women's Aid (1981: 3), in the introduction to its "Family Violence" booklet stated in 1981:

> In the five and a half years since, over two thousand women have sought and been given refuge, with over fifteen thousand children ranging from babes in arms to teenage boys and girls. The majority of women who come return to their husbands and a minority of these will make a successful fresh start together. However, most women return home because they have no option. They are financially dependent, homeless and burdened with children. Some of these women return to Women's Aid many times.

Up until the early 1970s the family law statutes in Ireland dated from the Victorian period, when women were afforded little legal recognition within marriage in general. Domestic violence was a completely hidden crime – few spoke about it, from the women who experienced it, to the public and to political representatives. If a woman was subjected to domestic violence, in effect there was nowhere to go and no laws to protect her. Women's Aid was set up as a service provider and it concentrated all its energies on providing a badly needed safe space

Women Against Violence Against Women march, Dublin, 13 October 1978 (BL/F/AP 883/20, Attic Press Archive)

VIOLENCE — SOLVING THE PROBLEM

The first Irish conference on Violence Against Women was held in Galway May 20-21st. The main areas of discussion were rape, women battering and psychological violence. The following are the highlights of the weekend.

Rape

It was generally agreed that rape is an aspect of the overall oppression of women in this society. The usual image of a rapist as a psychopath was rejected but there was some disagreement on the statement that all men are potential rapists. However, it was agreed that all women, with without regard to age, are potential rape victims and that this fact has tremendous effects on the way we live our lives. As women we are expected to exercise continual censorship on ourselves: in the way we dress where we go, what time we are out, who we are with. In other words, we live in a totally different world from men, a far more restricted one. This is particularly the case for thos those of us who live alone.

If we fail to exercise this continual censorship, we are told that we "asked for it" if we are attacked. This, we felt, is an aspect of the image of woman in th this society as passive and without independent sexuality. Women are supposed to restrain the supposedly "uncontrollable" sexual urges of men. And if we fail to, then again the results are said to be our fault. These false images of men as aggressive and hypersexual, women as passive and asexual are in turn used to mould boys and girls into the expected stereotypes.

As well as discussing rape from a theoretical point of view and from personal experience, we spent much of our workshops deciding how we could deal with this aspect of our oppression.

Methods we discussed included: having a positive attidue that we can deal with situations; learning methods of self-defence; holding Reclaim-the-Night marches such as women have done in England and elsewhere; attacking images in the media, especially in advertising, which exploit women as consumer objects; going in groups into areas/places which are dangerous for individual women. But the most definite decisions emerged from discussions of the work and the experiences of the Rape Crisis Centre Group in Dublin. Also, in the context of groups operating outside Dublin, a letter we had received from a Dundalk Women's Group was of great benefit.

The Dundalk women don't have the resources to set up a Rape Crisis Centre so they have decided to be available, on a rota basis, to help individual raped/battered women in the town by being with them when the they make statements to the Gardai, etc. Limerick and Galway women felt that this idea was particularly useful to them.

The Rape Crisis Centre Group described the ideas which they have developed on counselling raped women and run running a centre. They also promised to organise a weekend seminar on these matters when the groups in Galway and Limerick feel ready to begin work on rape.

Besides the workshop discussions on rape, Kate Crowley, from the Campaign Against Rape, gave a talk to the conference on the law in relation to rape. Kate's suggestions were that:
a) the victim's statement be treated as irrebuttable unless serious doubt can be cast on it (as happens in some civil actions)
b) the victim have the right to choose her own prosecution (paid for by the state) and that she and her prosecution counsel conduct the case. This would mean that she could consult with her lawyer: in such a subjective case this could only be to the advantage of the victim.

Woman Battering

In the area of woman-battering, the Galway Conference was also of great significance because it was the first time that representatives from all the existing refuges for battered women in Ireland, met together. Women who are involved in the efforts to establish a refuge in Galway were also there.

In a talk to the conference, Joan Neary, information officer for the National Women's Aid Federation in Britain, described how that Federation operates. She said that any Hostel which joins the Federation (and there are now 130 of them) must accept their basic philosophy, which is that women-battering is not just an individual problem of a particularl family but it is symptomatic of the whole role of women in society.

This perspective means that Hostels in the Federation place great emphasis on the development of constructive alternatives, based on the idea of self-help. The Hostels are not seen merely as emergency accomodation but as the beginning of a new way of life. They are run by the women who live in them, not by any full-

7

Article on violence in *Wicca* 12 (c. 1979–80) (BL/F/AP/1498, Attic Press Archive)

the dates and times are
unconfirmed.

conference on violence —

Arising out of the January National Women's Conference held at Trinity College, Dublin, a special conference on women and violence will be held in Galway on the weekend of May 19-21. Topics to be discussed will include the areas of battering, rape, etc., attitudes towards violence against women (the media, legal and medical attitudes, etc.) and, most important, discussuions will be held on what can be done. The conference is intended to be action-oriented; for example, the establishment of rape crisis centres around the country will be decided. Any one wishing to attend should contact:

Eva O'Donovan
Conference Planning Collective
42 Oaklands, Galway

Galway conference on violence, advertised in *Wicca* (BL/F/AP/1, Attic Press Archive)

for women and children who were frightened, often in danger, and with nobody else to turn to. Gradually, refuges were established in other locations around the country, staffed and funded by voluntary collectives.

In the 1980s greater rationalisation of the refuge service began and the Irish state began to fund refuges, which gave Women's Aid leaders the time and space to become advocates for political reform. In the 1980s the state began to provide funding and professional staff for the Dublin refuge service, and by 1985, 12 groups located in the main urban centres in the country were receiving a modest amount of financial support from the State. Women's Aid began to split its energies between providing services for battered women and their children, and working towards political change. The provision of services to women remained the core of the organisation's work, however. Service provision informed and gave the organisation the front-line expertise which it used to complement its professional research, lobbying and campaigning work. The organisation today continues to provide services directly to women as well as campaigning for political and legal reform.

Prior to 1976, women seeking protection from her husband's violence could only bring charges under Victorian law, the Offences Against the Person Act 1861. In 1976, barring orders were introduced for the first time under the Family Law (Maintenance of Spouses and Children) Act 1976. A violent husband was prevented from entering the house for three months. Often there was very ineffective implementation of the law – where a husband breached it, the wife had to go to court again; in the meantime she had no protection. The Family (Protection of Spouses and Children) Act 1981 introduced the right to a protection order. A protection order was a court order restraining a man from abusing/threatening his wife during the interim period before a barring order was obtained. The situation was improved around barring orders, with their duration increasing from three to 12 months. It became a criminal offence to breach a barring order and police were given power of arrest without a warrant. At same time, gardaí were instructed to overcome traditional reticence about becoming involved in rows between husbands and wives.

Legal Developments in the 1980s and 1990s

1986

Funding of a common research project between Women's Aid, Dublin and the Boys and Girls Welfare Society, Cheshire, Northern Ireland and Women's Aid, Belfast was provided to conduct a survey of attitudes towards violence in the family.

1991

Women's Aid began seeking reforms in three major areas:

*   police be given powers of arrest when called to domestic violence disputes;

*   cohabitees to be included; and

*   improvement in the legal aid scheme.

Also, in 1991, Women's Aid begin training garda recruits on how to respond to domestic violence situations.

1993

Research by Women's Aid and St James's Hospital was conducted. This was one of the first studies to look at the identification of and response to women who attend accident and emergency departments as a result of domestic-violence injuries. This research showed the nature of the violence inflicted (attempted strangulation, sexual assault, burns/scalds, loss of consciousness and fractures); the fact that many women were prevented from seeking medical attention for some time by the abuser; and that for many women, the injury which brought them to the hospital was not an isolated incident, but part of a long history of domestic violence.

The Domestic Violence and Sexual Assault Investigation Unit of the Garda Síochána was set up.

1994

The gardaí introduced the Garda Síochána Policy on Domestic Violence Intervention.

"Silent No More" was published by Women's Aid. The research documented the experience and support needs of women who have left abusive relationships.

1995

Women's Aid published "Making the Links", the first major Irish research into the prevalence and nature of domestic violence. It showed that almost one in five (18%) women had experienced abuse by a current or former partner. It also showed that the main two reasons why women did not leave violent situations were economic dependence and having nowhere else to go. Of the women who had experienced violence, 64% said their children had witnessed it.

Women's Aid's extensive "Flowers, Chocolates and Multiple Bruising" advertising campaign.

1996

The Domestic Violence Act 1996 strengthened the powers of arrest of police authorities in domestic violence incidents.

The law was extended to give cohabitees protection from violent partner and parents protection from violent children over 18.

Safety orders were available as an alternative to barring orders.

Health boards were provided with powers to apply for protection order, on behalf of adult/child victims of domestic violence.

WOMEN
in
IRELAND :

'Fighting the Backlash......

Defending the Gains.'

The enclosed information was compiled and written by an ad hoc group of women active in women's issues in the twenty-six counties of Ireland. The articles reflect the areas of involvement of the writers and are not a comprehensive or complete account of the present situation for Irish women. The areas covered are · Women Prisoners in Armagh Jail; Women in Education; Women and Employment; Women on Trial — the Joanne Hayes Case; Violence Against Women; Divorce; Women in Rural Ireland; Women Strikers at Dunnes Stores. Due to lack of resources, there are many gaps, such as Reproductive Rights, Sexuality, Discrimination in the Social Welfare Code and Training etc., but it was felt that some information is better than none and will supplement other existing material on the position of women in Ireland today.

The ad hoc group of women activists initially came together to organise the 1984 Irish Womens Conference, which was attended by over 600 women from all over the country and from all walks of life. The issues included in this document were among those raised at the conference.

June 1985

The movement's agenda, 1985 (BL/F/AP/1482/6, Attic Press Archive)

Safety order could last for up to five years.

Barring order could last for up to three years.

1999

Women's Aid publish "Safety and Sanctions," based on research into the monitoring of the Domestic Violence Act 1996. The research showed that women accessing the legal system experience high levels of violence. The grounds cited in 50–60% of civil applications involved physical violence. The grounds included long histories of repeated violence, physical injury, threats to kill and violence during pregnancy. The sanctions for abusers were found to be limited and ineffective, with only an average of 3% of offenders receiving a sentence when breaching a court order.

Source: Women's Aid

Irish feminists have worked to an equivalent extent in the arena of sexual violence. The first Irish Rape Crisis Centre was set up in 1977 in Dublin. Issues addressed by Irish Rape Crisis Centres today include deconstructing the range of myths and attitudes about rape and sexual abuse, which feminists discovered were deeply embedded in Irish culture through rape crisis work in the 1970s.[13] Rape, as a crime, was and is notoriously underreported (Fennell, 1993). In addition, the fact that so few reported rape cases result in conviction has been the focus of several campaigns to reform the legal system. Rape and violence were pivotal questions for Irish feminists from the 1970s onwards, primarily through the provision of services and campaigns (through women's refuge, rape crisis services and anti-pornography campaigning).

By the end of the 1980s, there was a tremendous advancement of related agencies for women, including the Well Woman Centre, Women's Aid, and the Rape Crisis Centre.[14] Many of these groups were set up or run by women who had originally come to feminism through groups like the CSW, the IWLM and IWU. Others were part of a new generation of activists who were too young to participate in the 1970s, but who came to feminism later through the anti-amendment campaign and other initiatives in the early 1980s. Caroline Fennell (1993: 151) suggests that feminists who started out in radical framework of rape crisis provision subsequently adopted a rather paradoxical position "seeing the law as oppressive of women (classically the cross-examination of a rape victim in a witness box), while yet heralding its potential as a vigorous feminist instrument (rape law reform)."

In the 1990s the Irish public was shocked by the emergence of stories of institutional sexual and physical abuse experienced by incarcerated children in Ireland and elsewhere in the 1950s and 1960s. The whole area of woman-centred refuge and sexual assault that was first established by the Irish feminist movement in the

1970s has since expanded. The remit of rape crisis work now incorporates the assault of men and children alongside the crime of the rape of women.

Conclusion

When Mary Robinson, a lawyer and activist in the women's movement, was elected President of Ireland she provocatively made a specific reference to women in her election speech: "Mná na hEireann...instead of rocking the cradle, we have rocked the system." The election of a long-standing feminist activist as President of Ireland was an extraordinary achievement in the history of feminism internationally. Since the 1960s Robinson was a leading figure in several feminist campaigns and legal cases, including the political and legal campaigns for contraception and law reform.

Yvonne Galligan (1998) focuses on the development of the relationship between feminism and the state in Ireland. By the 1980s, the feminism that had consolidated the women's movement in the previous decades had moved from the margins to the mainstream. The professionalisation and mainstreaming that occurred across the women's movement affected both liberal and radical feminist groups. Organisations like the Rape Crisis Centre, which were originally radical in orientation, gradually mainstreamed and professionalised. The availability of state funding for some women's organisations in the 1980s was an integral factor in this trend.

For Galligan (1998), when Ireland transformed from being a predominantly rural society into a more industrial and modernised society, from the 1960s onwards, women in Ireland developed a considerable political voice. Long excluded from participation in the formal political arena, they organised to make new, challenging and specific demands on government. Analysis of the relationship between feminist representatives and political decision makers shows how Irish women developed the effective political skills required to represent women's interests to government. The political activity of the women's movement in the Republic of Ireland contributed to the dismantling of a range of discriminatory policies against women, and the political system slowly moved to accommodate the feminist agenda.

However, notwithstanding the fact that Irish women have benefited from the mainstreaming of second-wave feminism in the spheres of employment and law reform especially, change has neither been universal in all areas or realised in all Irish women's lives. Chapter 7 explores how social inequality and class differences among Irish women were highlighted and politicised in other radical sections of Irish feminist activism and the alternative feminisms that were mobilised are highlighted.

Case Study

Joanne Hayes: The "Kerry Babies" Case

Joanne Hayes, Tralee, Co. Kerry 24 January 1985 (photo: Clodagh Boyd)

In April 1984, three months after the events at Granard (see p. 65), what came to be known as the "Kerry Babies" case hit the headlines.[15] The body of a baby with stab wounds was found on the shore in Cahirciveen, Co. Kerry. A murder hunt was launched, and a young woman and her family who lived at Abbeydorney, near Tralee, were taken in for questioning. McCafferty (1985: 13) describes the way in which this investigation was carried out: the gardaí interrogated large numbers of women in the locality who were suspected of being sexually promiscuous.

Joanne Hayes was an unmarried woman, and was having a relationship with a married man, Jeremiah Locke, by whom she already had one child. Under interrogation, she confessed to infanticide. Members of her family confessed to having transported the baby's body 50 miles away and thrown the bag containing the body into the sea. Her mother and aunt also signed confessions admitting complicity in this affair. However, the body of another baby was then discovered on the Hayes farm. Joanne Hayes had claimed in custody that she had given birth to a baby in a field at her home, that the baby had died, and she had buried it. Gardaí concluded that she had given birth to twins, continuing to prepare a murder case against her. Then, forensics showed that the babies had two different blood groups. Hayes and Locke were both type O, as was the Tralee baby. The baby found in Cahirciveen was blood type A. Still, gardaí insisted that Hayes had made a voluntary confession, and continued to come up with a range of possibilities to prove that she had given birth to twins by different men. Following several more anomalies in the case, and the disappearance of the bag in which the Cahirciveen baby was found, charges against Joanne Hayes were eventually dropped when the case came to court.

The case gained considerable public attention, and a journalist for the *Sunday Independent* published an investigative piece following the collapse of the case in court. Using copied garda files, this article revealed the lengths to which the force had gone to obtain confessions and the "right" forensic evidence to prove Hayes's guilt. Questions were asked in the Dáil, and a tribunal was finally established to enquire into the "Kerry Babies" affair in 1985. Serious questions had been raised about garda methods during the investigation, including their methods of interrogation and gaining false confessions from an entire family.

However, in effect, the tribunal put Joanne Hayes on trial for the second time, and this time she was interrogated in the full media glare over a period of three months. In order to vindicate themselves, the gardaí set out to prove that Joanne Hayes had had sex with two different men on the same night within hours of each other, and had conceived two babies of different blood types. Thus, the gardaí, the state, the court-appointed psychiatrist, and the public at large, were allowed to interrogate Joanne Hayes' sexuality, lifestyle and, crucially, her morality. Finally, an expert witness took the stand to confirm that Hayes could not have given birth to a baby of blood group A. Despite this vindication, the tribunal report condemned Hayes, rather than the gardaí. Justice Lynch concluded that she was the one to blame – after all, it was she who had led a married man astray, conceived two children outside wedlock, concealed her second pregnancy, and buried her dead child in a field.

Demonstrations were organised locally by the Tralee Women's Group to show support for Joanne Hayes and her family during the tribunal. Gradually, they were joined by a number of other women's groups from all over the country, and a protest march was held in Dublin. The slogan

Support march and rally for Joanne Hayes, Tralee, Co. Kerry 24 January 1985 (photo: Clodagh Boyd)

"who's on trial?" became central to these protests as feminist groups pointed up the way in which cross-examination was used both in the initial arrest and the subsequent court hearings, to publicly parade Hayes's sexuality, and thus discredit her. The tribunal judge, Justice Lynch, condemned such demos as an insult to the judiciary, threatening protesters with fines and imprisonment.

Following the tribunal, Joanne Hayes returned to her quiet life on the farm in Abbeydorney with her daughter Yvonne. Two books were published about this case in 1985, Nell McCafferty's *A Woman to Blame* and

Published by Attic Press

Hayes's own account of the case, *My Story*. Intersecting as it did with a number of other cases in the early 1980s, the public controversy over the Kerry Babies case illustrates the dangers for Irish women who violated the moral order during that period. More importantly, it marks a key point of transition in an Irish society already beginning to move away from the hegemony of Catholic conservatism, particularly in the arena of women's sexuality.

Notes

1 Files BL/F/AP/1–83, of the Attic Press Archive, relate to the personal involvement of Róisín Conroy and the development of women's rights in the Irish Labour Movement.

2 File BL/F/AP/34, Attic Press Archive: the ICTU *Working Women's Charter* (1981).

3 File BL/F/AP/1358, Attic Press Archive, relates to the activities of the Women's *Ad Hoc* Election Committee (1981) – a group that came together to identify issues relevant to Irish women in the subsequent general election campaign and to access the policies of the parties and the candidates on these issues. File BL/F/AP1499 contains *The Women's Political Association Newsletter*, no. 21, 22, 25, 27.

4 Files BL/F/AP/51–61, Attic Press Archive: Includes material in relation to equal pay and the ITGWU (c.1972–1978). Includes "Make Sure You get Equal Pay. Guidelines for women workers and trade union representative on how to make a claim under the Anti-Discrimination Pay Act 1974"; files relating to the establishment of the Labour court with reference to women's rights in industry; file relating to agitation for the implementation of equal pay legislation and better working conditions. Files BL/F/AP/1206–1218, Attic Press Archive, contain various documents relating to employment equality in the period 1970–1982.

5 File BL/F/AP/62, Attic Press Archive: Relates to inequalities in the Irish social welfare system (1975–76). Includes *Womanworker*, issue no. 1, produced by trade union activists and supporters of Irishwomen United, which contains a request for support for their forthcoming "mass lobby of the Dáil" (20 October 1976). Also contains press cuttings and typescript notes including "Aspects of Discrimination Against Women in Our Social Welfare System".

6 Files BL/F/AP/1312–1327, Attic Press Archive, relate to the Campaign for a United Social Welfare Code (1981–1982). Includes material relating to legal action between the state (at the prosecution of Róisín Conroy regarding her inability to qualify for unemployment assistance under current legislation) and the Minister for Social Welfare, Ireland and the Attorney General.

7 Files BL/F/AP/66–73 of the Attic Press Archive contain material relating to children's rights and family law in Ireland (1974–1989).

8 File BL/F/AP/1303, Attic Press Archive, contains material relating to Cherish (c.1976–1987), an association of single unmarried parents established to provide mutual support for single parents.

9 File BL/F/AP/1494, Attic Press Archive, contains editions of *The AIM Group Newsletter*, nos. 10–17 (1975–77). File BL/F/AP/1504 contains *Women's AIM*, nos. 1–3, 5–9, 11, 12, 14 (1979–1984).

10 Files BL/F/AP/76–78 of the Attic Press Archive contain material in relation to the campaign for divorce in Ireland for the period 1972 to 1982, including newspaper articles relating to the work of the Action Information Motivation (AIM) group.

11 File BL/F/AP/1330, Attic Press Archive, contains material (80 items) relating to the organisation and press coverage of the "Women Against Violence Against Women" march in Dublin (13 October 1978).

12 File BL/F/AP/1280, Attic Press Archive, contains material (35 items) relating to the Divorce Action Group's (DAG) campaign (1981–1986) to legalise divorce in Ireland. Includes press releases, campaign flyers from both the pro and anti-divorce campaigns, a DAG newsletter, an ICCL submission to the Joint Committee on Marriage Breakdown, a DAG submission to the New Ireland Forum, and Labour party campaign flyers supporting the introduction of divorce legislation.

13 File BL/F/AP/1328, Attic Press Archive: details campaign for the introduction of new legislation on rape in Ireland (1975–1980), with reference to the Council for the Status of Women,

Campaign Against Rape Group, and the Women Against Violence Against Women march in Dublin (1978). Includes "Submission on Rape in Ireland" by the Council for the Status of Women (October 1978).

14 File BL/F/AP/1141, Attic Press Archive, includes first report from the Dublin Rape Crisis Centre (1979). File BL/F/AP/1240 relates to the workings of the Rape Crisis Centre Group (c.1977); includes a resume of policy and membership of the group, and documentation relating to the necessity of adequate record keeping and the "tentative" extraction of information from victims. File BL/F/AP/1242, Attic Press Archive: First and second reports of the Dublin Rape Crisis Centre (1979 and 1981). File BL/F/AP/1243, Attic Press Archive, includes a submission for funding for the Dublin Rape Crisis Centre (c.1981), which details the work and aims of the centre.

15 File BL/F/AP/765, Attic Press Archive: the "Report of the Tribunal of Inquiry into the Kerry Babies Case" (69pp.). File BL/F/AP/1367 details the Campaign Against the Kerry Tribunal Report – including circular letter detailing the convening of meeting to launch the campaign (8 June 1985).

Chapter 4
Feminist Cultural Projects

Pat Murphy, Nell McCafferty, and Róisín Conroy at booksigning following publication of
Women in Focus, 1987 (BL/F/AP/412, Attic Press Archive)

The area of feminist culture(s), specifically the kinds of cultural production that emerged during the second-wave women's movement in Ireland, is one which remains largely under-researched and under-represented. In discussing "culture" here, we intend to address issues of artistic representation, and to examine the ways in which second-wave feminist activism in Ireland constructed a counter-culture that critiqued and subverted mainstream values.

It might seem very clear now, as it did to feminist activists at the time, that there was quite a distinct "feminist culture" during this period, that it was vibrant and recognisable throughout the 1970s and early 1980s, ranging from iconic songs to literature, from street theatre to film and video groups, and from visual arts to specific styles in food and clothes. However, arriving at definitions of just what that feminist culture consisted of, is a difficult task – do we focus on what tends to be seen as "high culture" (theatre, visual arts, literature) or concentrate on elements of street or "popular culture" (feminist newspapers, slogans on t-shirts, protest chants)? The division of culture into "high" and "popular" proves impossible during a period where a poem written by an activist is chanted by a crowd at a protest march, is later published in a feminist newspaper, and goes on to form part of the collection of an emerging writer.[1]

Furthermore, is it possible to describe the kinds of cultural production associated with the Irish feminist movement as a singular *culture*, which can be categorised as one whole aspect of the feminist activisms of the period? Is it possible to reflect on this "culture" as a specific space, cut off from other aspects of culture and society? Elements of other alternative movements and cultural forces on the national and international stages – such as folk music, co-operative living, vegetarianism, left-wing ideologies and protest marches – as well as the demands and influences working within the various cultural arenas themselves, intersected with the spaces being opened up to feminist scrutiny in this country, influencing what could be described as "feminist cultures".

Given that this is such a vast area, this chapter will provide a survey of the general area of cultural production, focusing on *some* of the cultural work specific to the women's movement. Clearly, much work has already been done on some aspects of late twentieth-century Irish feminist cultural production, specifically in the realms of literature[2], film[3] and the visual arts.[4]

For example, in the visual arts in Ireland it is possible to see distinct trends and changes that came about in this field as a direct result of second-wave feminism. Many women artists were activists who belonged to feminist groups, and some established groups and initiatives specifically to promote and collectivise the work of feminist artists during this period. An ad in the first issue of *Wicca* (1977) states:

> Women artists will exhibit their work in the gallery of the Project Arts Centre, 15 May to 9 June. Approx. 20 women – non-professionals, professionals and students working in a variety of mediums – have been selected by a panel to have their work shown. Work by women is frequently rejected by male-run institutions and galleries because they work in "unacceptable" mediums such as ceramics and fabrics and they are not always neutral, intellectual and formal, say the organisers of the exhibition. (BL/F/AP/1498, Attic Press Archive)

The Women Artists Action Group (WAAG) was formed by Pauline Cummins in 1987. The main aim of the group was to provide a forum for women artists, who had up until this point "reacted [to the feminist movement] alone, in their studios" but without any space for collective action ("Art Beyond Barriers", WAAG, National Library of Ireland, Ir. 700: 106). Other artists, such as Louise Walsh and Geraldine O'Reilly, worked within community-based programmes to bring about change. Just as the feminist movement influenced the work of these artists, their work informed and commented upon the changes in Irish society brought about in part by the feminist movement. Installations such as "Sounding the Depths" (Walsh and Cummins, Irish Museum of Modern Art, 1992) challenged and interrogated representations of the female body, and the way in which women had been positioned in Irish culture and society. Similarly, Rita Duffy's work in the 1980s – particularly "Mother Ireland" and "Mother Ulster" (1989) – undermines the colonisation of women by the various hegemonies and state powers on this island.

This kind of work reached the wider culture and society, not only in Ireland but internationally. This movement is reflected in other areas of cultural production that emerged from, or in tandem with, the Irish women's movement, such as the National Writers' Workshop, which Eavan Boland facilitated in 1984 and which was aimed at encouraging women's literary work. Even within areas addressed by scholarly work, such as Irish women's writing, the effects of these key feminist initiatives tend to be neglected. The absence of scholarly research and writing on the specific theme of cultural production *vis-à-vis* the Irish women's movement, is addressed in this chapter. Elements of a second-wave feminist culture represented in the documents surveyed in the Irish women's movement research project, which have not emerged in other studies of cultural production in the period, are revealed.

Graphic Feminisms

The kinds of material held by feminist archives are somewhat different from those found in more traditional archives, which tend to focus on conventional documents. The "documents" in these archives can sometimes run to three-dimensional objects such as badges, signs and whistles, as well as banners and t-shirts – a reminder of the kinds of objects which narrate the cultural histories of activist movements.

A key element of this archival material is what could be described as "graphic feminism" – the posters, flyers, newspapers, cartoons, magazines, graffiti and banners, as well as slogans on t-shirts and badges which played a central role in the activism of this period. Graphic material was a focal point of feminist activism during the period of this study, and is situated at the point where visual culture and activist propaganda meet. Images on posters were direct, vivid and memorable: for example, the image on the cover of the IWLM document *Chains – or Change?* mentioned in Chapter 1. Posters in the archives advertise key events such as the first public meeting of the Irish Women's Liberation Movement at the Mansion House in 1971, meetings of the Society for Sexual Liberation in the late 1970s (mentioned in Chapter 6) and a range of other meetings, demos and conferences. Flyers and pamphlets in the archive advertise meetings, but also disseminate booklists of further feminist reading and provide information relating to contraception, abortion and equal pay issues.

Some of the "documents" aim to intervene in graphic images that were already in the public domain – such as advertising and billboards. For example, stickers printed with the words "This is Offensive to Women" and "Sexism" were designed to be stuck across advertisements on hoardings and billboards. Similarly, in almost all of the feminist magazines available, there were reproductions of this kind of billboard advertising defaced by feminist graffiti.

Chains – or Change? The Civil Wrongs of Irishwomen, **IWLM manifesto 1971 (BL/F/AP/1518, Attic Press Archive). (See also pp. 26–27)**

Billboard reproduced in *Women's News*, September 1986 (*Women's News* Collection)

The wealth and range of this material is exceptional. Some of these documents are sophisticated, produced by professional photographers, artists, cartoonists and writers, and printed in colour on high-quality paper. Much of this material however, is home-made, produced by local groups and activists using typewriters and reproduced by hand-operated Gestetner copiers, sometimes with line-drawings also done by hand. As many such groups operated on low (or no) budgets, a lot of this material was reproduced on what is now rapidly disintegrating poor-quality paper, as well as on recycled/reused paper.[5] Because of the conditions within which the material was produced, there is a sense of immediacy about many of these documents which advertise meetings and actions. However, the low resolution of reproduced flyers, for example, has rendered them difficult to read over time. The fact that they have been in use means that they are often covered in handwriting – minutes from the meeting, phone numbers of group members, or notes relating to other ongoing actions may cover them – adding to the information pool but also distracting from the main document. And many are undated. These are far from the carefully preserved manuscripts of officialdom. Much of this ephemeral material was not really considered worth keeping, or preserving – items such as flyers, ticket stubs and programmes were frequently kept by accident, or for sentimental reasons.

Furthermore, because this kind of material originates in political activism, which was anti-establishment, these concerns are reflected in the material. Many of the flyers deliberately give no indication as to the group or organisation which produced them; in other words, they could not be traced back to the activist group

Arja Kajermo's cartoons appeared in a variety of publications, including *In Dublin* (reproduced with permission of the artist). (n.d.) c. 1987

or individuals either by researchers today, or more crucially, by the offices of the state or anti-feminist groups at the time.

As mentioned in the introduction, some of this material cannot be specifically located within the feminist culture of the period, but belongs to counter-cultural movements at work. For example, the cartoons of Arja Kajermo, which were published in *In Dublin* as well as in feminist publications, make reference to the artist's feminist agenda but also make incisive comment on other sacred cows of Irish society. Cartoons were another feature of the "graphic feminism" of this period. In particular, the range of Spellbound postcards available in independent bookshops and "alternative" shops around the country, were common currency and recognisable to many people both within and outside the reaches of activist feminism.

Spellbound has...
- a range of 75 black and white feminist/satirical/political postcards
- a range of 8 full-colour folding cards carrying images from the Women Artists' Action Group Slide Library
- a range of four full-colour folding cards designed by Dublin-based artist Jane Daly carrying images which combine the women's symbol with celtic designs.
- a range of silk-screen printed t-shirts including a a new design devised by members of Spellbound Co-operative: It carries the names of over a hundred Irish women; artists, musicians, writers, dancers, film-makers, storytellers, politicians, revolutionaries, educators, actors, activists, athletes, doctors, explorers, adventurers, pirates, goddesses, academics, and inventors.

...and much more

Spellbound products are available at outlets all over the country including, Waterstones (Cork & Dublin), Books Upstairs, The Pen Corner (all in Dublin), Sheela Na Gig (Galway), Quay Co-op (Cork), ...
For further information, catalogues and order forms, contact Stephanie at the address below.

SPELLBOUND
A WOMEN WORKERS' CO-OPERATIVE • 23-25 MOSS STREET, DUBLIN 2. TEL. (01) 712149

Spellbound postcard advertising their products. (n.d.) c. 1992

These cards, produced by a women's co-operative, inserted feminist ideas and jokes into mainstream circulation, and presented a radical alternative to the versions of Ireland represented in the John Hinde greeting cards then widely available. Some of the cards they produced derived from the slide library of women artists' work collected by the WAAG.

The influence of "graphic feminism" internationally is also clear in the production of much of the visual material in these archives. For example, well-known images such as the "woman's symbol", or that of Rosie the Riveter, and slogans such as "Women Hold up Half the Sky" were widely disseminated. Attic Press used the work of an American feminist cartoonist, bülbül, among others, in the *Women's Diary and Guidebook*. Similarly, the dissemination of the Radicalesbian (*sic*) manifesto "The Woman-Identified Woman", discussed in Chapter 6, carried both its textual message and the visual image of two women kissing across international boundaries.

The immediacy of this material has already been mentioned, but its casual and provisional nature deserves attention. Produced in response to the fluid nature of feminist activism throughout the 1970s and 1980s, just as activist feminist groups began to merge into mainstream organisations, so too did this material change. Today, many feminist and other activist groups and projects continue to use logos and graphic material to get their message across. However, created in a context of

limited budgets and basic technology, documents from the 1970s and 1980s are worlds apart from the glossy reports and posters commissioned by women's groups and centres today, with covers designed by graphic artists or desktop-published in-house using scanned photographs and artwork.

Furthermore, there was a somewhat different attitude to the ownership of material, both textual and graphic, produced in this period when individual authorship, or the design and ownership of an image, was less important than the political impact its widespread use could effect. Earlier feminist groups reproduced imagery and design across international and organisational boundaries without much regard for the ownership or copyright of such graphics. The widespread dissemination of the "woman symbol" is one example of this, but many of the images mentioned above were similarly reproduced, as were cartoons, often without the names of individual artists attached to them. Similarly, feminist articles were frequently reproduced without headings, or the names of authors forgotten – always assuming they were printed on the original documents in the first place. This is indicative of the

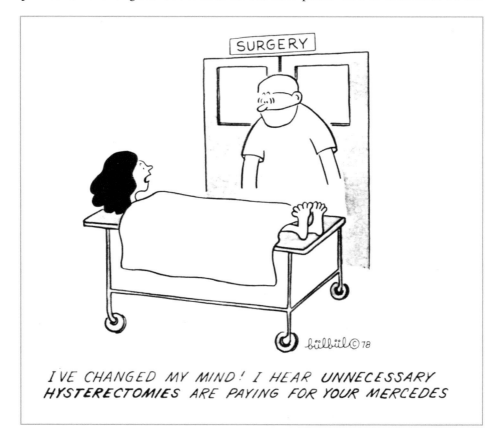

bülbül's cartoons, a feature of many feminist publications of this period, including the IFI/Attic Press Diary Guidebook. (reproduced with permission of the artist). 1978

I USED TO BE
A GOOD LITTLE GIRL
UNTIL I DISCOVERED
THE
IRISH WOMEN'S
DIARY 1984

Frontispiece, IFI/Attic Press Diary & Guidebook

importance of group identities over individual ownership of material or copy-rights, and it also reflects the sense of solidarity and common cause fostered and experienced by feminist activists in a variety of countries.

Feminist Newspapers and Magazines

The number of journalists involved in the early days of the Irish women's move-ment gives us an indication of the role played by the media in second-wave femi-nist agendas.[6] The journalism of key figures such as June Levine, Mary Anderson, Mary Maher, Nell McCafferty, Janet Martin, Nuala Fennell and Mary Kenny, among others, both in feminist publications and the mainstream press, were central to the consciousness-raising revolution of the 1970s and 1980s. Rose comments:

> The importance of the women's pages of the national newspapers as a source of inspiration in the struggle to end discrimination has lost ground to the mushrooming pressure groups and politically-inclined women throughout the country who are becoming more and more vocifer-ous in their demands. Recognising this fact, the pioneering "Women First" of the *The Irish Times* appeared for the last time in October 1974 with the explanation that "there no longer appears to be any justification to confine women's affairs to a purely women's section of the newspaper",

and that in future coverage of women's affairs would be given in the general body of the newspaper. (Rose, 1975: 78–79)

Apart from the column inches covered by feminist and women's issues in the mainstream press, Irish feminists soon recognised the need to publish their material in magazines and newspapers of their own making, which were not driven by commercial or other mainstream interests. A variety of feminist publications began to appear in this country from the mid-1970s on, some of them with short runs or produced as one-off issues such as *Anima Rising*, the Galway feminist collective newsletter (1978), or *Elektra*, the Trinity College Dublin Women's Group Magazine (1980). Others were produced from within mainstream publications, such as the *In Dublin Women's Issue* (November 1978) or addressed feminist issues within the publications of other groups, such as *Quare Times*, a lesbian and gay magazine from the early 1980s. Some of the groups publishing these magazines managed to sustain publication over a number of issues. For example, there were 13 issues of *Wicca* produced by a voluntary editorial group in Dublin with very few resources, financial or otherwise. With only one exception, Belfast's *Women's News*, which is now in its 19th year, none of them have survived to the present day.

One of the first magazines to be produced by feminist activists in this period was the *Fownes Street Journal*, published by an offshoot group of the IWLM.[7] This covered key areas of activism ongoing at that time, such as the November 1972 submission to the Commission on the Status of Women, which began:

> The married woman in Ireland who works in the home has no legal or economic identity. She is not entitled to payment or salary, either from her husband or the state. In a society where financial reward is the measure of each member's contribution, it is significant that the housewife is valued at nothing. (BL/F/AP/1110/1, Attic Press Archive)

It goes on to list key feminist demands, such as those outlined by the IWLM. Articles carried by the *Fownes Street Journal* included pieces about equal rights at work and equal pay, gender stereotyping in schools and the workplace, women's roles in the home, and the trap of the family romance and romantic love. Many articles were unsigned but in later issues some of the pieces were written by activists such as Ruth Riddick and Ruth Jacob. Advertising in the magazine also tied in with feminist thinking at the time – for example, an ad for jewellery reminded readers "you don't need to get married to get a ring". A questionnaire for readers in September 1973 asked questions such as:

> Are you trained to do any other work besides what you are doing at the moment?; Do you belong to any of the active groups in your area?
>
> Where do you stand on the big issues affecting women? (e.g. Contraception/Abortion/Divorce/Equal Pay for Equal Work/Equal Taxation/Equal Educational Opportunity/Day Care Centres/Mixed Schools)
>
> Do you think the name of each writer should appear with each article?

Women's News, 19 September 1986, issue co-produced in Cork and Belfast (*Women's News* Collection)

Quare Times, spring 1984 (BL/F/AP 1533/3, Attic Press Archive)

These questions address key Irish feminist concerns of the early 1970s. The *Fownes Street Journal* was very simply produced: typewritten pages were reproduced in black and white, and there were few illustrations or photographs. Later magazines and newspapers from the feminist movement developed from this early project in feminist journalism, which showed Irish feminists the importance of making their ideas readily available to their constituent groups and beyond.

In 1975, *Banshee* was set up by members of IWU who "felt it was necessary to start producing a feminist paper as soon as possible" (report from the editorial committee, May 1976, BL/F/AP/1142/10). Like the *Fownes Street Journal*, *Banshee* focused primarily on the main campaigns IWU were involved in. Crucially, the production of *Banshee* reveals the level at which feminist ideas and theoretical perspectives were worked out within the activist movement of the period. The 1976 editorial committee commented that its content:

> reflected an awareness of the oppression of women in its many forms – cultural, social, economic, political, and physical. However, in the absence of a coherent ideological base, specifying the causes of that oppression, the analytical content of the magazine is as diverse as the various tendencies within the movement. (BL/F/AP/1142/10, Attic Press Archive)

After publication of *Banshee* 1, and in response to criticism from outside the editorial group about the way in which articles were solicited from individuals, the editors endeavoured to publish articles written collectively or coming out of workshops on the issue involved. This underlines the suspicion with which individual opinion, as opposed to ideas and policies arrived at collectively, was regarded by feminists at that time. The editorial group, which seemed to range between five and nine women over the course of the newspaper, agreed to either outline IWU policy on the issues in question, or to state clearly that they had no policy on that issue – which is possibly one of the reasons why their editorial meetings "never lasted less than four hours, and on a couple of occasions lasted six hours" (BL/F/AP/1142/10, Attic Press Archive).[8] As a result of this high level of consultation and discussion, *Banshee* reflects the issues and agendas of importance to those involved in feminist activism in Ireland 1975–1976, such as the family, reproductive rights, socialist feminist and class activism, and lesbian feminist issues, to name just a few.

In 1977, *Wicca* was set up to fill the void left following the demise of *Banshee*; but unlike either of the earlier magazines discussed above, *Wicca* was not linked to any particular feminist organisation. This is reflected in an editorial in issue 8:

> *Wicca* is the only voice of feminism being heard in the 26 counties. We have not up to now had a solid permanent women's movement to support us. In actual fact we have had very little support. Naturally this isolation shows in the magazine. (n.d.) c. 1978 (BL/F/AP/1498, Attic Press Archive)

The editorial group of *Wicca* again reflects the collectivist principles of *Banshee*, with over 40 women listed as being involved in the magazine's production over its lifetime, and the fluidity of this group is also reflected in the way in which members come and go over the issues. Members of the editorial groups who produced *Wicca* include Geraldine Moane, Wendy Wells, Carmel Ruane, Brigid Ruane, Oonagh Mac Namara, Miriam McQuaid, Mary Phelan, Joni Sheerin (later Crone), Mary MacNamara, Anne Marie Walker, Ethel Galvin, Doreen McGouran, Róisín

Advertisements in *Fownes Street Journal*, November 1972 (BL/F/AP/1492, Attic Press Archive)

Cover of *Banshee 2* (n.d.) c. 1976 (BL/F/AP/1123, Attic Press Archive)

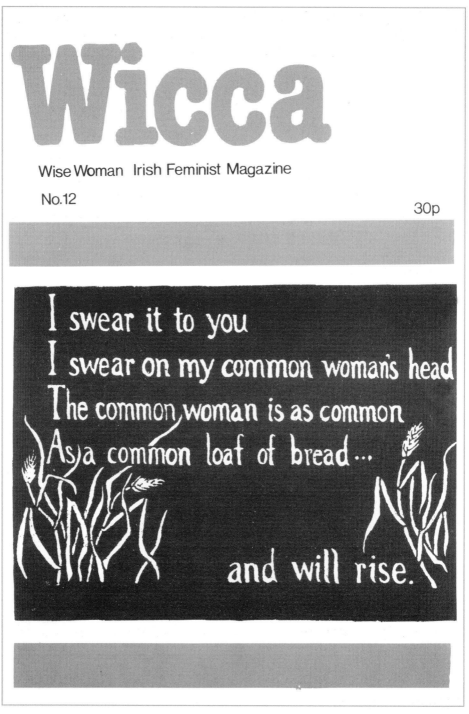

Cover of *Wicca 12* **(n.d.) c. 1978 (BL/F/AP/1498, Attic Press Archive)**

Boyd, Clodagh Boyd, Ann O'Brien, Sandra Stephen, Kate O'Brien, Anne Speed, Liz Holmes, Sarah O'Hara, Deirdre Cullen, Orla Rylands, Jean O'Keefe and Nora Greany. In *Wicca* 8, the editorial group describe this membership:

> *Wicca* is an open collective of about 12 permanent members. There is a floating membership and involvement of about 20 women … There are no qualifications for joining the collective other than being a woman committed to the general principles of feminism. (BL/F/AP/1498, Attic Press Archive) (n.d.) c. 1978

Key issues given voice in *Wicca* include the Armagh Prison campaigns, the Contraception Action Campaign (CAP), equal pay, strikes, trade unions, abortion, the Carnsore Point protests (which successfully campaigned against the proposed nuclear power plant the ESB wanted to establish in Co. Wexford), women in prisons, lesbian sexuality, disabilities and prostitution, as well as articles on women's rights internationally.

Unlike its predecessors, a concerted effort was made by the *Wicca* team to deal with cultural matters relevant to feminists – they interviewed the film critic Laura Mulvey following her paper in Dublin, focused on women in the Irish music scene, and reviewed publications such as *The Wall Reader* (Boland, 1979) and feminist writing by Adrienne Rich, among others. The final issue of *Wicca*, number 13, focused solely on feminist fiction, poetry and music, and included an article by Mary Dorcey on writing.

Today, the available collections of feminist periodicals are an important record of feminist theory and activism in the 1970s and 1980s, and provide us with valuable insights into the ways in which feminist issues were raised and discussed during the period. Furthermore, the way in which many of these publications were produced are a good example of the decision-making and working methods of some of the activist groups in Ireland at that time. The editorials in many of their magazines are open about the methods of production, and the decision-making processes involved in selecting articles. Feminist activists involved in these magazines worked to demystify the skills and techniques involved in journalism. They illustrated that anyone could learn to publish a magazine; provided opportunities to women who wanted to write, create artwork or take photographs to publish their material; and worked together to learn the skills of magazine production. Much of this knowledge would later be put to work by some of the same women in the fields of literature, art, photography, television and radio production, and publishing.

Feminist Publishing

Over the past 30 years, feminist writing in and about Ireland has grown exponentially. These texts have placed Irish feminist issues in a global context in the fields of literature, sociology, the arts, politics and the law, among others. In particular, feminist publications and books have reached many constituencies that otherwise

Members of the *Wicca* collective, 1978 (photo: Clodagh Boyd)

may have remained unaffected by feminist ideas. Frequently, feminist ideas have tended to focus on political lobbying, or been confined to the woman-centred activities of specific activist groups. However, feminist publications in the public domain also have an important part to play in consciousness raising.

Anne Crilly, a member of the Derry Film and Video Co-Op, gives an indication of the dearth of published material in this field:

> Sometimes I think women, particularly in Ireland, forget that it was only just over fifteen years ago that there was hardly any books out on women in Ireland. I mean there has been a massive explosion in women's studies and books on women in Ireland in the last fifteen years, but when I was researching *Mother Ireland* in maybe the period 1983–85, there was only a couple of books. There was Margaret MacCurtain's book, *Women and Irish Society*. There was another book came out about women and Irish art by Eiléan Ní Chuilleanáin. And there was also Margaret Ward's book, *Cumann na mBan, Unmanageable Revolutionaries*. That was it, you know, that was the total. And now so much has been done. (Thompson, 1998)[9]

A key factor in the development of feminist writing specific to Ireland was the establishment of feminist publishing projects at the end of the 1970s. Pioneers in feminist publishing in Ireland in the late 1970s and early 1980s include Catherine Rose, Janet Martin, Louise C. Callaghan and others involved at Arlen House; Róisín Conroy and Mary Doran of Irish Feminist Information (IFI) and Attic Press; and later editors at Attic, Mary Paul Keane, Ailbhe Smyth, and Gráinne Healy.

Arlen House was the first feminist publishing house in Ireland. Established in 1975 in Galway by Catherine Rose, one of its early publications was Janet Martin's

ARLEN HOUSE

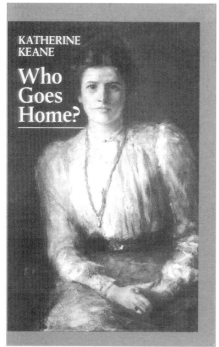

1984

repr. 1987

repr. 1980

1985

A selection of Arlen House titles

Essential Guide for Women (1977). The impact of this radical initiative in Irish publishing history was palpable, and as Rose comments:

> [There's] no harm in reminding ourselves that we had to hold our breath in 1977 when *The Essential Guide* was first published. Legal opinion at the time was that publisher and author were risking the then statutory fine and imprisonment for the publication of material which could be seen to advise the use of contraception or abortion. (*In the Cauldron: Arlen House List of New Books for Autumn* 1980 (BL/F/AP 419/52, Attic Press Archive)

On her move to Dublin in 1978, Rose was joined by others interested in this project, and with the help of Eavan Boland, Margaret MacCurtain, Janet Martin and Terry Prone, Arlen House became firmly established as an independent publishing house with a strong interest in feminism. An ad in *Wicca* 5 sends out a call:

> Artists, high on creative energy, low on sexist attitudes: you might like to work part-time with us. We're an all-female feminist company and we need people who can illustrate books, design jackets. Experience with layouts and paste-ups a help. Write with details to: Janet Martin. (BL/F/AP/1498, Attic Press Archive)

The main focus of the press was women's writing, and thus Arlen House became the champion of out-of-print work by Irish women writers such as Kate O'Brien, Janet McNeill, Nora Hoult and Anna Parnell, as well as new poetry collections by Eavan Boland, Rita Ann Higgins and Mary Rose Callaghan, among others.

Also in 1978, Irish Feminist Information (IFI) was set up by Róisín Conroy and Mary Doran.[10] In what could be seen as a direct result of the production of the kinds of materials outlined in the "Graphic Feminism" section above, they wanted to set up a publishing and distribution service for activist groups. The idea was to provide a service to facilitate the growing number of feminist and left-wing groups who wanted a wider forum for their printed material. IFI would set up a distribution network for the material countrywide, through independent bookshops, co-ops and healthfood shops, and send out the material to women's groups and individuals. Their main interest was in women's material and other political material that had little or no attraction to existing publishing houses or bookshops.

They also wanted to provide flyers and leaflets themselves with information for feminists, and began by putting together a list of feminist groups and services, with a particular focus on health services for women. Conroy and Doran pooled their own finances, got a small bank loan, and initially published a women's calendar in poster form, which they later developed into the IFI *Women's Diary and Guidebook*. The diaries were an immediate hit. Many women talk about their surprise at seeing a menstruation chart printed on the inside cover of the diary – putting this kind of information into the public domain was a first for IFI. Similar kinds of publications produced by IFI during this period included the *Books Upstairs Women's Health Catalogue* (1982), which provided listings of material specific to an Irish context

The IFI *Women's Diary & Guidebook* later became the *Attic Guidebook & Diary*

and focused on the area of "self-help" remedies, which they pointed out "will be particularly of use to women who are at present more isolated from existing health and welfare agencies" (BL/F/AP/170/4, Attic Press Archive). The relevance of this kind of information is highlighted by June Levine in *Sisters* (1982), who discusses her experience of getting pregnant while on the pill:

> Many general practitioners in Ireland dispense contraceptive advice, mainly the pill, without having any special training. Some drugs prescribed for ailments do interact with the pill. Many Irish women, myself included, came by this information only when it was published in the first edition of the *Irish Women's Diary*, produced in 1980 …. They printed a chart from *Spare Rib*. Drugs which can interact with the pill are certain antibiotics and some of the drugs which act on the nervous system. At the time I became pregnant I was taking prescribed antibiotics and "nerve pills". (Levine, 1982: 97–8)

The fact that this kind of information was not available in the public domain before IFI distributed the diary underlines the secrecy and taboos surrounding the area of women's health up to this time.

In addition to publishing, IFI was also at the centre of support and development for other feminist initiatives ongoing in the early 1980s in Dublin, such as *Wicca*, mentioned above, the Women's Centre in Dame Street and the Women Against Sexist Education group. They also became involved in a training initiative by setting up the Women in Community Publishing courses, with the assistance of the Women in Publishing group.[11] Having secured state funding from AnCo,[12] this course was set up to train a group of women in community publishing skills. Both the skills offered by the course and the high levels of unemployment at that time, are reflected in the numbers of women who applied – 85 applicants competed for 12 places on the course (BL/F/AP/305/1–4, Attic Press Archive). Members of WIP advised the Women in Community Publishing course in the planning stages of the course, participated as ongoing consultants, and supported them in carving out a new niche in publishing. Patricia Kelleher describes the course aims:

> It was an attempt to deprofessionalise publishing and to co-operate with the state without being co-opted. It was inspired by an awareness that even though the project was small and insignificant in itself, it was connected up to a bigger process of change engaged in by many women's groups and people seeking alternatives. It was political, ideological, but above all practical. (BL/F/AP/305/1–4, Attic Press Archive)[13]

Participants on the courses produced programmes for women's conferences, flyers and leaflets. Furthermore, several key booklets in terms of Irish social change and social history were produced either during the courses or as a direct result of course projects, such as *If You Can Talk … You Can Write* (produced with KLEAR), *Singled Out: Single Mothers in Ireland* (produced with Cherish), the *Missing Pieces* (1984–1985) booklets, which reclaimed important figures in Irish women's history, and the facsimile pack *Did Your Granny Have a Hammer?* (1985) on the Irish women's suffrage movement.

Having built up a base for their business, both financially and in terms of skilled personnel, IFI began to think about expanding its project, and mooted the idea of establishing a feminist publishing house. Gathering together a group of fellow-activists, Conroy and Doran suggested a business venture where they would each buy a share in this new publishing house, to be run by Conroy. Thus, 1984 saw the founding of Attic Press, Ireland's only feminist publishing house, and a landmark in activism and publishing for several generations of Irish feminists. The novels and social texts published by Attic made feminist ideas accessible to new generations of Irish feminists, and for the first time, culturally specific feminist material was available to Irish women on a wider scale than heretofore. Throughout the 1980s and early 1990s, Attic Press published contemporary works by writers such as Nell McCafferty, Eilís Ní Dhuibhne, Eithne Strong, Evelyn Conlon, Ronit Lentin and many others. A Women's Studies list was also established by the press in the 1990s, which produced key texts in the field of feminist education, such as *The Irish Women's Studies Reader* (Smyth, ed., 1993), as well as focusing on feminist recovery projects such as such as Daisy Swanton's *Emerging from the Shadows*

This 1985 facsimile pack was produced by the Women in Community Publishing Course, in conjunction with Rosemary Cullen Owens and Attic Press.

1989

1994

1986

1988

Attic Press titles

1991

1987

1992

A STORY OF PROSTITUTION

June Levine a

A LINK IN THE CHAIN
Hilda Tweedy

*The Story of
The Irish Housewives Association
1942 - 1992*

MAD & BAD FAIRIES

1987

Fairytales for

SMAS
TIM
A HISTORY OF T
SUFFRAG
1889 - 1922

Rosemary Cullen Owens

1984

LIFTING THE LID

HANDBOOK OF FACTS AND INFORMATION
ON IRELAND

ula Barry

1986

Attic Press titles

MS MUFFET AND OTHERS

'A funny, sassy, heretical collection of feminist fairytales'

1986

(1994). Attic also published important social histories, such as June Levine and Lyn Madden's *Lyn: A Story of Prostitution* (1989), Ursula Barry's *Lifting the Lid* (1986) and the LIP pamphlets series.

It continued to publish the *Women's Diary and Guidebook*, which was popular with many women, including those who did not necessarily consider themselves to be feminist. The importance of these groundbreaking publishing houses in Ireland should not be underestimated. They provided a vital link between the ideologies and theories of feminist groups and the wider reading public, and it is clear that the availability of feminist texts disseminated radical social ideas throughout Irish culture and society. This link between theory and practice was bolstered by the role played by those women involved in Attic Press in activism on the ground, and the publishing house was at the centre of many campaigns throughout its lifetime, for example, in relation to the Kerry Babies case, among others. In terms of the work of individual writers, the fact that their work was published not only encouraged women's cultural production in this and other areas, but could also be said to have wrought changes in mainstream publishing, as houses began to realise the viability of publishing work by women writers.

Attic Press ceased to operate as a publishing house in the late 1990s, although Cork University Press bought the imprint and continue to stock and sell the remaining Attic titles. On the whole, in more recent times the kind of feminist material entering the public domain tends to be dominated by academic material of one kind or another. While there are some exceptions, the general tendency has been to remove feminist ideas from the public domain and to render them inaccessible to all but academic readers, which could possibly be seen as an element of the backlash against feminist ideas in the mainstream and evidence of a new kind of activism in academe.

Conclusion

The work of Irish feminist cultural projects in the 1970s and 1980s exemplifies the wider aims of Irish feminist activism in the period. Artists and activists worked against the marginalisation of women, and opposed the closed nature of many cultural arenas by working in collective and interdisciplinary ways. Focusing on issues such as gender, sexualities, race and national identities, these women raised awareness of feminist issues in the Irish cultural arena, and generally, in the public domain. By creating fissures in traditional notions of gender roles, and of Irishness, they were central to the reshaping of Irish identities which has taken place over the past 30 years.

If anything, this exploration of the available material relating to second-wave cultural projects in Ireland illustrates the need for further research and writing in this field, in which a full-length study has yet to emerge. There are a number of key questions yet to be explored, such as the impact of these radical publications coming out of feminist activism on the work of activists themselves, and in the wider public domain. For example, in relation to community politics in the 1980s and 1990s, many community development projects and community education schemes either used material published by Attic Press or were able to avail of these publications in compiling their own education packs. As yet there has been no analysis of this kind of diffusion of feminist ideas into the mainstream in Ireland, and as such, we cannot speculate as to the long-term effects of the production of these publications. Apart from the dearth of scholarly research, autobiographies and memoirs written by activists and artists involved in this period have yet to emerge on any scale[14]; these may further illuminate areas such as the changes wrought by feminist ideas in the arena of cultural representation, and the perceived impact of this during the period itself. Furthermore, as work continues to emerge internationally relating to feminist activism and politics during the 1970s and 1980s, there is room for comparative studies on the effect of international feminisms on Irish activist and cultural spheres.

Notes

1 The work of writers such as Evelyn Conlan and Mary Dorcey has been particularly associated with the emergence of Irish feminist activism in the 1970s and 1980s.

2 Examples include, Fogarty (2002); Fogarty (1999); Boyle Haberstroh (1996); Meaney (1991); Smyth (1997); St. Peter (2000); and Wills (1993). At the time of writing, at least three other scholars – Patricia Coughlan, Anne Owens-Weeks and Rebecca Pelan – are engaged in full-length monographs in the field of Irish women's writing.

3 For example, Farley (2000); Meaney (2004); and Pettit (2000).

4 See Robertson (2000) and Robertson (1995).

5 Eco-awareness was also a feature of early feminist activism.

6 Gillespie (2003) has recently documented articles published by this group of journalists.

7 File BL/F/AP/1492, Attic Press Archive, contains various feminist newsletters (1973–1988), including: *Fownes Street Journal* 1.2, and *Rebel Sister* 5 (May 1976). File BL/F/AP/1498 contains *Wicca* 1–4 and 7–13. File BL/F/AP/1517 contains copies of *Bread and Roses* (UCD Women's Liberation Group Magazine) 1, 3–6.

8 File BL/F/AP1174, Attic Press Archive: file of publications from IWU (1975). Includes editorial reports and notes on the distribution of *Banshee*; and the IWU newsletter no. 2. File BL/F/AP/1182 relates to IWU's distribution of *Banshee* after a decision was made by the Censorship Board to ban this feminist publication. This file contains 23 items concerning the issue, including two reports from the editorial board.

9 Titles mentioned by Crilly, which were published by Arlen House include: McCurtain and Ó Corráin (1978) and Ni Chuileanáin (1985). The Arlen Press imprint has recently been revived by Alan Hayes.

10 Files BL/F/AP/219–224 contain material in relation to the establishment of the Irish Feminist Information (IFI) premises at 48 Fleet Street, Dublin.

11 The Women in Publishing (WIP) group had been set up in 1982 by some of the Arlen House team, Mary Paul Keane, (Wolfhound Press), and Sarah O'Hara (IPA), and they organised workshops on production, editing, and marketing.

12 Now FÁS, a government agency set up to facilitate training in industry in the 1960s.

13 The Attic Press Archive contains several files in relation to Women in Community Publishing Course and Group, Women's Community Publishing Co-operative and Women's Community Press (c. 1982–87). See files BL/F/AP/292–391.

14 June Levine's (1982) *Sisters: The Personal Story of an Irish Feminist* and Nell McCafferty's (2004) autobiography *Nell* are as yet the only full-length publications in this area.

Chapter 5
Feminism and Northern Ireland

International Women's Day Protest outside Armagh Women's Jail, 8 March 1980 (photo: Clodagh Boyd)

The emergence of a distinctive second-wave women's movement in Northern Ireland has been well documented in recent years by feminist writers and activists (such as Ward, 1991; McWilliams, 1995; Evason, 1991; Rooney, 1995; Rooney, 1999; Sales, 1997; and Roulston and Davies *et al*, 2000). The development of the women's movement in Northern Ireland has been complicated and shaped by the impact sectarianism, religious differences and violence have had on women's lives since the late 1960s. Feminist researchers and activists have demonstrated how women's organisations in the North were interconnected to the universal goals and strategies of second-wave feminism. However, there have been few systematic attempts made to study, reveal and compare either the links or divisions in Irish feminist politics North/South from the 1970s to the present.

Clearly, the signing of the Treaty and Partition (establishing the "six county" entity of Northern Ireland) had a profound effect on the development of Irish feminist politics across the island from the 1920s on. In particular, the institutional development and ethos of two distinct nation-states on the island has created a particular context to women's lives on both sides of the border. For example, in the decades after independence, feminist activists in the Republic of Ireland witnessed the acute marginalisation of the women's movement in Irish public life and the introduction of a series of conservative pieces of legalisation, which served to restrict women's lives in a number of areas. By the late 1960s, the onset of the conflict in Northern Ireland created further differences in how women "lived their lives" north and south of the border in Ireland.

This chapter provides a general survey of the development of feminism and the women's movement in Northern Ireland over the last three decades. In addition, how the question of "the North" was treated in the women's movement in the South is explored. Evidence of vibrant debates about the political situation in Northern Ireland (such as the Armagh women's prisoners campaigns and the H Block crisis) in the wider women's movement is evident. At the same time, a reluctance to even consider "the North," in particular the demands of Northern Republicans, is evident in the recent history of Irish feminism in the South. Echoing the debate that took place during first wave of feminism in Ireland, it was argued that feminists who give up their autonomy to go into anti-imperialist and republican organisations have to subjugate their needs as women for the good of "the greater cause" (McWilliams, 1993: 95). Paramilitary violence in any shape or form was rejected as a means of achieving Irish unity by a significant majority within the women's movement. Furthermore, with the onset of over three decades of violent conflict in the late 1960s, the women's movement in the North was affected and shaped by a complexity of circumstances and divisions which Southern feminists often felt ill equipped to deal with.

Nevertheless, important alliances did develop independently of nationalist politics between feminists North and South during the second wave of the women's movement. For example, important links in the women's movement have developed between pro-choice campaigns, lesbian activists and organisations such as Women's Aid and the Rape Crisis Centres on a North/South basis. At the same time, some activists in the South openly sympathised with the discriminations experienced by Northern Catholics throughout the period of the Troubles (by supporting the civil rights movement, for example) but chose not associate or participate in Republican campaigns/organisations, while some women were active both in the women's movement and nationalist politics in Ireland as members of Republican organisations. Republican feminism is undoubtedly a long-standing position in the history of the Irish women's movement.

However, the relationship feminist politics should have with national liberation struggles is a highly contested issue globally, including in Ireland. Numerous feminist activists and writers have been highly critical of the dominant conceptualisation of women in nationalist representations, movements and ideologies (see Yuval Davis, 1997). Others have adopted a more positive interpretation of the relationship between feminism and nationalism (Coulter, 1993 for example). The appearance of new documentary evidence in recent years demonstrates that Republican feminism and anti-Republicanism are both significant dynamics in the recent history of the Irish women's movement. At the same time, it is evident that Republican

Front cover of *Women's News*, Issue 2 (April 1984) (*Women's News* Collection)

feminists managed at various stages to embrace nationalist causes while maintaining impressive alliances in the wider women's movement and the cause of Irish women. The Irish case therefore demonstrates there is never a neutral relationship between nationalism and feminism in any given context and that nationalism is a key dynamic of *difference* in the women's movement.[1]

Feminism in Northern Ireland

Evason (1991) writes that between 1970 and 1975 there were few women's groups in Northern Ireland in the wake of the political crises of the late 1960s and early 1970s. Three core groups emerged: the Lower Ormeau Women's Group, which was formed in 1972 and existed for less than a year; the Queen's University Women's Liberation Group, which met between 1973 and 1975; and the Coleraine Women's Group, which was started in 1974 and comprised mainly of university students and academic staff. The Coleraine group was initially a consciousness-raising group. It expanded its membership to other staff and women from a nearby housing estate and increasingly became involved in a number of specific campaigns (including a campaign for the extension of sex discrimination legislation in 1975, which was already implemented in Britain; the absence of abortion legislation in Northern Ireland; domestic violence; rape; and rights for divorced or separated women). In 1977, the group proliferated and became Coleraine Women's Aid. This occurred partly because of many women's concern to specialise on this issue and through networks forged with Women's Aid groups in Belfast and Derry. The group also proliferated into the newly formed Women's Law and Research group, which focused on the divorce campaign.

The capacity of the movement grew substantially from 1975 until the early 1980s. The Northern Ireland Women's Rights Movement (NIWRM) was established in 1975, following a women's film weekend in Queen's University Belfast, and became a focal umbrella movement organisation. It fostered close links with the trade unions and support from a wide range of organisations. A Women's Charter for Northern Ireland was drawn up by the NIWRM and included the following demands: equal opportunities in education, training and work; equal pay; family-planning services; maternity leave; and childcare facilities. Conflict arose over the tactical advantage of explicitly demanding a women's right to choose abortion. A provision was finally included in these demands calling for a parity of rights with women in England according to the 1967 Act.

Two groups with a more radical focus were offshoots from the NIWRM – the radical feminist Women's Aid group, which argued for the abandonment of hierarchical organising and structures; and the Socialist Women's Group, which diverged from the concerns of radical feminists to demand an acceptance of socialism as a precondition for women's liberation. In addition, they were concerned with an appropriate response to the Peace People (originally the Peace Women's Movement), which the NIWRM initially supported.

NORTHERN IRELAND WOMEN'S RIGHTS MOVEMENT

CHARTER

WOMEN'S CHARTER FOR NORTHERN IRELAND

The Northern Ireland Women's Rights Movement has been active since 1975 in campaigning for an extension of women's rights throughout Northern Ireland. The Movement accepts that some advances in both legislation affecting women and its implementation have been achieved, nevertheless it believes that many areas of inequality remain which must yet be challenged.

The Movement realises that legislation on its own cannot change attitudes towards women, but feels that progressive legislation in conjunction with education and agitation can create a climate that is conducive to change. In such a climate women themselves can be encouraged to develop an awareness and to build up the confidence necessary to challenge the prevailing social attitudes that discriminate against them. The NIWRM firmly believes that all women should have the opportunity to realise their full potential as human beings in our society.

The Northern Ireland Women's Rights Movement is committed to the building of a non-sectarian women's movement throughout Northern Ireland. It rejects a situation in which women, and in particular working-class women, are doubly exploited - both on the basis of their gender and due to their economic position in society. Furthermore we believe that the struggle for women's rights is an integral part of the struggle for human rights, which will result in a society in which women and men are released from crude stereotypes and limited ideas of what they are, and may be.

The NIWRM asserts its position as an active participant in the international struggle for women's rights - we believe that the gains already made must be defended and extended. Finally, we support those organisations that are campaigning for a world that will be free from the threat of nuclear annihilation, as we recognise that our best efforts in the field of women's rights can be reduced to ashes by nuclear militarism. We put forward the following Charter to encapsulate our Demands.

Northern Ireland Women's Rights Movement Charter 1975 (BL/F/AP/1482/5, Attic Press Archive)

We pledge ourselves to work for -

EQUAL OPPORTUNITIES IN EDUCATION AND TRAINING

The NIWRM believe that there is a need to implement a vigorous campaign to eliminate those attitudes that would seek to differentiate between the education of boys and girls. In the area of training a programme of positive discrimination is demanded in order to encourage women to enter non-traditional areas of work.

we demand

* positive efforts to eliminate the widespread sex discrimination which exists in schools in Northern Ireland by means of in-service training for teachers and special courses for tutors.
* a common curriculum for boys and girls based on relevant needs.
* the phasing out of single-sex schools and, where possible, the amalgamation of boys and girls schools, with consideration of programmes for positive action to alleviate the present effects of previous discrimination.
* the provision of integrated schooling and teacher training outside the control of specific religious denominations.
* the extension of continuing education facilities and adult education in the community, particularly where such provision takes note of the educational and practical needs of women.
* day release to be made available to all, especially women.
* return to work and re-training courses to be made available to women re-entering employment both by programmes of positive action and by an extension of facilities within Government Training Centres.

EQUAL OPPORTUNITIES IN EMPLOYMENT

In advocating the following demands the NIWRM is aware of the need for a radical restructuring of the economy in order to reverse the current trend towards growing unemployment.

we demand

* equal opportunities in employment and promotion regardless of sex and marital status.
* the effective implementation of legislation covering the area of equal pay for work of equal value, and the re-valuing of jobs that have been traditionally regarded as 'women's work'.
* a national minimum wage below which no worker should fall and which is set at both a realistic level and guaranteed against inflation.
* effective machinery to ensure the provision of acceptable Contracts and Conditions of Employment, and implementation of agreed rates of pay.
* a situation in which the conditions of employment and benefits for part-time workers should be no less than those for full-time workers, pro-rata to the hours worked.
* parity of working conditions for women and men to go hand in hand with improved protection at work.
* adequate parental and special leave when required for the care of dependants alongside guaranteed maternity and paternity leave with an automatic right of return to the job held prior to leave.
* the unionisation of all women employed outside the home, whether on a full-time or part-time basis, and the recognition by Trade Unions of the rights and needs of their female members.

IMPROVED HEALTH AND FAMILY PLANNING SERVICES

Health services are recognised as an essential public provision which the NIWRM will fight to protect against the undermining effects of privatisation.

we demand

* the individual right of control over one's own body, irrespective of marital status.
* the availability of a free and comprehensive Family Planning Service for all people - whether married or single.
* the provision of adequate sex education in schools and Training Centres.

Northern Ireland Women's Rights Movement Charter 1975 (BL/F/AP/1482/5, Attic Press Archive)

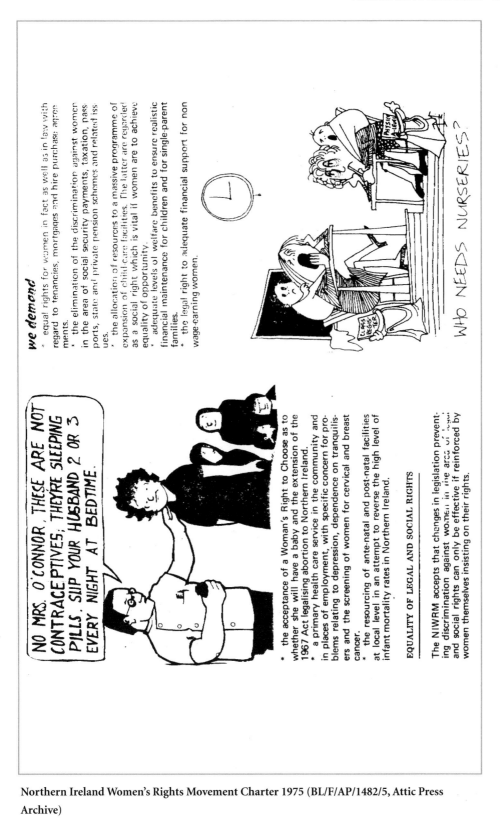

Northern Ireland Women's Rights Movement Charter 1975 (BL/F/AP/1482/5, Attic Press Archive)

THE RIGHT TO PERSONAL SECURITY

Many women's organisations have highlighted aspects of violence towards women. The NIWRM recognises that women in Northern Ireland bear a particular burden due to the political tensions and violence within our society.

we demand

* the rejection of both pornography and of media images which exploit the portrayal of women in a sexist manner.
* the recognition that the definition of rape should be extended; that rape within marriage should be acknowledged and that the legal test of consent should be firmly established on an objective rather than subjective basis, where at present the belief of the man is the deciding factor.
* the provision of facilities and support for the victims of Domestic Violence and Incest.
* the elimination of sexual harrassment at work and an effective trade union campaign to raise awareness concerning the issue of sexual harrassment.
* the need for adequate financial compensation to the victims of rape, incest, domestic violence or assault.
* an end to the extensive use of the degrading practice of strip-searching female prisoners and acceptable prison facilities for education, employment, recreation health and the care of children.
* the recognition that everyone in Northern Ireland has suffered as a direct result of sectarian violence, of paramilitary activity and due to harrassment by the security forces. The NIWRM accepts that women, and working-class women in particular, have borne the brunt of that violence.

THE INTERNATIONAL PERSPECTIVE

In recognition of the possible nuclear annihilation which threatens the world on a daily basis, the NIWRM seeks to identify with progressive women's movements throughout the world.

* the rejection of divisions between people based on colour or creed, particularly the abhorrent system of apartheid.
* the maintenance of the neutrality of the Republic of Ireland and its continued rejection of NATO.
* the unilateral nuclear disarmament of the United Kingdom and the withdrawal of cruise missiles based there.
* an end to the dangerous escalation of the stockpiles of nuclear weapons and the re-establishment of international multi-disarmament

In conclusion, the Northern Ireland Women's Rights Movement seeks to promote these demands by means of campaigns, research projects, pressure groups and local action. It seeks contact and solidarity with women's organisations that support the ideal of a non-sectarian women's movement. This movement will only be built by a combination of women organised at their place of work: by women active within their trade unions and by women who have come together around particular issues of concern in their local communities. To all such women - both active concerned individuals and organised groups - the Northern Ireland Women's Rights Movement pledges its committment and seeks support.

Northern Ireland Women's Rights Movement Charter 1975 (BL/F/AP/1482/5, Attic Press Archive)

Tensions emerged within and between groups in the Northern Irish women's movement over feminist ideology, class politics and more specific issues (including support for the Armagh women from 1979 on). This resulted in the formation of new groups, such as the Belfast Women's Collective, which attempted to mobilise on a broader front than the Socialist Women's Group. The Women Against Imperialism group (1978) and the Northern Ireland Abortion Campaign (which held its first conference in 1980) were offshoots from this organisation. In 1980 a Women's Centre was opened in Belfast by the NIWRM, which continued to actively campaign on a number of issues throughout the 1980s.

Throughout the 1980s, many of the groups formed in the previous decade persisted and grew, including the Northern Ireland Women's Aid Federation, the Women's Law and Research Group, and lesbian groups. Other organisations, such as, Women Against Imperialism, Women in Media, the Northern Ireland Abortion Campaign and the Belfast Women's Collective, were short-lived and had proliferated by the mid-1980s. However, the women themselves who were involved did not "disappear" and many became involved in new campaigns and specific areas into the 1990s. The first Rape Crisis Centre and the Northern Ireland Women in Education group were set up in 1982. The first edition of *Women's News* appeared in 1984 and is still published. In addition, there has been a flowering of women's activity and enthusiasm in Derry in recent years at a number of levels. In the 1990s women have been increasingly active at community level in Northern Ireland. There are now, for instance, a number of community women's centres in Belfast and in Coleraine and Derry. The Falls Women's Centre, the Shankill Women's Group, Ballybeen Women's Centre and the Lower Ormeau Women's Information/Drop-in Centre all have strong identities.

Eileen Evason (1991) suggests that while some groups within the women's movement have been absorbed with wider political events in Northern Ireland at all stages since the 1970s, many others focused on feminist issues to which they gave priority. The women's movement in Northern Ireland may have taken a distinct course of its own, but clearly feminists were not entirely insulated from other developments in Anglo-American feminism, for instance. In addition, while the Southern women's movement was often divided on the question of identifying with feminist Republican issues in particular, there were several alliances with feminist campaigns, in Dublin especially (for example, the establishment of the first Rape Crisis Centre in Dublin was linked to the "Free Noreen Winchester campaign".

While feminist activism in Northern Ireland has a striking regional dimension, which until recently was dominated by over 30 years of violent conflict, in other respects it followed a similar path to the second-wave women's movement both in the rest of Western Europe and on the island. It initially took the form of an organised, autonomous and radical women's movement in the mid-1970s; more mainstream activism and alliances with the state developed in the 1980s; locally based women's groups "mushroomed" in both Protestant and Catholic working class communities in the 1980s; and a women's party (the Northern Ireland Women's Coalition) was established in the 1990s. Since the 1980s, locally based women's groups have emerged North and South. Furthermore, the consolidation of women's studies in Northern Ireland in this period has provided the breeding ground for diversifying and expanding feminist scholarship and education. The Northern Ireland Women's Coalition in large part grew out of community-based and women's studies initiatives in the 1990s.

Group meeting at the Belfast Downtown Women's Centre, in *Women's News*, October 2001, Issue 128 (*Women's News* Collection)

Staff of *Women's News* participating in a march in Belfast (*Women's News* Collection n.d.)

Peace campaigner Pat Arrowsmith addresses a rally outside Armagh jail, 8 March 1981 (photo: Clodagh Boyd)

Women on Trial/Women Are Angry march, Dublin, 23 March 1985 (photo: Clodagh Boyd)

Case Study

Noreen Winchester

Noreen Winchester was released from Armagh Women's prison on Friday 21st of April. She had served two years of a seven year sentence for the manslaughter of her father. Following the rejection of her appeal against the sentence, a Free Noreen Winchester campaign was started in Belfast at the instigation of Belfast Women's Aid and led by Ms. Audrey Middleton. Campaigns also got underway in Dublin and Holland. Feminists everywhere were overjoyed to hear of Noreen's release.

We hope, however, that the questions that were beginning to be raised about Noreen's case will not now be dismissed. Her trial and appeal highlighted the urgent need for new legislation on rape. Through the publicity it received, Noreen's case also opened up the previously taboo topic of sexual violence in the family. She had been regularly raped and beaten by her father from the age of eleven until she at last retaliated. How many more young girls are still in this hideous situation?

According to Women's Aid both north and south the incidence of incest in Ireland is very high. Within the past month, two women came to Dublin Harcourt Terrace refuge because of their husbands incestuous attacks on their young daughters. Limerick Women's Aid have come across similar cases. Women's Aid wishes to assist any girl or woman who has had such an experience. The notice board on the last page has the phone numbers of refuges in several cities.

Rape of daughters by fathers is common. Sexual assaults on daughters begin around the age of eight and fathers frequently rape a number of daughters in turn, moving from one to another as the older reaches puberty, to avoid pregnancy. The unique aspect of Noreen's situation is that she defended herself. Because rape within a family is not considered rape, but either the expected sexual fare for the despotic husband, or as incest, a situation too taboo to be discussed, Noreen and Annie, her mother, were stopped from approaching authorities or enlisting the help of neighbors. And Belfast isn't a rape crisis centre. Economically dependent, they had no money and no where to go; Annie could not support all the children and Noreen couldn't leave them to be beaten. Noreen Winchester was a victim because of her father's physical strength, economic strength and the society that makes the husband the head of the household, domestic matters private, sexual matters taboo.

The punishment of Noreen brings into

Article in *Wicca* 1 documenting the Noreen Winchester campaign 1978 (BL/F/AP/1489/1, Attic Press Archive)

Belfast victory rally outside the City Hall- celebrating the release of Noreen Winchester. Left of frame is Karen McGinn (Women's Aid Belfast)

"IT'S GREAT TO BE FREE...I SAW A DOG LAST NIGHT FOR THE FIRST TIME IN AGES AND I'M GOING OUT SHOPPING TODAY, WHICH WILL BE GREAT FUN. I WON'T HAVE TO EAT WITH PLASTIC KNIVES AND FORKS FOR A WHILE. I WISH I COULD BE WITH EVERY ONE THIS AFTERNOON BUT AT THE MOMENT I AM BUSY MEETING LOTS OF FRIENDS OVER HERE—EVEN IF IT IS DIFFICULT TO UNDERSTAND THEM. WHEN I COME BACK I WANT TO GET A JOB HELPING PEOPLE WHO ARE IN THE SAME WAY THAT I WAS. THANK EVERYBODY FOR THEIR SUPPORT."—note from Noreen Winchester read at the Belfast celebration.

Noreen Winchester's mother, Annie, was 16 when she married Norman Winchester and was already pregnant. In subsequent years, she had a total of 16 children while holding down a job as a stitcher in a clothing factory in Belfast. However, her husband, who had a fondness for socialising and drinking, essentially pocketed the money she earned and the family lived in abject poverty. Regular beatings started soon after the marriage and before long violence and abuse was part of the Winchesters' lives. Over time, Norman Winchester's abuse of Annie Winchester steadily deteriorated and grew more severe in character.

Noreen Winchester was the eldest child and by the time she reached 11 years old her father was sexually abusing and raping her. At that stage, eight of the 16 children born to the family had died, most in the first months of infancy. The horror Noreen Winchester suffered has been publicly documented (see most recently, Kiely, 1999: 215–229). Winchester raped and physically assaulted his daughter on a regular basis and the suffering she experienced is immeasurable.

In December 1974, when Noreen reached 17, the situation became too much for her mother Annie. Annie left the family home and ultimately confided in her sister as to what had been taking place in the family home. Winchester subsequently dissuaded Annie from filing for divorce, but he gave her permission to take three of the children to her new home. However, he refused to part with Noreen, who would accompany her father to a new home at 27 Hunter Street, in Sandy Row, along with her sister Tina and three brothers.

From April 1975 until March 1976 Norman Winchester terrorised the five children who lived with him. He cut virtually all ties between the children and the outside world and neighbours remained unaware as to what was taking place. Each Sunday, the four younger children were, however, allowed out, and Winchester raped his daughter Noreen. Winchester's abuse of his oldest daughter ultimately drove her to despair. On the night of Saturday, 20 March 1976, Winchester came home drunk and fell asleep on the settee. Noreen lived in dread of each Sunday, when her father had intercourse with her. On that evening, 18-year-old Noreen took a bread knife from the kitchen and approached her father from behind. She struck him a total of 21 times (Kiely, 1999: 222). With the help of her siblings, Noreen dragged the corpse to a nearby alley and left it there.

The police immediately concluded that Winchester was the victim of a sectarian killing but remained suspicious as to the exact reason for the killing. Meanwhile, the children began living with their mother again and months went by. The RUC gradually began to turn its attention to the family and the Winchester children eventually confessed to the crime under questioning in August 1976. The trial of Noreen Winchester began in February 1977. During the initial days of the trial, the truth about life with Norman Winchester at 27 Hunter Street did not emerge. Noreen's defence counsel advised her to plead guilty to manslaughter in order to lessen her sentence. The judge then dismissed the jury and the trial developed differently.

In court, Noreen's 13-year-old brother provided a vivid account of the degree of control exercised over his sister and he spoke of the starvation and constant abuse they experienced. As regards the circumstances of the killing, he confessed all. The extent to which the killing of Norman Winchester was murder or premeditated became a subject of public debate. The fact that Winchester was asleep when initially stabbed and the manner in which the body was disposed of raised several questions about Noreen's motive in the trial. Sarah Nelson wrote in the *Irish Times*: "… why does a normal girl with no history of crime, aggression or disturbance suddenly act out of character?" (Kiely, 1999: 225). Nonetheless, despite clear knowledge of the horrifying circumstances in which the Winchester children

lived their lives, Noreen Winchester was sentenced to seven years in prison for the killing of her father.

The trial did gain a lot of public attention, however. Many did not share the opinion of the court and a committee was formed to appeal the case in April 1978. The group picketed City Hall in Belfast and collected signatures for a petition, which was delivered to the Secretary of State for Northern Ireland. The "Free Noreen Winchester" campaign was formed by Women's Aid, which worked to protect and support battered and abused women. The Alliance Party, the Northern Ireland Women's Rights Movement and the Association of Legal Aid Centres subsequently joined the campaign. While the campaign to free Noreen intensified, support for criminalising the killer of Norman Winchester also emerged, notably from his family. Winchester was described by some as a decent man who merely liked a drink and social life, and not as the violent and abusive character his wife and children described him as.

```
"ITS GREAT TO BE FREE...I SAW A DOG LAST NIGHT FOR THE
FIRST TIME IN AGES AND I'M GOING OUT SHOPPING TODAY, WHICH
WILL BE GREAT FUN.  I WON'T HAVE TO EAT WITH PLASTIC KNIVES
AND FORKS FOR A WHILE.  I WISH I COULD BE WITH EVERY ONE
THIS AFTERNOON BUT AT THE MOMENT I AM BUSY MEETING LOTS OF
FRIENDS OVER HERE--EVEN IF IT IS DIFFICULT TO UNDERSTAND
THEM.  WHEN I COME BACK I WANT TO GET A JOB HELPING PEOPLE
WHO ARE IN THE SAME WAY THAT I WAS.  THANK EVERYBODY FOR
THEIR SUPPORT."--note from Noreen Winchester read at the
Belfast celebration.
```

Documenting the Noreen Winchester Campaign, *Wicca* **1 1978 (BL/F/AP/1489/1, Attic Press Archive)**

A hearing was eventually held in the Northern Ireland Appeal Court and presided over by the Lord Chief Justice, Sir Robert Lowry. He concluded that while the original trial judge had been correct in his ruling, there was nothing to prevent the Government exercising the ancient right of the English monarch to pardon a convicted crime. In due course, he submitted his recommendation for mercy to Buckingham Palace.

Noreen Winchester gained her freedom in April 1978, aged 21. A story of years of hidden brutality and violent incest was out in the open. Many more stories were to come out in Ireland in subsequent years.

Feminism and Republicanism

The changing political situation in Northern Ireland following the emergence of the civil rights movement in Derry in 1968 was unavoidably contentious in the ideologically vibrant radical feminist groups, which emerged in the 1970s. In the South, although North/South connections were important between Republican-feminists, there were often constrained links between the two parallel movements. Sympathetic Southern nationalists expressed solidarity with the women prisoners in Armagh, for example, while many other activists in the South were vehemently opposed to Republican politics in any shape or form.

Considerable evidence of this debate and associated conflict exists in recent Irish feminist history.[2] The Armagh Prisoners campaign was widely debated through radical publications like *Wicca* and in the later Women Against Imperialism group, which organised North/South:

> The fact that women patriots are engaging in a separate struggle with the British adminis-
> tration in pursuit of status as political prisoners, even to the point of death, has had
> widescale repercussions within the women's movement and in society as a whole... Whilst
> the Armagh prisoners have declared themselves that they do not wish to be supported as
> women, but as patriots, nevertheless the fact that women are standing in the forefront of
> this struggle has raised the issue of political status in a very sharp way in the women's
> movement. (*Wicca* 13 (1977): 14/BL/F/AP/1498, Attic Press Archive)[3]

Many feminists North and South were unwilling to see state violence against women prisoners and activists as a legitimate feminist issue, a position that was actively opposed by Republican-feminist activists.

Movement archives document how differences occurred, within both the IWLM and in IWU, among activists who defined their feminism in terms of Republican politics and those who criticized any involvement with nationalist causes. Many held the view that historically Irish nationalism had proven itself to be as central to the subordination of Irish women as British colonialism. Nationalism is the basis of a long-standing conflict that dominated the first wave of feminism in Ireland, when dispute over whether to campaign for the right of Irish women to vote for a British parliament or to secure Irish independence first divided the women's movement. In the 1970s, feminists involved in Republican politics also saw their cause differently to other factions, in groups like IWU. For some women, opposition to Republicanism was in itself enough of a reason to be a feminist, in the first instance. The national question was therefore an integral movement dis-course and dynamic in radical feminist groups and created vigorous dialogue, dif-ference and exchange in several organizations, on questions such as the definition of an Irish identity, the legacy of British colonialism in Ireland, the civil rights of Northern Catholics and the legitimacy of the Irish nation-state.

The question of women and Irish nationalism essentially remains highly con-tentious in Irish feminism and it is unlikely that a consensus will easily materialise.

Women in Prison — Armagh

IN THE LAST ISSUE OF WICCA WE GAVE DETAILS OF THE LIVING CONDITIONS OF THE WOMEN IN MOUNTJOY PRISON. THE OTHER MAJOR DETENTION CENTRE FOR WOMEN IN IRELAND IS ARMAGH JAIL IN THE NORTH.

In May 1976 Mr. Mason removed special category status which had previously been granted to prisoners convicted of crimes that are widely acknowledged as political crimes. Since then all the

crushing the spirit

less bars ...same tyranny

" When a Government puts people in jail for their political opinions, we do not ask the nationality of that Government, we are always on the side of the victim of State tyranny .... "

MARIE-LOUISE Berneri
Feminist and political activist 1918-1949

4

Armagh Prisoners Campaign, article in _Wicca_ 5 (c. 1978) (BL/F/AP/1498/5, Attic Press Archive)

Armagh

War affects women. Within Northern Ireland, and, occasionally, during the overspill into the South, women have been killed and maimed and bereaved; more often, they have been left as sole providers of their families, while male relatives were jailed or buried; more often again, they have presided over the living death of families torn asunder by a combination of all these things.

and we agreed from the start, south of the Border, that we would not discuss Northern reland. We chose not to begin with a split, but to find common ground, build upon it, gather the strength of the movement around us and then ... and then ... we held our breath and put Northern Ireland off until tomorrow.

Tomorrow is upon us now. I t is

the framework of marriage - the Irishwomen's Liberation Movement did not think, at its launching in the Mansion House, to demand divorce.

We have to take the first step North now because there is an exclusively female group there whose desperate situation commands our attention and demands from us a response. They are the Republican

Women have been involved in roles that have gone far beyond nurturing those who depend on them - they have taken part in daily protest, engaged in politics, taken up arms on one side or the other, joining the ranks of the IRA, the RUC, the UDR, the UDA, the UVF and the British Army.

How could they have done otherwise? The war affected them and they took sides as they saw fit!!

Feminists have been paralysed in face of the war in Northern Ireland. That too is understandable, because the women's movement was born out of an instinctive gut reaction to oppression and there was no ready made body of intellectual belief to which we could collectively subscribe. We began only yesterday

upon us, as it has not been upon any other feminist movement around the globe. Ireland is the only country in the entire world within whose borders there is at once an extant, strong feminist movement and a war. It is upon us now to develop a theory of feminism and war. Obviously it will be impossible to develop such a theory overnight. Men have been at, and controlled, war since time began and have found no adequate solution. There is no rational reason to believe that any solution we attempt will be instantly successful.

Equally, there is no rational reason now for avoiding the attempt. We have to take the first stumbling step, as we took the first step only yesterday, ten years ago, by pitching our demands for liberation within

women protestors of Armagh jail, who are, in the broadest sense, prisoners of war. They are in jail because the actions they took, or are alleged to have taken, or were convicted of taking though they patently did not do so, resulted from the war that has convulsed Northern Ireland for more than a decade. All of these 32 young working-class women were children when that war began. They are children of our time, who emerged from infancy to the sound of gunfire, went to school through the blasting of bombs, entered their teens to the tread of tanks, and are passing their early adult lives now to the sound of silence, in the odour of shit.

P.T.O.

13

Various feminist newsletters and magazines documented the conditions of female prisoners in Armagh (c. 1978–80) (BL/F/AP/1498, Attic Press Archive)

women in armagh prison

There are 30 women in Armagh prison, in a modern concentration camp how & if we support them is now a soul searching question for Irish feminists. We are now forced to explain what we mean when we say we are feminists, we are forced to take a stand. Irish women finding themselves in a neo-colonial state, need to examine the tenets of international feminism & to forge a theory which will help & guide us in our struggle for control over our lives.

There seems to me to be parallels between the way in which imperial-ist nations oppress other peoples in order to maintain their state of power as the way men oppress women in order to maintain their advantaged position. Thus Irish women have a double oppression & I believe one cannot be struggled against without confronting the other. A feminist vision of the future runs counter to the exploit-ive & parasitical nature of imperialism.

When I stepped off the bus, on International Women's Day, this year, in Belfast, the reality of Imperialism hit me in the shape of the shock & paranoia, I felt at my first sight of the occupying army mingling with shoppers. I stayed the weekend, yet there is no way my mind can grasp the fear & tension of daily life there. Because of this, we women in the 26 counties end up with easy rhetoric about the monstrosity of armed struggle. many women claim that they do not believe in violence. Who does — but there have been so many centuries of violence done to women & continue to be that it makes nonsense of what some so-called pacifists say when they state that all violence is the same.

This implies that a woman who injures/kills her husband /father after years of torture & rape, that the two acts are morally the same.

I believe that because of our history of oppression & our exclus-ion from the active political world that we have developed "female values" of nurturance & caring & that we, like the women in Armagh prison, only take to acts of violence , when we have

been put to the end of our endurance. To the women who recognise the violence that is being done to us, & who claim that we must find different methods of struggle, e.g. non-violent action. I respect their sincerity. However the Civil Rights Movement is a glaring example of how the violence of the State can 'gas' hundreds of people of the streets. In the meantime I cannot assure non-violent feminists that if the war spreads to the 26 counties, or if I am attacked in the streets of Dublin that I will not defend myself by violent action .

Yet I reel with confusion. I believe that many other feminsts have gone through the same period of confusion & the movement has become entrenched on both sides. On one side women who support the Republican movement & who promulgate the importance of the anti-imperialist war & on the side women who claim the war has nothing to do with feminism & so what if we have a socialist republic--the position won't change.

It should be obvious from the above that I believe that feminism is of necessity anti-imperialist . Consequently we must be involved in the anti-imperialist struggle & despite the patriarchial attitudes which are rife within the Republican Movement feminist must work longside such groups. However this must be on our terms. I believe it is necessary for us women to organize seperately & autonomously to forge a feminist theory & a feminist practice which is relevant to our situation, only then can the anti-imperialist movement become feminist.   *Bríd.*

18

Article in *Wicca* magazine (c. 1978–80) (BL/F/AP/198/5, Attic Press Archive)

BRUTALITY

Women in the 6 Counties have been politically and militarily active throughout the events of the past 10 years. They have been raided, beaten, and imprisoned. But a new "refinement" has been recently adopted by the RUC as part of their interrogation techniques.

Women interrogated at Castlereagh during the past few months report that as well as being physically threatened and hit around the head (which causes less marking), they were also threatened with sexual abuse.

One woman from Short Strand whose case is now being studied by Amnesty International, was taken to Castlereagh with her baby. She was first threatened that the child would be taken from her and put into care. The next day, after the child had been collected by a relative, a policewoman asked if she had ever been raped. The policewoman then went out of the room, turning out the light. Two men came in and tried to force her down on a table top. As she struggled the policewoman came in laughing and turned on the light again.

The same woman was also subjected to abusive remarks from policemen when she asked for a sanitary towel as her period had started.

Another woman was taunted about a recent miscarriage. The police said she had a miscarriage because she panicked when planting a bomb.

These incidents are not unique--but they are becoming a far more common occurance. They give us an insight into the police's attitude towards sex--that it is a weapon for intimidating and humiliating women.

Women are not remaining silent--more and more are speaking out against this latest manifestation of

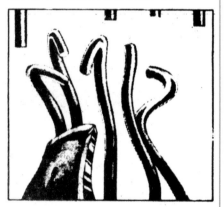

brutality. We are investigating the cases of women who have suffered similar treatment and in our next issue will feature a major article on women and brutality.

---from "Women's Action" by the Belfast Women's Collective. To contact them about the magazine, to hire their video film on nurseries or book Wayward Women, a women's theater group, write to 52 Broadway Belfast.

Report from the Belfast Women's Collective in *Wicca* (c. 1978–80) (BL/F/AP/1498/5, Attic Press Archive)

Women marching in Northern Ireland in *The Other Woman,* **November–December 1973**

Clara Connolly writes: "The republican feminist agenda is a thorn in the flesh of both the republican and feminist movements in Ireland. It is an agenda with a long and still-developing history" (1995: 111). Clár na mBan, a Republican feminist group, began in the early 1990s with a series of informal meetings held by women working within an anti-imperialist perspective. The group held a major conference in 1994 in response to the absence of women's voices in the critical political developments of 1993, notably the Hume/Adams talks and the Downing Street Declaration. A major theme of the conference was the exclusion of women from all male-dominated political structures, mainstream and Republican/nationalist politics. Clara Connolly (a member of Clár na mBan) repeated, in an article published in 1995, many of the same issues that historically have shaped the difficult relationship between feminism and nationalism in Ireland:

> For many years, republican and Southern feminists have been in involved in a war of mutual recrimination. Northern Irish republicans, and their allies in the South, have accused mainstream feminists of ignoring the conflict in Northern Ireland, and the effects of the British occupation on Northern Irish Catholic women. Southern feminists, in conflict not only with the Church but with Irish nationalist representations of women, have been hostile to what they see as the hijacking of feminism for nationalist ends. (Connolly, 1995: 118)

However, quite a dramatic transformation of the two "pillars" Connolly identifies – the Catholic Church and official nationalist ideology – has occurred in recent years. Because of recent social and political change, new directions and possibilities in Irish feminist debate are now consolidating. For example, unexplored

Mo Mowlam meeting local feminist activists in Belfast (c. 1995) (*Women's News* Collection)

opportunities for dialogue between Protestant activists in Northern Ireland and Southern feminists may arise. Crucially, however, the longstanding absence of all women's voices in the formal political process in Northern Ireland remains manifest. Quite apart from the dominant dilemmas faced by the British and Irish governments and the male-dominated Northern Ireland Assembly, the differences which exist among Irish women will also need to be addressed, both within feminist politics and in the mainstream, if the peace process is to succeed.

The Northern Ireland Women's Coalition

In recent years, the Northern Ireland Women's Coalition (NIWC) has created a distinctive space for women on the political agenda in Northern Ireland. The Women's Coalition was thrust onto the political stage in 1996, when two delegates were elected to multi-party talks on the future of Northern Ireland. Just six weeks earlier, women from all walks of life met to discuss how women's voices could be heard in these crucial negotiations. At the negotiating table, Monica McWilliams and Pearl Sagar sought to bring a new approach to traditional problems in Northern Ireland. The Coalition called for the creation of a Civic Forum, support for victims of violence, integrated education and mixed housing. The NIWC delegates were the only female signatories to the Belfast Agreement. Since the Agreement was signed and endorsed by the people of Northern Ireland in a referendum, the Coalition have worked for its full implementation as the only way to secure a peaceful future for Northern Ireland:

> Traditional political parties will bring their fixed agendas on the constitutional question to
> negotiations; the Women's Coalition is dedicated to drawing together the different views,
> ideas and options to achieve a workable solution. Over the years of violence women have
> been very effective in developing and maintaining contact across the various divides in our

society. They have created a space for discussion and for an honest exchange of views. In doing this women have seen themselves as agents of change. (NIWC Manifesto, published in the Irish Journal of Feminist Studies, 1998: 2)

The Women's Coalition is a cross-community political party working for inclusion, human rights and equality in Northern Ireland. Members are both women and men and from nationalist, unionist and other backgrounds. The Coalition's policies are based on the needs of all traditions as well as women's common interests. Until recently, represented in the Northern Ireland Assembly and at Local Council level, the Women's Coalition aims to work towards the implementation of the Belfast Agreement. The Coalition is plural in orientation, however, and aims to widen participation in politics by ensuring the voices of young people, older people, ethnic minorities, women and community and voluntary groups are heard.

Case Study

Monica McWilliams

Monica McWilliams is a founding member and representative
of the Northern Ireland Women's
Coalition. McWilliams' political
story is, in several respects,
embedded in the growth of academic feminism in Ireland and
its links with both mainstream
politics and community politics.
Elected to the Northern Ireland
Assembly in 1998, she represented South Belfast, which has a
constituency of 60,000 people.
Dr McWilliams is also a professor
of women's studies and social
policy at the University of Ulster,
where she introduced the first
accredited access courses for
women returning to education.
She was awarded the doctor of
humane letters from Lesley
College, in Massachusetts, for her

NIWC Member Monica McWilliams
(***Women's News* Collection**)

work on the impact of political conflict and domestic violence on women's
lives in Northern Ireland. Her publications include several pieces relating
to the Northern Ireland Peace process and two books on domestic violence.

As a signatory of the Good Friday Agreement, she was awarded the
National Democratic Institute Award and the John F. Kennedy Leadership
and Courage Award. In 1999, she received the Frank Cousins Peace Award
and Boston Immigration Center's Woman of the Year Award. McWilliams's
peace-building activities include co-founding the Northern Ireland
Women's Coalition to increase the representation of women in Northern
Ireland's political process. Monica McWilliams played an instrumental role
in the multiparty negotiations that led to the Belfast Agreement. The NIWC
was central in negotiating the establishment of the Civic Forum and the
Agreement's commitment to victims of violence in Northern Ireland.

Conclusion

In recent years, much has been written in Ireland and elsewhere about feminists striving for common ground while recognizing difference. Eilish Rooney (2000: 178) writes that: "Feminists seeking to mobilize women on the basis of their common interests face particular problems in the north of Ireland." Major issues particular to Northern Ireland have had to be tackled by women, as well as the basic struggles against economic exploitation and sexual oppression mobilised by feminists elsewhere (McWilliams, 1993: 95). Monica McWilliams wrote in 1993:

> …it remains the case that the oppression caused by the present political impasse is deeply destructive to all women. Some are psychologically scarred by the deaths of, or injuries to, loved ones, whilst others are emotionally drained trying to cope with the daily tensions of living in the midst of such intense political conflict. Women on both that nationalist and loyalist sides have faced the destruction of family life when husbands, brothers or sons have been arrested under the emergency Prevention of Terrorism Act, tried by Diplock (non-jury) courts and held for long periods without trial on remand. Women have also been subjected to the humiliating and degrading treatment of strip-searching… simply living in the insidious atmosphere of sectarianism and violence on a daily basis can cause increased anxiety in itself… These multiple layers of oppression affect the psychological and physical well-being of women in Northern Ireland; some affect women living in nationalist areas more, while others affect Catholics and Protestants equally. (McWilliams, 1993: 95)

The experiences of Protestant, Unionist, Loyalist, working- and middle-class women and those of Catholic, Nationalist, Republican, working- and middle-class women therefore interweave and conflict in multifaceted ways in the Northern Irish context. In a recent extensive collection on women and politics in Northern Ireland, Eilish Rooney (2000) explores how the crude, homogenising assumptions of particular labels and language are applied to "women" in Northern Ireland – Unionist and Loyalist, Nationalist and Republican, working-class and middle-class. And yet she argues that, paradoxically, these forms of identification seem unavoidable in order to explore the political differences that frame women's lives. In other words, "difference matters".

In recent decades, while North/South co-operation has occurred in some areas (such as in the campaign to extend the Abortion Act 1967 to Northern Ireland and in the arenas of rape crisis and refuge provision), feminists in the South have concentrated on maintaining opposition to church-state authority and control, in the Irish political mainstream. Outside of the arena of Republican feminism, feminist writers and activists in the south have said little about women's experience in Northern Ireland and many have avoided the issue (for a discussion, see Mulholland and Smyth, 1999). Furthermore, the experience of Protestant women and activists in Northern Ireland has received minimal attention in Irish feminist writing to date. More exploration of the disparate national and international dynamics that have shaped women's lives in Ireland is necessary in feminist scholarship in order to create a greater understanding of all the issues raised in this chapter.

Notes

1 See *Feminism Versus Nationalism: Women's Liberation Ireland 1971–1973* by Mary Flynn (source: BL/F/AP/1138, Attic Press Archive).

2 File BL/F/AP/1306, Attic Press Archive, includes leaflet produced by the Women's Committee of the Communist Party of Ireland (1978), calling for support for Armagh Women Prisoners.

3 File BL/F/AP/1511, Attic Press Archive, contains *Women's News*, nos. 5, 6, 9, 14, 24 (September 1984–March 1987).

Chapter 6
Lesbian Activism

Poster advertising the Sexual Liberation Movement (Irish Queer Archive). (n.d.) c. 1970s

The Ireland I live in now is so far removed from the Ireland of twenty years ago it might be a different country. And the Ireland of my childhood remembered from this perspective seems like another planet.

Mary Dorcey. Interview.
(O'Carroll and Collins, 1995:35)

Introduction

The emergence of the second wave of the women's movement in Ireland tends to be associated chiefly with campaigns concerning reproductive rights and equality in employment. Against this backdrop, the ways in which the women's movement became a focus for the sexual liberation of women in Ireland from the 1970s onwards has received little attention. For much of the twentieth century, Irish society was dominated by repressive social and cultural attitudes to sexuality in general. The women's movement addressed this silence in a number of different ways – in particular, consciousness-raising groups became a forum for Irish women to express and discuss their sexuality in a more open fashion. Consciousness-raising groups were some of the first "safe spaces" in which Irish lesbians and bisexual

The Lesbian Movement

There have always been lesbians active in the radical feminist movement but it is only recently that they have emerged as a separate group. In September 1977 a women's disco was started in the Tailor's Hall, when Irish Women United, which used to use that place for fund raising socials, ceased to exist.

Since then, the women's disco has moved to the Pembroke Inn to the Parliament Inn and, just recently, back to the Pembroke Inn where women meet every Thursday to dance to the current top 40.

About 40 women attend weekly, and most of them are lesbians, but heterosexual women are welcome and are assured that this is not the female equivalent of a pick-up in Zhivagos . . . it's just a place to dance to your heart's content.

Liberation for Irish Lesbians was formed in September of last year. There is no formal membership, but about 20 women attend each meeting. They are feminists as well as lesbians, which is not as obvious as it seems. According to LIL organiser Joni Sheeran, there are some lesbians who see feminism as a vaguely irrelevant political concept. It is these same women who tend to conform to the traditional "butch" and "fem" roles in lesbian relationships.

Radical Irish lesbians feel they have more in common with radical feminists than with homosexual men. The now defunct Irish Gay Rights Movement had

LIL's Joni Sheeran

a membership of 300 men and three women. The Movement split over the question of whether it was a political pressure group or a social organisation.

More recently, the National Gay Federation has been formed with a clear commitment to political action. LIL is affiliated to the NGF and is participating in the new Hirschfeld Centre in 10 Fownes Street, Dublin 2. With the

centre in operation as a meeting place, LIL expects its membership to grow. At last year's Gay Women's Conference, 81 women attended and it is these women LIL hopes to attract to the Hirschfeld Centre.

The main problem for Irish lesbians, according to Joni Sheeran, is one of recognition. Until recently, homosexuality was identified as a male problem. This has worked to the advantage of gay women in that there are no laws against lesbianism in Ireland, but it also means that many isolated Irish lesbians see no way out of their isolation.

For these women, LIL has organised a phone service, called "Tel-a-friend", every Wednesday from 8 to 10 at 710608. They hope to expand this service and have convinced some organisations like the Samaritans to refer people to them. Joni Sheeran says this kind of supportive feeling is really unique to the lesbian movement and doesn't exist, to the same degree, in the women's movement.

For the future, Liberation for Irish Lesbians hopes to utilise the spacious, four storey Hirschfeld Centre. There is talk of setting up a sports club, establishing a library and beginning a wide range of discussion/research groups. Of course, the women's disco will continue. In the Hirschfeld Centre there will be mixed gay discos. Through the Centre gay men and women, who seldom have much in common, hope to fight their mutual oppression together.   **P.B.**

40 MAGILL APRIL 1979

Extract from Pat Brennan article, "Women in Revolt", in *Magill* 2.7 (1979) (BL/F/AP/1139/34, Attic Press Archive)

women began to define and address their sexuality in a more open way for the first time in 1970s Ireland.

Lesbians have been part of numerous campaigns for political liberation in Ireland, yet very little is known about the development of lesbian feminist activism in Ireland, or the women who were involved in it. In general, there is a dearth of research on lesbian political activism both in mainstream Irish history and in Irish women's history. This lack of scholarly work, combined with a paucity of relevant sources/collections in Irish archives, adds to the general invisibility of lesbian lives in contemporary Ireland. The emergence of lesbian feminism as an important strand of the second-wave women's movement in Ireland will be explored and documented in this chapter.

Despite the fact that the Irish lesbian community is noted for its political activism,[1] academic, political and media analysis has focused more on gay men than on lesbians. The public face of activism in the lesbian, gay and bisexual (LGB)[2] communities in Ireland in the late 1980s and early 1990s was mainly focused on service provision around the HIV/AIDS crisis and on rights-based activism (principally the campaign for the decriminalisation of male homosexuality).[3] Although many lesbians participated in this work, women did not have the same kind of public or media profile as their gay male counterparts, and many made deliberate choices for one reason or another to work "behind the scenes." According to Hug: "Irish lesbians commanded less of our attention since no laws and no papal pronouncements have attacked them" (1999: 238). However, this chapter will demonstrate in some depth that the reasons for lesbian invisibility in Irish society are more complex and are rooted in pervasive gendered societal attitudes to Irish women and their sexuality, which have received limited attention in Irish studies to date.

The difficulties for Irish lesbians in being publicly "out", particularly in the early days of lesbian feminist activism, are attested to by many of those involved. Joni Crone describes the Irish lesbian community in the 1980s as "an underground minority, a subculture whose members have been unwilling or unable to court publicity, because to do so may have invited violence, rape or even death" (Crone, 1995: 61). She goes on to discuss the difficulties of being identified as lesbian in the late 1970s, when she was involved in organising the first lesbian conference in Ireland:

> It was only quite late in the proceedings that we realized that if we called the event a "lesbian conference" most of the organizing collective would be unable to attend because "walking through the door would be a public statement" ... it was sobering to discover that most of the lesbian women we knew were leading double lives. At home, at work, and even within the Women's Movement, they were open about their feminism, but they disguised their sexual identity. Our compromise solution was to call the weekend a "Women's Conference on Lesbianism". This meant that women of every sexual persuasion were free to attend. (Hug, 1995: 64)

Albeit based on motives of self-protection, defining a space or event as a "women's space" opened it to the participation of all women, irrespective of their sexual orientation. Describing the Toronto lesbian community in the 1970s, Becki Ross points out that groups formed during this period were "officially open to all women, and were not referred to as lesbian spaces; the word 'lesbian' did not appear in their names", even where the membership and direction of an organisation was based on lesbian energies (1995: 55). The Women's Place, a resource centre on McCurtain Street in Cork,[4] and the Galway Women's Camp chose to define their space in this way, rejecting the boundaries imposed on lesbians by mainstream society.

Although there has been a sea-change in Irish attitudes to the LGBT communities in the past 20 years, some of the old prejudices still pertain, particularly for women. So for example, although current equality legislation guarantees protection against discrimination on the grounds of sexual orientation,[5] there have been few cases taken so far involving lesbians. To make such a case involves taking a public stand, and clearly few lesbians are ready to take this step. Yet collectively, for the past 20 years or more, lesbians have been involved in a number of initiatives aimed at improving local resources and services for the LGBT communities.

Groups such as Lesbians Organising Together (LOT) in Dublin, Lesbians in Cork (L.INC) and Lesbian Education and Awareness (LEA), a national group based in Dublin, have attracted government funding for projects designed to tackle the invisibility of this community.[6]

In her study of lesbian community activism in Toronto, Ross describes a scenario which may be familiar to lesbians in Ireland:

> Among those of us privileged to be out and to have access to [community] resources, there is little collective knowledge of how they came to exist, who was responsible for their genesis, and how fragile they continue to be. When I came out, even the immediate lesbian past seemed remote; I joined a collective state of unknowing that is both personally disabling and politically dangerous. (Ross, 1995: 4)

An understanding of what it is to be lesbian or bisexual, how that changes over time and place, and an awareness of the issues and struggles faced by lesbians and bisexual women in different social contexts has been available to Irish women in a variety of textual forms since the late 1960s. However, in terms of a specific history of what it is to be lesbian and bisexual in Ireland, research and writing in this field is only in its early stages.[7]

Lesbians and the Women's Movement

Despite their active involvement as participants in the early days of the Irish women's movement, lesbian issues were not on the core feminist agenda. Solidarity between women was a feature of the early feminist years, and in order to present a unified front to the dominant culture differences between women, such as sexuality, were perceived as problematic elements with the power to distract from the main focus of the movement, or even to destroy it from within. Feminists who became involved in the Irish Women's Liberation Movement (IWLM) tacitly agreed to leave their "difference(s)" at the door, or at least, not to publicly own them. Mary Dorcey remembers: "I came back to Ireland. I went to the Women's Movement (then in its second year). I met wonderful women. I was enchanted by the exhilaration, the self-confidence, energy, wit, anger, vision but, to my surprise, no one declaring themselves lesbians or speaking about it" (1995: 35). The first group to specifically address lesbian and gay issues was set up in 1973 following an open meeting in Dublin. Here Dorcey describes seeing a poster advertising the organisation:

> "The Sexual Liberation Movement Meets Tonight at Eight O'Clock". Bewildering and ludicrous as it seems from this vantage point, that night twenty-two years ago was the first time I think the word "sexual" was written anywhere in public. The Women's Movement had been in action for one year, the Pill train had taken place, and I had seen some of the group on the *Late Late Show*, but while they demanded the right to legal contraception, I don't remember that anyone talked about sex. (1995: 35)

Poster advertising the Sexual Liberation Movement (Irish Queer Archive) c, 1970s

Following this meeting, lesbians involved in the women's movement began to discuss their sexuality more openly. The newly formed Sexual Liberation Movement (SLM) held a public meeting in 1973, the first of its kind in this country, addressed by the psychiatrist and politician Noel Browne and Babs Todd, an English lesbian activist, on the subject of gay rights.

Not having been named within the IWLM charter of "seven minimum demands", lesbian experience was finally referred to, albeit somewhat obliquely, in the Irishwomen United (IWU) charter when sexuality was added to the demands, with feminists calling for: "The right of all women to our own self-defined sexuality." IWU acted as an umbrella organisation for a range of different kinds of feminist groups and issues, and there were many lesbian feminist activists involved in it.

Lesbian Feminist Activism

In order to understand the formation of lesbian/bisexual communities in Ireland, it is perhaps more useful to replace our perception of "the" lesbian feminist movement with a more fluid concept of interacting groups and social scenes in different geographical locations. This problematises efforts to either subsume lesbian activism under the umbrella of "the gay movement", or to depict lesbian activism as a single social movement, with common goals and a shared vision. During the 1970s and 1980s, some lesbians and bisexual women chose to work with gay men towards gay rights, some continued to work within mainstream feminist activist groups, and others set up groups that were women-only or lesbian-only.

Of course, many lesbians and bisexual women moved in and out of these different groupings, or worked on a variety of campaigns under different umbrellas at different periods. Irish lesbians were also involved in the anti-nuclear movement and, at local level, in a variety of other activist initiatives. There seems to have been little formal co-operation between IWU and those involved in the Irish Gay Rights Movement (IGRM) set up in 1974 – on the whole, lesbians tended to work within the feminist rather than the gay-rights movement.

It is evident both from the documentary evidence of this period and from talking to a number of activists involved in different groupings at the time, that the wider Irish women's movement was not prepared to address the issues and experiences of lesbian feminist activists in Ireland in the late 1970s/early 1980s, or at least not to do so publicly. Although there was never the sense of bitter division apparent within feminism internationally, particularly in the USA, the question of lesbian feminism became one of the points of dissonance within the Irish women's movement.

One of the early contributing factors to the establishment of distinct lesbian groups and communities was the growing disaffection among lesbians with the wider feminist movement. Irish lesbians who continued to work on political campaigns in tandem with their heterosexual sisters (and brothers) frequently found

WOMEN'S CONFERENCE ON LESBIANISM

☿

Following the National Women's Conference in January we have organised this Conference to discuss a wide range of issues relating to lesbians and lesbianism.   This is the first Conference of its kind to be held in Ireland. Lesbianism has not been explored by public debate or within the women's movement here.   Lesbians have been in the vanguard of the fight for radical change – the struggle for an autonomous lifestyle for women will not be complete while lesbians are oppressed, therefore, we should not be disclaimed publicly or in the context of women's liberation.   We feel this Conference will break down the barriers of silence and ignorance surrounding lesbian sexuality.

Workshops from Saturday to Sunday will include:-

COMING OUT – THE-CHURCH AND LESBIANISM – ROLE PLAYING – SOCIAL CONDITIONING AND THE FAMILY – MONOGAMY, POSSESSIVENESS AND JEALOUSY – SEXUALITY AND SEXUAL FANTASIES – LESBIANISM AND FEMINISM – SEPARATISM.

other pracital workshops include Dance, Theatre, Motor-cycle Maintenance, Video.

A Social has been organised for Friday night at the Resources Centre and a disco/party for Saturday evening.   An Art Exhibition will be held over the weekend.   Women are invited to bring their own work on Saturday morning to sell or display.   A bookstall will also be set up – all publications welcome.

We invite all women to participate in a sharing of lesbian experience and sensibilities, rather than in defence of your own sexuality – whatever it is!

VENUE: Trinity College, Dublin.

TIME OF REGISTRATION:

   Friday: 8.00 p.m. (evening) at
           The Resources Centre,
           168 Rathgar Road,
           Dublin 6.
           (BUSES 15, 15a, 18)

   Saturday: 9.00 a.m. onwards at
            Trinity College.

FEE: £1.00

REPLIES TO BE SENT TO:-

WOMEN'S CONFERENCE PLANNING COMMITTEE,
c/o 3a VERGEMOUNT HALL,
CLONSKEAGH ROAD,
DUBLIN 6.

DATE: 26th to 28th May, 1978.

ACCOMMODATION: available, bring sleeping. bag if possible.

FOOD: available throughout i.e. breakfast & snacks

CRECHE: available free at Trinity Saturday & Sunday 10.00 - 6.00 only

NOTE: *Evening creches not available.   Volunteers urgently needed.   If YOU need creche facilities be sure to let us know well in advance as we need an indication of numbers. Also you must supply your own nappies, feeds, toys etc*

LESBIANISM IS BLOOMING   PATRIARCHY WILL NEVER BE THE SAME

Flyer for the first Irish Conference on Lesbianism, held at Trinity College Dublin, May 1978 (BL/F/AP/1116, Attic Press Archive)

Lesbians in The Irish Feminist Movement

The Irish Women's Liberation Movement has existed for ten years. The organisation formed in 1970 has disintegrated, the individuals involved have changed but a broad based movement working for women's rights continues.

Kate Millet's visit to Ireland on October 14th brought together socialist feminists, radical feminists, middle-of-the-road feminists, active and not-so-active feminists, and lesbian feminists. Kate Millet is a highly respected writer, activist, feminist who has 'come out' as a lesbian. But why has it taken ten years before the word 'lesbian' could be uttered in public at an Irish feminist meeting? Why, even in the most radical group yet - Irishwomen United - was the existence of lesbians ignored? The last line of their charter in small print reads:

7. The right of all women to a self-determined sexuality.

This may be interpreted as thinly disguised recognition and support for lesbianism. But veiled references and tokenism after years of activism is just not good enough. For ten years we have struggled alongside our sisters for contraception, divorce, justice for deserted and battered wives, equal pay and every legal and social issue that has arisen. We've given a large degree of energy, ideas, time and commitment. Most of the time these issues have not been central to the lives of lesbians. We have never demanded:

1.   The right of lesbian women to a self-determined sexuality.
2.   The right of lesbian mothers to custody of their children.
3.   The right of lesbians to equal opportunity and protection in employment.

4.   The right of lesbians to protection under the law.
We're a long way from this last demand since in Ireland, legally, we don't even exist!

In the United States in 1971, the National Organisation of Women (N.O.W.) voted to support lesbianism legally and morally. They accepted lesbianism as a valid lifestyle. This did not happen overnight. It was the result of a consistent, determined struggle by lesbians within the movement. When will we see the day the Irish Housewives Association for instance, or the W.P.A., the Council for the Status of Women or any women's group accepts lesbianism as a valid lifestyle? And why should they? Because lesbians are in any and all of these groups and in trade unions, offices, factories, convents, on buses, in restaurants, on the streets - *WE ARE EVERYWHERE.*

At the Kate Millet meeting I challenged Irish feminists to recognise the contribution lesbians have made within the movement here. The response was overwhelming. That surely indicates the degree of support and solidarity which is present just below the surface but still not articulated. Lesbianism as a women's rights

issue has not yet been confronted, debated, discussed or endorsed. After ten years of activism the time has come for you, as a lesbian, to 'come out' to yourself, and to your sisters and make the concept of Irish Lesbian Feminism a reality.

Source material: *"Sappho was a Right-on Woman"* by Sidney Abbott and Barbara Love. Paperback published by Stein and Day, New York. Category: Sociology/General.

Recommended reading: *"Sexual Politics"; "Flying"; "Sita"* all by Kate Millet, available Books Upstairs, 10 South King Street, Dublin 2.

Contacts: Tel-A-Friend, telephone information and counselling service for gay women and men. Women's night Thursdays 8 - 10 p.m. Phone 710608.

"Sita's" womens disco; Liberation for Irish Lesbians (L.I.L.); National Gay Federation also meeting place, coffee bar, cinema, discos, all at the Hirschfeld Centre, 10 Fownes Street, Dublin 2 (behind the new Central Bank in Dame St.). Also lesbian group meets Mondays, 8 Marlboro St., 8 p.m. sharp.

Joni Sheerin.

Article by Joni Sheerin/Crone in *Elektra* **(Trinity College Dublin Women's Magazine), November 1980 (BL/F/AP/749, Attic Press Archive)**

a lack of support when it came to organising on issues directly related to lesbian lives and experiences. The first Irish lesbian conference, mentioned earlier, was held in Dublin in May 1978, and the flyer announcing the conference touches on some of these issues.

> Lesbianism has not been explored by public debate or within the women's movement here. Lesbians have been in the vanguard of the fight for radical change – the struggle for an autonomous lifestyle for women will not be complete while lesbians are oppressed, therefore we should not be disclaimed publicly or in the context of women's liberation. We feel this conference will break down the barriers of silence and ignorance surrounding lesbian sexuality …. We invite all women to participate in a sharing of lesbian experience and sensibilities, rather than in defence of your own sexuality – whatever it is! (BL/F/AP/1116, Attic Press Archive)

The impact of this conference was palpable, as Crone notes: "The 1978 conference was significant for the boost it gave to lesbian pride, and had a lasting effect on the community. Lesbian feminists now recognised the contribution we had already made to the Women's Movement since 1970" (Crone, 1995: 65). The first Lesbian Line collective came together in September of the same year, and delegates from the lesbian conference joined with a group working on family violence to plan a campaign for a broad-based women's centre (Crone, 1995: 65).

This growing confidence also had an impact on lesbian involvement in the wider feminist movement, as lesbians began to realise that their issues and experiences were being ignored or sidelined by the wider movement. Joni Sheerin (later Joni Crone) put this forcefully in a review of a Kate Millet lecture in Dublin in 1980:

> Why has it taken ten years before the word "lesbian" could be uttered at an Irish feminist meeting? Why, even in the most radical group yet – Irishwomen United – was the existence of lesbians ignored? … Veiled references and tokenism after years of activism is just not good enough. For ten years we have struggled alongside our sisters for contraception, divorce, justice for deserted and battered wives, equal pay, and every legal and social issue that has arisen. We've given a large degree of energy and ideas, time and commitment. Most of the time these issues have not been central to the lives of lesbians. (*Elektra*, November 1980/BL/F/AP/749, Attic Press Archive)

There were positive responses from heterosexual feminists to this challenge, which, as the writer comments, "indicates the degree of support and solidarity which is present just below the surface but still not articulated".

However, for some lesbians and bisexual women this was cold comfort, and their response was to turn away from mainstream feminist organising and to work on projects within their own communities, sometimes in collaboration with gay men. Emphasis was placed on establishing social networks for lesbians around the country. For example, an ad in the second issue of *Wicca* mooted the idea of holding a women's camp, and advertised for women to join the collective organising it.[8]

'THE FIRST OF MANY'

The first Women's Conference on Lesbianism to be held in Ireland took place the weekend of May 26th to 28th at Trinity College, Dublin. Workshops on Saturday and Sunday ranged from subjects as diverse as Matriarchy and Motorcycle Mechanics to Women and Alcohol and a fascinating workshop on Parthenogenosis and Cloning (both forms of asexual reproduction, one producing all female offspring and the other both male and female.) Needless to say current research is concentrating on cloning to produce more males, which has frightening implications not only for the women's movement but for our entire sex. The Lesbianism and Feminism Workshop was repeated as was Coming Out and Self Defense. Friday evening's opening music session and registration saw a much smaller turnout than expected and panic stations for the planning committee But by Saturday afternoon the attendance had picked up and we had a few surprises, including Monica Sjoo's offer to do a workshop on Matriarchy with slides of her paintings. We were also able to show a film made by a New Zealand women's collective which showed a much larger choice of careers for school leavers than the usual secretarial positions or the caring professions. Saturday night at The Universal Folk Club was an exciting event. We had brought Ova, a women's band, over from London. They played some fantastic rhythmic music, which got everyone up dancing. They helped to make this conference a success as they gave an open air music workshop the next day, so thanks to Rosemary, Sally and Jana.

The hot sunshine throughout the weekend may have contributed to the warm, relaxed atmosphere among women at the conference, which I'm sure I was not alone in feeling. Smaller numbers also made for more intense workshops and it was easier to keep track of everyone when we needed to communicate the few surprise changes in our schedules. Sunshine, trees, and circles of women discussing topics of intense personal significance certainly makes for warm, calm, open communic-

ation. This was especially evident during the Lesbian Sexuality workshop in which lesbians and heterosexual feminists discussed varied aspects of female and lesbian sexuality.
Lesbians and feminists did not confront each other and what emerged was a lot of positive interchange and mutual support. The lesbianism and feminism workshop for instance, agreed that Irish lesbian feminists should not form a separate movement of their own but should remain an integal part of the Irish feminist movement.

The follow-up session on Sunday evening was a short affair. On the finance side we just broke even. The National Women's Conference in February attracted about 300 women, nearly a third of whom were lesbians so we planned for at least 100 women--we got 81.
The Conference recognised the urgent necessity for a women's centre in Dublin as a contact point for all women's groups in Ireland. A group was formed to organise this project which would include a gay women's centre and to contact other women's groups who have already expressed an interest in running a centre. A suggestion was made that for the next Irish women's conference on lesbianism, papers should be circulated beforehand. This was agreed to but it was also suggested that in the meantime a number of less formal get-togethers should take place. Names were taken for a proposed Feminist Skill Sharing Weekend and there was much support and enthusiasm for a type of Women's Festival in September/October which would include women's art, films, theatre and dance. The weekend concluded with the big clean-up and back to the playing fields for a soccer match. This first Women's Conference on Lesbianism in Ireland was exciting, informative, and fun. We are already planning the next one for autumn '78 or early '79. See you there.

Joni Sheerin

painting by Monica Sjoo

13

Joni Sheerin, review of the first Women's Conference on Lesbianism (Dublin May 26th–28th). Painting by Monica Sjoo, who gave a seminar on Matriarchy, using slides of her work in *Wicca* 2 (1978) (BL/F/AP/1498, Attic Press Archive)

Similarly, near the back of *Sapphire*, Ireland's first gay publication, which was produced by gay men in Cork, there is a notice which reads:

> Since the formation of the Cork Branch of the IGRM the gay women in this city have been considering setting up a social scene for themselves … The first women's meeting will take place on Monday 30 January '78 at 8.00 pm and hopefully will continue on each subsequent Monday at the same time. (*Sapphire* January 1978/Irish Queer Archive)

Protest march following the Fairview Park killing, 19 March 1983 (photo: Clodagh Boyd)

On the whole, Irish lesbians continued to coalesce with gay men's groups throughout the 1980s, despite privately acknowledging the difficulties of such co-operative work. This tendency to maintain co-operation with other groups may have also been as a result of a lack of resources and community space, which could be accessed by them as part of wider "gay and lesbian" organisations. However, it is possible to see a discernible lesbian presence growing in strength and visibility

Lesbian and Gay Pride March, Dublin 1984 (photo: Clodagh Boyd)

within the lesbian and gay, *and* feminist movements, where lesbian feminists were involved at grassroots level, forming groups, exploring ideas, finding and redecorating premises, devising policies and organising events.

One of the largest displays of the growing public confidence of the Irish lesbian and gay movements came in 1983 in response to the judgement in the killing of Declan Flynn in Fairview Park. A gay man, Flynn had been chased and beaten to death by a gang of youths in August 1982. At the trial, the judge endorsed the homophobia of his attackers, by giving the gang suspended sentences, and commenting that: "this could never be regarded as murder". Following their release, the gang held a victory parade in Fairview Park, which was countered by a protest march organised by the Dublin Lesbian and Gay Collectives. Lesbian and gay marchers were supported by their parents and friends, a number of feminist groups, as well as the trade union movement (*Dublin Lesbian and Gay Men's Collectives*, 1986: 195–197).

However, that same year the lesbian and gay movement divided as a direct result of the anti-amendment campaign. Lesbians, and some gay men, joined the campaign to call for a rejection of the 1983 Abortion amendment. However, this resulted in a split in the movement when the National Gay Federation (NGF) refused to formally affiliate with the Women's Right to Choose Campaign, despite the vote of its members in favour of affiliation. Crone describes the fallout from this decision:

at the Women's Disco, every Saturday night, Summer 9-11 pm,
Winter 8.30 - 10.30 pm, J. J. Smyth's music Lounge, 12 Aungier Street,
Dublin 2. Price IR£1.50. All women welcome.

Advertisement for the women's disco upstairs at J.J. Smyth's (Irish Queer Archive). 1986

FEEL LIKE A WEEK IN THE SUN, IN THE
company of other women, swimming, re-
laxing, playing music...? Then how
about a women's festival and camp?
We'd like it to happen this summer at
the end of August or the beginning of September.

At the moment, we're only four women, so we need some more
help to get the Festival together. We have not got a definite venue, and we're looking for any women who are into
music and would like to come and play; for tents; ideas
about food, transport, etc.

The women in Denmark hold a camp every summer, and its a
nice idea as a way of getting women together for a celebr-
ation, as an alternative to the intense conference work-
shops.
Cotact us if you'd like to help organize, whatever part of
the country you're in:
Eleanor Lamb, Knockmahon House, Old Youghal Rd.,
Mayfield, Cork. Tel 51674 or
Gabi Froese, 9, St. Mary's Rd., Galway or
Eva O'Donovan, 42 Oaklands, Salthill, Galway or
May Phelan, 168 Rathgar Rd., Rathmines, Dublin6

IN SISTERHOOD,
ELEANOR, EVA, GABI AND MARY

Advertisement for the first Irish Women's Camp in *Wicca* 2(n.d.) c. 1977 (BL/F/AP/1498, Attic
Press Archive)

Ruth Jacob and Liz Noonan, lesbian political candidate, at the Bolton Street election count February 1982 (photo: Clodagh Boyd)

> A minority of influential and vocal gay men cited a subclause in the original document detailing the aims and objectives of NGF which gave the steering committee a right to overturn decisions of the members in exceptional circumstances, "in the best interests of the organisation" *(sic)*. This betrayal of lesbian and heterosexual women who had campaigned previously for gay male law reform resulted in lesbians leaving the NGF. And it was the last time that many of us chose to work in any official capacity in solidarity with gay men. (Crone, 1995: 68)

Not all lesbians and gay men chose to work separately following the anti-amendment campaign. Some of those who left the NGF at this point belonged to the Dublin Lesbian and Gay Collective (DLGC), which, like the Cork Gay Collective, had a strong radical and socialist agenda, as well as taking an openly pro-choice and anti-amendment stance.

Coming Out in Public

The beginning of the 1980s is the point where we begin to see the emergence of specific lesbian communities in Ireland. The organisations and groups they started and belonged to were mainly urban-based during this period. Deirdre Walsh's account of this period gives a flavour of lesbian activism in Cork in the 1980s:

> Discussion groups, action groups, sprung up all over around issues affecting women's lives: contraception, abortion, divorce, sexual freedoms including lesbianism. It was the first time it felt

safe for me to march under a Lesbian banner with other straight women's groups in an International Women's Day march down Patrick Street in Cork … There was, for a time, an incredible feeling of, dare I say it, "sisterhood". It was the first time for me, and also for many other women involved, of solidarity based on our gender, and it was as powerful as it was idealistic. (Walsh, 2000; 6)

Walsh also describes the first lesbian political meeting in Cork, in November 1984, which gave rise to both the Cork Lesbian Line and the Cork Women's Fun Weekend.

In Dublin, the hub of the lesbian social world was Saturday night in J.J.Smyth's. Venues such as J.J.'s were not only crucial in terms of providing a space for women to meet and socialise, but also had a significance as a meeting point for "political" lesbians. The confidence of the lesbian community in Ireland was also apparent in the appearance of a home-grown lesbian culture in the 1980s: lesbians involved in traditional music, the visual arts and literature began to appear on the scene, for example, Mary Dorcey's work began to appear in print. Bands such as "Brazen Bitch", "Standing Ovulation" and "Loose Women and the Clitorettes" (which had

Protestors outside RTÉ studios condemn the appearance of lesbian nuns on *The Late Late Show*, 1985 (photo: Clodagh Boyd)

some lesbian members) began to play at lesbian and feminist events such as the All Ireland Women's Conferences. These were followed by later groups such as "Zrazy" and "Bust".

Despite these advances, mainstream Irish society was not quite ready for the revolution. Dorcey's public radical feminist statement made headline news:

> I spoke at Women's Week in University College Dublin on sexuality. I spoke as an open lesbian describing heterosexuality as sado-masochism and declared: "if feminism is the theory, lesbianism is the practice". It was like a Roman arena. I was the Gladiator. I just about escaped with my life … *The Irish Times* ran a front-page headline "Self-Confessed Lesbian Denounces Heterosexuality". (O'Carroll, 1995: 36)

Similarly, Joni Crone describes the reaction to her appearance on *The Late Late Show* in 1980, the first Irish lesbian to be interviewed:

> I did suffer personally but not professionally … I suffered rejection from my family, received threats of violence and experienced ostracism. My parents had feared that their house would be set on fire or that they would be shunned by the neighbours … The positive effects of this event, an Irish woman coming out on national television, were as wide-ranging as that earlier conference. (Crone, 1995: 66)

Anne Maguire describes Crone's television appearance as "an incredible act of bravery" (Maguire, 1995: 200) and Emma Donoghue mentions the encouragement it gave to other Irish lesbians to come out (Donoghue, 1995: 169).

There was a much more extreme reaction to a public discussion of lesbianism in 1985, when two lesbian nuns from the USA appeared on the *The Late Late Show*.[9] A storm of controversy erupted – Buswell's Hotel refused to provide their accommodation, death-threats were phoned in to RTÉ, and a police escort had to be arranged to and from the studio. All of these stories put into context the bravery of locally based lesbian activists who were willing to "come out". Joni Crone concludes:

> "Coming out" as an Irish lesbian involves undoing much of our conditioning. It means recognizing the external and internal barriers which prevent us taking charge of our lives, and resolving to become autonomous human beings, independent persons with a right to life, a right to love, a right to control our own bodies, a right to live free from harassment in our work and our homes, a right to choose who we love, how we love, and if or when we want to become parents. (1995: 61)

Lesbian Nation

For every lesbian in a position to come out in Ireland in the 1970s and 1980s, there were many more staying in the closet, or emigrating. The 1995 GLEN/Combat

New York Radicalesbian Manifesto, 1970 (BL/F/AP/1455/17, Attic Press Archive; also in Canadian Women's Movement Archive)

Poverty report on poverty in the Irish lesbian and gay community showed that almost 60% of respondents had emigrated at some point in their lives, and that sexual orientation was a key factor in their decision: "Because I could not survive where I did not belong, I left" (Maguire, 1995: 210).

As a result of these migrations, there were cross-currents between Irish feminist communities and those in other countries: "We kept in close touch with events in the USA. We felt part of an international movement. Alix Dobkin sang what became a theme song: "Every Woman Can be a Lesbian", and we knew she was right. All around us women were coming out and joining in" (Dorcey, 1995: 36)[10]. Many lesbians who left became involved in a variety of political groups in London and other cities abroad – and the exchanges between individuals there and their friends "back home" gave much-needed support, literature and theoretical perspectives to those who stayed in Ireland. For example, the typescript of the text of the New York Radicalesbian manifesto "The Woman-Identified Woman" is part of the Attic Press Archive (BL/F/AP/1455/17). This text was widely reproduced in a variety of feminist publications throughout the USA, Canada and the UK in 1972, which highlights the influence of lesbian theory and politics from the USA on lesbian communities closer to home. The influence of feminist theory originating in the USA on the local movement is apparent in the language and politics of early Irish lesbian activists – for example, when asked to define lesbian difference,

Dorcey replies: "the early 1970s phrase "women-identified-woman" probably expresses it" (1995: 33).

Other women lived abroad for several years, and then returned to Ireland, where they became involved in feminist activism. Presenting a somewhat different perspective on 1980s Ireland to the general feminist pessimism in that period, these women talk positively about the rapid changes in Irish society. Those who emigrated and later returned were in a position to compare the Ireland they had left with the one they returned to. Nikki Keeling describes this development in the 1980s: "It was good to be a part of the lesbian presence and to be there when women went away and for those that came back expecting Ireland to have nothing for lesbians and bisexual women. I was proud of the scene and the progress we'd made" (Keeling, 2001: 5).

One of the principal and longest-running groups started during this period in Ireland was the national Lesbian Line telephone support network, which began in the early 1980s. *Women's News* in Belfast received a grant from Co-Operation North in 1984 to facilitate cross-border initiatives, which facilitated an exchange between the Lesbian Lines North and South. These links were built on in the course of the 1980s, and a subsequent exchange in 1988 organised by Geraldine McCarthy and Lorraine Stefani at the Cork and Belfast Lesbian Lines won a Co-Operation North prize (Walsh, 1995:174). The success of this dialogue can still be seen today in the networking between lesbian groups and individuals throughout the island. Helen Slattery, an activist involved in the setting-up of the Cork Lesbian Line, captures the excitement of this period:

There used to be great travelling done between cities at that time, for Lesbian Line meetings as well as other events. International Women's Day meant a trip to Belfast to their strip-search protests ... then it was Cork for the Fun Weekend in May, and Galway for the Women's Summer Camp. We made strong connections then because we were at the forefront of the lesbian movement, and the connections made with many of those women then are as strong now as if they were only made yesterday. (Slattery, 2001: 5)

The Cork Women's Fun Weekend became a focal point for many lesbians living abroad to "come home" for the weekend. Commenting on the 1990 Women's Weekend, one woman described it as: "a stamp of encouragement for women all over Ireland, and those who have emigrated abroad to keep in touch and establish a network" (*Gay Community News,* July 1990). Despite the falling-away of many of the more political activities in the intervening period, the Cork Women's Fun Weekend is still going strong – which is maybe an indication of the secondary status of political discussion/activism in many LBT communities today, both in Ireland and abroad.

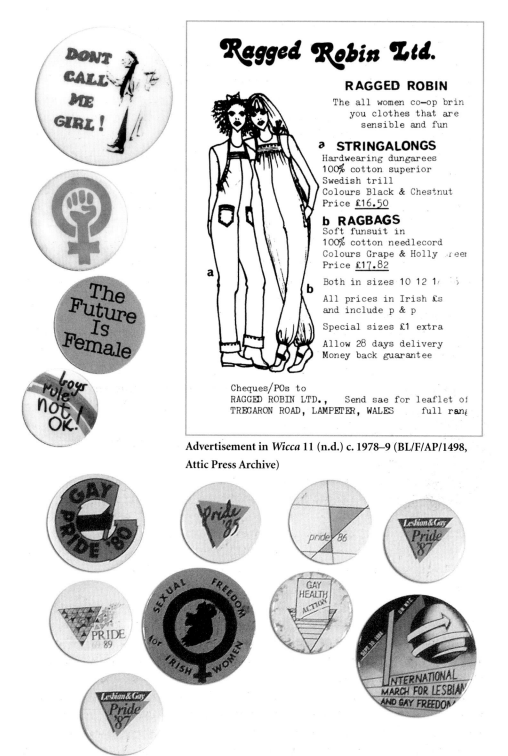

Advertisement in *Wicca* 11 (n.d.) c. 1978–9 (BL/F/AP/1498, Attic Press Archive)

Badges from the Attic Press Collection (BL/F/AP/1588) and the Irish Queer Archive

Lesbian and Gay Pride March, Dublin 1983 (photo: Clodagh Boyd)

Identity Politics

A central part of the community-building projects of the early 1980s was the investment in identity politics – the deployment of categories such as "women" and "lesbians" during this period were a call to arms to those who self-identified as feminist/lesbian. Phelan points out that such use of language by lesbian feminists is conscious: "Arguments and definitions are proposed less with an eye to eternal truth than with a view toward their concrete implications for community membership and political strategy" (1989: 136). Texts such as "The Woman-Identified Woman", mentioned above, gave a theoretical perspective to this work, suggesting that lesbians use the terms of their oppression to redefine the world, rather than themselves. The process of "coming out", self-identifying as lesbian redefining the terms of engagement, were all ways in which lesbian feminists revolutionised the known social world.

Members of the Irish lesbian and gay communities meeting Mary Robinson, President of Ireland, at Áras an Uachtaráin, 1993 (photo: Chris Robson)

Nonetheless, in their efforts to construct a new political and social movement, lesbian feminists – just as their straight sisters before them – downplayed or ignored the differences within their communities. Thus, exclusion and the silencing of "other" voices are not only charges that can be levelled at the mainstream environment "outside" these communities as they were constructed in the 1970s and 1980s. Phelan points out: "Any sense of the plurality of lesbian lives was lost in the construction of 'the' lesbian – the unified epistemological and volitional agent ... The political lesson we may learn from this, then, is that the real danger facing us is not one of doctrine, nor of behaviour, but more fundamentally of the impulse to totalization" (1989: 138). Irish lesbian communities are only now beginning to look at the kinds of ways they organised in the past, who was included and who was excluded in various groups.[11]

Conclusion

We want a feminist revolution. This means we want to create a non-patriarchal, communal, pan-sexual world. (By pan-sexual we mean a world where sexuality is a free expression of love and is not restricted by gender or age. In this world terms like homosexual, heterosexual, bisexual, male, and female would become irrelevant in all walks of life.) (*The Other Woman*, 1973)

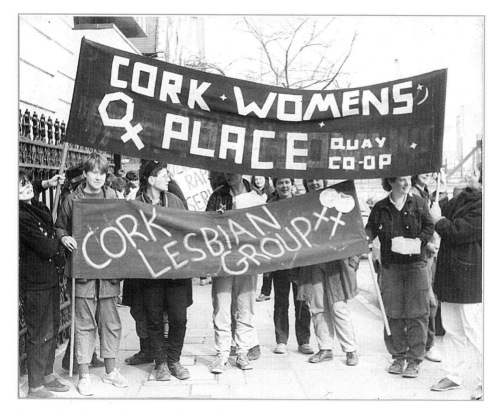

International Women's Day March in Cork, 8 March 1985 (*Women's News* Collection)

Internationally, the lesbian feminist project of the 1970s and 1980s sought to explode the binaries of sex and gender, and to question so-called "heteronormativity". Although the revolution as envisaged was never fully realised, in terms of raising awareness of lesbian/bisexual experiences, the activism of this period was crucial. This is particularly apparent if we compare it to the experience of the generation just preceding lesbian feminist activism – older Irish lesbians remind us of the high rates of depression and alcoholism among single women whose sexual identities were impossible to reconcile with the heteronormative environment they inhabited in the 1940s and 1950s. A marked difference between contemporary LBT communities in Ireland and those in other Western countries can be discerned in terms of the age profile of such groups – there is not a visible presence of "out" lesbians/bisexuals over the age of sixty in this country, which is telling.

The Irish lesbian community grew in terms of numbers and resources in the 1990s, and groups such as LOT, LEA and L.INC have continued the community building and service provision initiated by earlier groups beginning in the late 1970s. Key moments of Irish lesbian activism include the first legal case to openly award custody to a lesbian mother in May 1992; the 1992 award-winning lesbian and gay float in the Cork St Patrick's Day Parade, alongside the ongoing Irish Lesbian and Gay Organisation (ILGO) campaign to march in the New York Parade; the first annual Lesbian Lives conference organised by WERRC in 1993, now in its tenth year; the high-profile visit in February 1993 to Áras an Uachtaráin to meet President Mary Robinson; the 1999 LEA/NOW billboard campaign which was the first such use of advertising space; and more recently, the 2003 visit of President Mary McAleese to the L.INC resource centre. The difference for the contemporary generation of activists is the visibility of lesbian role models in the wider society, the already-existing groups and services in the larger urban centres nationally, and the consolidation of Irish lesbian culture in the intervening period. Those pioneers who set up groups, resource centres, committees within other organisations and ran workshops focusing on lesbian/bisexual issues, made space for several generations of women to accept their own sexual identities, whether lesbian, bisexual, or heterosexual.

Irish lesbians have long been active in a variety of organisations and movements to bring about social and cultural change. The long-established legacy and community development skills of the Irish lesbian movement are evident in the equality agenda and discourse of the Irish state today (such as in the objectives of the recently established Equality Authority). While the ongoing development of LGBT communities and cultures in a variety of locations is indicative of a thriving and active community moving into the twenty-first century, remembering the past and recovering the "hidden histories" of lesbian and bisexual activism in Ireland will ensure that contemporary struggles can be read in the context of the groundbreaking politics and activism of earlier periods.

Notes

1 Ger Moane (1995) points out, for example, that Dublin and Cork Lesbian Line delegates have been very active in the Council for the Status of Women. Council motions urging the government to introduce anti-discrimination legislation were passed in 1987, 1988 and 1989, and the Council was active in lobbying for the law reform passed in 1993 (O'Carroll and Collins, 1995: 92–3).

2 This commonly used acronym, referring to the lesbian, gay and bisexual communities, is employed throughout this chapter. The addition of "T" refers to the inclusion of the transgender community.

3 The following files in the Attic Press Archive relate to the issue of LGBT rights in Ireland. As these sources were extremely scanty, and tended to relate almost wholly to the question of gay rights and law reform, or to LGBT questions from the perspective of the right-wing group Family Solidarity, we supplemented them by recourse to documents at the Irish Queer Archive, and discussions and conversations with lesbian activists. Files BL/F/AP/1298–1301, Attic Press Archive, contains material on gay rights in Ireland (1976–1990). File BL/F/AP/1300, Attic Press Archive, contains material relating to lesbian and gay rights (c.1980) including: programme of women's poetry organised by the Gay Sweatshop; a flyer for a lesbian custody conference held in Sheffield; articles "Feminism and Lesbianism" and "The Rights of Lesbian Women and Gay Men'; and a publicity sheet from David Norris relating the Campaign for Homosexual Law Reform. File BL/F/AP/1301, Attic Press Archive, contains *The Homosexual Challenge: Analysis and Response*, by Family Solidarity, Dublin (1990) 64pp.

4 This was established when Cork lesbian feminists left the women's space in the Quay Co-Op, which they had set up in co-operation with a variety of radical groups.

5 The Employment Equality Act 1998 and the Equal Status Act 2000 outlaw discrimination in employment, vocational training, advertising, collective agreements, the provision of goods and services and other opportunities to which the public have access, on nine distinct grounds: gender, marital status, family status, age, disability, race, sexual orientation, religious belief and membership of the Traveller Community.

6 LOT obtained a grant of £50,000 from the Department of Social Welfare in 1995, and the LEA/NOW project was the first lesbian project in the EU funded under the New Opportunities for Women (NOW) programme. LEA/NOW received £550,000 in two tranches of funding in 1995 and 1997. The L.INC resource centre was the only LGBT group to receive a Millenium Award of £10,000, and the only lesbian group funded under the Equality for Women measure of the Department of Justice, Equality and Law Reform in 2001 (£121,000). This funding is indicative of institutional recognition of lesbian community activism at state and EU level, and an awareness of the need to build up community services for Irish lesbians.

7 The first designated Lesbian Studies course was run by the LEA/NOW project and included modules on Social/Policy Analysis, History, Literature, etc. Recovery work on lesbian social history is now beginning to emerge from women's studies centres around Ireland, ably supported by the annual *Lesbian Lives* conference, and *Lesbian and Queer Theory* courses run by WERRC at UCD. Such work, both practical and theoretical, provides support structures to the ongoing activism in lesbian and bisexual communities in various parts of Ireland and internationally. This work is also indicative of a transition from early lesbian feminist activism, which prioritised experience, to more recent efforts to analyse and problematise received versions of lesbian experiences and identities. There are very

few texts relating to Irish LGBT social history, with *Out for Ourselves: The Lives of Irish Lesbians and Gay Men* (Dublin: Dublin Lesbian and Gay Men's Collectives and Women's Community Press, 1986) and Íde O'Carroll and Eoin Collins" study *Lesbian and Gay Visions of Ireland* (London: Cassell, 1995) being the only full-length studies in this area.

8 The Irish Women's Camp, formerly the Galway Women's Camp, continues to be held in July each year.

9 The women, Rosemary Curb and Nancy Manahan, were on a book tour to promote their publication *Breaking Silence: Lesbian Nuns on Convent Sexuality*. London: Columbus, 1985.

10 Dobkin was a US-based folksinger whose album, *Lavender Jane Loves Women* was released in 1973.

11 Recent initiatives such as the WERRC Anti-Racism workshops for the LBT communities, and the investment of L.INC, the Cork LBT group and resource centre, in transgender issues, are some examples of this.

Chapter 7
Feminism, Community and Class

Telephonists strike for equal pay in *Banshee* 7 (c. 1976) (BL/F/AP/1123, Attic Press Archive)

Critics of Irish feminism and feminists have always charged that the women's movement was essentially an interest group of well-educated, middle-class, Dublin-based feminists who secured extra rights for already privileged women while "ignoring" their working class and rural sisters. Chapter 3 indicated how critics also assert that feminists have focused entirely on the position of educated women in the workforce and slighted those women (the majority) who choose to work primarily in the home as mothers.

While internationally most of the gains of second-wave feminism have benefited white, Western, middle-class, metropolitan women *more* than some other groups of women, this assumption should not negate the long-standing

IRISH TRANSPORT AND GENERAL WORKERS' UNION

itgwu

EQUALITY FOR WOMEN

A Discussion Paper presented to
Annual Delegate Conference 1980

ITGWU discussion paper on equal pay, 1980

work and strong connection between considerable sections of Irish feminism and
the left, as well as the legacy of working-class and rural-based feminism that exists
in Ireland and elsewhere. Furthermore, extensive documentary evidence suggests
that working-class and middle-class feminists have worked together in numerous
socialist and other radical campaigns, to challenge the dominant class structure
and social inequalities that have shaped women's lives in Irish society. Since the
1980s, working-class and rural women have found a new voice in Irish feminism
in the arena of community development. This chapter will address these important issues and debates.

Feminism and Socialism

Despite the fact that it has a rich and established history throughout the twentieth
century, the potency of socialist feminism is understated in both established
accounts of the Irish women's movement and in mainstream Irish labour history.[1]

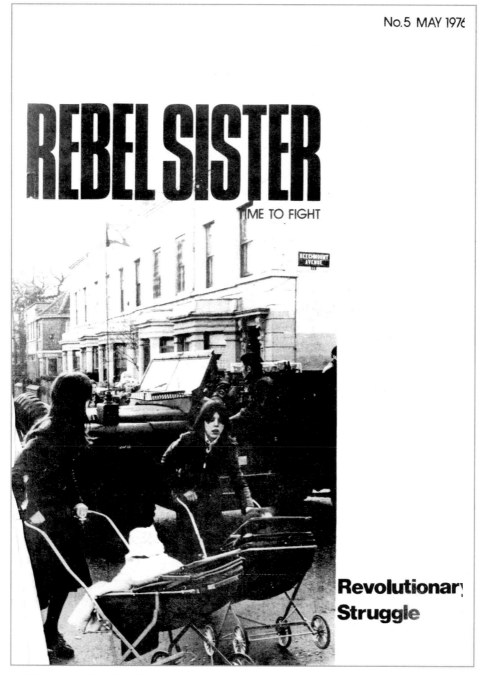

No.5 MAY 1976

REBEL SISTER

TIME TO FIGHT

BEECHMOUNT AVENUE

Revolutionary Struggle

Rebel Sister socialist feminist magazine, 1976 (BL/F/AP/1492/4, Attic Press Archive)

IWWU advertisement n.d. (BL/F/AP/1589, Attic Press Archive)

Women's dole queue 1980s (BL/F/AP/1125, Attic Press Archive)

Cover of *Wicca* **magazine (c. 1979) (BL/F/AP/1498/2, Attic Press Archive)**

60p (inc. VAT) An Irish Socialist Review No. 9

AUG/SEPT 1983

IF
MEN
PREG
WO
WE
THIS

NO
MORE
IRISH
SOLUTIONS

GRALTON

ANTI-AMENDMENT
CAMPAIGN ON TOUR
NEW LOOK SINN FEIN
POLITICS IN
ST. TERESAS GARDENS

FREE PULL-OUT
GENEALOGY OF
THE LEFT

Cover of *Gralton* Irish Socialist Review, August/September 1983 (BL/F/AP/1529/2, Attic Press Archive)

takeoff!

This is the first issue of what we consider to be an integral part of a movement to mobilise widespread and concerted support amongst groups who have an alternative line.

Our idea is to initiate the search for the largest possible common ground between groups and to try and clarify the issues on which we can co-operate and help each other to push forward. We hope that this co-operation will eliminate the frustration, stagnation and overlapping which are characteristic of group isolation.

In this issue some of these groups introduce themselves, some with brief histories, others by explaining what they are concerned with.

We would welcome and print any constructive criticism or ideas on this issue and on what the future development should be, remembering that it is YOU not us who are responsible for its content.

The second function of this magazine is to provide an outlet for groups lacking in printing facilities or money. We hope shortly to acquire an offset machine for general use.

We´re BROKE!

To bring out this magazine we must break even, if each group in the magazine would contribute we could probably do this.

Thank-you

This magazine is yours, we thank those who have written for it and look forward to the participation of many more.

Irish Women United

How we began..

Irishwomen United began in April 1975 as a few individual women interested in the idea of building a conference to discuss a womens charter; what its demands should be and how a campaign should be built.

On June 8th at this conference the charter was drawn up and endorsed by about 100 women and Irishwomen United was established as a group. The charter is based on the essential right of women to self-determination of our own lives.

summary of charter demands

(1) Equality in education, state financed, secular, co-educational schools with full community control at all levels.

(2) Equality in work, the male rate for the job when men and women are working together, upgrading of jobs where the labour force is wholly female, the right of access to all types of employment.

(3) The removal of all legal and bureaucratic obstacles to equality and the right to divorce.

(4) Free Legal Contraception and state financed birth control clinics.

(5) The recognition of motherhood and parenthood as a social function, state support for community laundries, kitchens, eating places, free and well equipped 24 hour nurseries, adequate housing for all.

(6) State provision of funds for womens centres to be controlled by the women themselves.

(7) Control of our own bodies.

(8) Freedom from sexist conditioning.
This charter outlines the basic issues on which the diverse groups of women in Ireland are increasingly uniting. The recent refusal to implement Equal Pay and the farce of 'women's year' have only served to further unite us and increase our strength.

what we do

We work on the basis of general meetings, pickets, public meetings, workshops etc.
The following groups meet at 12 Lower Pembroke Street, all women are welcome.

Sundays, 4 p.m. General Meeting.

Mondays, 8 p.m. Study Group

Tuesdays, 6 p.m. Contraception Group.

Thursdays, 7 p.m. Education
8 p.m. Employment

Consciousness raising groups are also in operation.

Article on Irishwomen United in *Open Press* magazine, February 1976 (BL/F/AP/1528/3, Attic Press Archive)

Purpose

Women's Aid (Dublin) was set up to combat the complex and savage situation of violence in the family as it affects the wife and children. It is the battered wife and her children who directly and immediately concern our group.

Safety

Women's Aid runs a refuge house in the city centre to which any woman who is a victim of violence from her husband can retreat. More often than not she brings her children with her.

In the refuge centre she has a respite from any attacks by her husband and can use the opportunity to reflect on her plight. Here she meets other women who, like herself, have been subjected to protracted assault. Most of the battered wives we have known have found this helpful.

Services

During her stay in the refuge a woman has the opportunity to take free legal advice and medical or psychiatric aid, as well as the chance to consult with social workers. Her children are catered for by two full time playleaders who, with the aid of dedicated volunteers, run a playroom and take them on frequent outings.

Support

After her stay in the refuge a woman can move on to a Women's Aid Support House, living in safety apart from her husband in community with other battered wives who have come through the Refuge. Our main priority at the present time is to obtain a permanent Refuge and long-term Support House. Our present accommodation is only temporary

Future

It is the aim of Women's Aid to extend its service to cover all aspects of family violence, we are undertaking a detailed analysis of the statutory social services.

Remember

If you yourself know of any wife who is suffering physical violence do not hesitate to recommend us. Phone. 681583.

CONTACT is an Advisory Service for young people, it was begun in 1972 by the Sisters of Our Lady of Charity to "explore the needs of young people in the city centre, especially those at risk". Since then we have had over 7000 interviews with these people, and have developed the following approach:

a) We offer educational, vocational and personal guidance and case work help to young people between the ages of 15 and 25 who approach our service.

b) We refer, when we feel it is useful and when the client agrees, to suitable other agencies.

Contact

c) We collect and distribute information useful to young people.

d) We are continuing to study and identify the needs of young people, especially those 'at risk' in the Dublin of today.

Contact CONTACT at 13 Westmoreland St. Dublin 2. Tel. 784188 Open Mon - Fri , 10.00 a.m. to 6.00 p.m. (Closed 1.00 to 2.00) Ask for Freda, Teresa or Dave.

The main problems we have found among young people in the city are lonliness, having no work, and having nowhere to stay. We answer these by making young people our friends, by introducing them to others, and by putting them in touch for jobs and accommodation. Every person is important, we respect each person's individuality and independence and support them with information, encouragement and interest in developing their own lives.

CONTACT is a voluntary organisation and needs your help. Collectors are needed for our Flag Days on 2nd and 3rd April.

Article on Women's Aid in *Open Press* magazine, February 1976 (BL/F/AP/1528/3, Attic Press Archive)

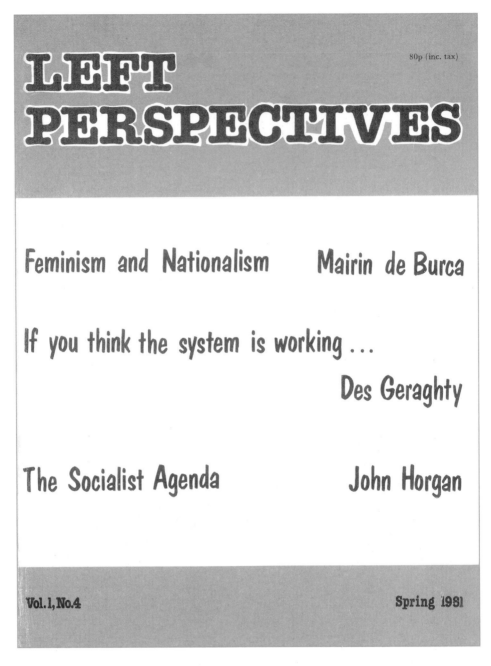

Cover of *Left Perspectives*, Spring 1980 (BL/F/AP/1528/4, Attic Press Archive)

Few liberation groups in the Western world have been given the opportunity that faces the Women's movement in Ireland. This opportunity exists in the form of the Report on the Status of Women. Objectively a lever with which to bring life to the Movement, the report will soon be discarded and shelved by the Trade Union bureaucrats and politicians. Containing 49 proposals on the position of Women in Irish society, the report actually compiled mainly by representatives of the status quo, presents a very great challenge to the movements of radical women. But we must first ask the question – How can these women meet this challenge? We must answer the question – Why is it such a challenge?

THE REPORT: ITS WEAKNESS AND ITS STRENGTH

A growing radicalisation of women throughout Europe, especially in Ireland has caused the capitalist class concern. Faced with a growing crisis of the Irish economy, the successive governments have had to take seriously, the question of women's status within the framework of the Common Market, the contraction and expansion of industry in certain areas has already become quite apparent. Light consumer manufacture is increasingly the area where industry is expanding. Women mainly provide the labour-power in these industries and will be required to do so for the next period. But the status of these women will have to be rationalised. That is to say, certain concessions will have to be made, in order to make greater profit. If women are the mainstay of the family, which is in effect, an area of

reproduction of human labour-power, to implement *all* the proposals would negate the advantages for the capitalist class. So to actually carry out the proposals would be *against* the interests of the status quo, i.e. the capitalist class.

Therefore, the womens movement *must* recognise that while the Report exists on paper, it is an absolute certainty, that nothing or very little will be, or indeed can be done with it – by the capitalist class. However, the

Report can do much for the womens movement. That is, if the movement recognises for itself, the *contradiction* between the Report and the possibility of its implementation; if it recognises the opportunity, this contradiction can present to our efforts to build the movement. Radical women in the movement, recognise and understand the oppression of women and why it is necessary to struggle. This Report is a practical example and presents real concrete opportunities.

UNITY CAN BE STRENGTH

For all the diverse elements in the womens movement, the report presents a solid base on which to unite. From the experience of other womens liberation movements, we can learn many lessons. Such movements have built their organisations around campaigns for basic human and civil rights, some of which automatically call into question the role of all state institutions concerning the position of the female sex. But *without* unity (on a principled basis) the womens movement in Ireland is and will remain tremendously weak and will fail to expand.

The Fownes Street organisation, consisting of several founder members of the original group has yet to realise this. Continuing to centre themselves on consciousness-raising meetings and around their journal (which is very lacking in an actual perspective) will not do anything to raise the consciousness of women outside the movement or draw women into the movement to any great extent. Women will be attracted to and involved in the movement that involves itself in the struggle for liberation,

not to a movement which stays outside that struggle. The remaining founder members of the first womens movement, must also realise, without a central axis, an movement will collapse in time. Their experience of two years ago, has proved this. Then, the movement was involved in every activity and demonstration taking place. But, without having defined for itself the central task, (Was it to fight for the right to family planning, contraception divorce, all of which are equally important issues) but without a truly democratic structure and effective leadership from the founder members initially, the movement floundered. But *to-day* a central axis presents itself in the from of the Report.

To other radical women, particularly in political organisations, in the Republican movement, in revolutionary socialist organisations, we would say; it is vital that the organisation take the question of womens liberation seriously and understand its important role in the struggle for revolutionary socialism.

But it is also essential that women organise themselves into an autonomous movement, capable of launching a country-wide campaign through which centuries of submission, and their tremendous lack of confidence will be eroded and replaced by confidence and self-determination. It is by experiencing first-hand the struggle involved, that women will gain a broader understanding of the very deep-rooted nature of their oppression.

The womens movement must unite in order to grow, to gain strength.

The RMG view of women's struggle, article in *The Plough – Towards an Irish Workers Republic* periodical n.d. (BL/F/AP/1528/8, Attic Press Archive)

EVE ADAM

The struggle for National Liberation and for re-unification of the country has been the main topic on the political front for the past 18 months. However, once more the economic aspect of the class struggle is due to appear. That is the whole question of the National Wage Agreement. Each time the debate has begun, we've seen an upsurge of interest and minor outbreaks of opposition to the proposals. This time, the opposition to the Wage Agreement have new "ammunition" to use in their fight. What is this, and how can it be used?

PRESSURE ON I.C.T.U.

We refer to the position of women workers in the Irish economy and their right to equal pay. With the entry of Ireland into the EEC the gross inequality of Irish women was highlighted, much to the embarrassment of the politicians. The government and employers were forced to pay lip-service to the question. One of the results of their "sham" concern however was a useful one, i.e. the "REPORT ON THE STATUS OF WOMEN".

The interim report published about 18 months ago, around the t... of the negotiations for the 2nd Wage Agreement revealed the outrageous discriminatory practices against women, both in terms of jobs available and rates paid. These revelations implicitly put pressure on the Irish Congress of Trade Unions to consider the question of women workers. However the final outcome of this consideration did not provide women with any real gains at all. Nor did it provide adequate steps towards procuring equal pay. IN FACT, the Equal Pay clauses in the agreement tied the hands of many female workers in their fight for equal pay.

A CLAUSE TO TRAP

The most obvious aspect of the current agreement which needs changing is the increment which workers received at the beginning of the agreement — £2.25 for women as compared to £2.50 for men !

Employers and Trade Union Officials have been saying for the past couple of years that the concept of a Wage Agreement helps the lower-paid workers! This is absolutely proved to be incorrect by taking a glance at the rates paid to female workers and the percentage increases payable under the agreement; a 9% increase on basic pay up to £30 per week.

– a 7½% increase on basic pay between £30 and £40
– a 4½% increase on basic pay on £40 and over.

In effect, workers earning £41 per week had the combined increase of 9½%, 7½% and 4% added to his pay packet, emerging with £3.29 extra per week. If we relate this to the average wage of female industrial workers, which is approx. £16 per week we see that the increase here totals approx. £1.44 per week! Most women were glad to get the £2.25 basic minimum allowed to workers, whose 9% increase on their basic wouldn't have meant that much anyway!

The equal pay clause included in the agreement was a result of the trade unions attitude towards the whole question. It established an attitude of "co-operation", with the "Rights Commissioner", appointed by the government to deal with the matter. This person, who not only has no experience of the methods of job evaluation employed, has no knowledge of the trade union movement, and no experience in the field of industrial relations at all! Besides, these glaring inadequacies which would be quickly condemned in other areas are only one aspect. In addition he has absolutely no power to initiate or act on his findings. His sole contribution is in the form of a report! For any person to present a case before him, the employer must be willing to participate in the procedures. What employer is willing to give away half the profits to cut off his source of cheap-labour, female labour.

Apart from these totally inadequate references in the clause, the biggest blow comes when the final stage is reached. Even if the employer agrees that a case for equal pay is legitimate, the agreement stipulates that unless the claimant is already in possession of 95% of the male-rate he shall receive no more than 17½% of the differential — not even of the male rate. Such an offer is a downright insult! A weeks travelling by bus would not be covered by this trivial sum.

EQUAL PAY — THE KEY

The whole concept of the move towards Equal Pay as contained in the Wage Agreement is an indication of the real nature of the Wage Agreement. The phrases "to abolish poverty" and "to increase the wages of the lower paid" means nothing and are exposed as hypocritical when related to the question of Equal Pay.

Oppositionists to the concept of a wage agreement can use the case of women workers as a typical example of the wage agreements complete failure in dealing with the problems of the working class. The question of equal pay for women must be used as a battering ram in the fight against a Wage Agreement. When our wages are increased by an average of 4% to deal with a cost of living which has increased by 20%, in the last two years, something quite radically different is needed.

A sliding scale of wages is the only solution to the problems of the working class. Besides this increased productivity should result in increased wages for the workers over and above their basic wages. Increased productivity for the employers during the last three years is something which has been totally ignored by the Bureaucracy in the Unions.

A WHOLE NEW DEAL

The Trade Union movement must realise the potential for struggle around the question of Equal Pay. Militants must use this betrayal of wage bureaucracy in their struggle against wage agreements. Women in the movement must insist on the Trade Union movement laying down the principles of job evaluation, to be strictly adhered to. These principles should be founded on the overall contribution that women workers make to the economy in general and industry in particular. The unscientific theories of employers must be thrown out as these are contrived in the interests solely of the employers. (b) Within the individual work place, those principles must be the only guideline to job evaluation undertaken. Any violation should be confronted by strike action. (c) If the employers refuse to co-operate in the procedures again strike action will be necessary (d) And if in the final result employers refuse to adhere to the right for equal pay — there is and can be no other alternative but to strike!

Trade Unionists must press the leadership to insist on legislation to protect women workers against the discriminatory manoeuvres of the employers, and to ensure that all increments contained in a sliding scale of pay should be paid to men and women equally.

A struggle is on the agenda, its up to militants to make it the strongest yet. The material is there, waiting to be used.

FOR A SLIDING SCALE OF WAGES!
FOR THE RIGHT TO EQUAL PAY!
FOR THE RIGHT TO STRIKE!
OUT WITH WAGE AGREEMENTS!

"Women can take the lead" article in *The Plough – Towards an Irish Workers Republic* periodical n.d. (BL/F/AP/1528/8, Attic Press Archive)

Furthermore, there are relatively few archives available in Ireland which document the relationship between feminism and socialism since the 1960s. The Attic Press archive contains some material on socialist feminism. While Republican, radical and socialist activists in practice overlapped in several second-wave feminist organisations and campaigns, Republicanism and radicalism have received far more attention than socialism in the historiography of modern Irish feminism to date. An integrated, twentieth century account of socialist feminism in the history of the Irish women's movement has yet to appear. This anomaly in Irish feminist studies is compounded by the current lack of a *systematic* debate about class in mainstream feminist politics. The archives and radical publications of several organisations reveal that class disparities among Irish women and the more general problem of social inequality in Irish society were in fact a critical concern in both the radical women's movement in the 1970s and the women's groups formed within the political left and the trade unions more generally. In addition, class has been widely scrutinised as a reality in Irish women's lives in Irish feminist studies and in social research.[2]

While some historians have pioneered analysis of working class women's lives in mainstream Irish history, class has not been fully advanced as a critical variable in the history of Irish feminist *politics*. Some work to date has looked at how individual feminist activists have been actively involved in the trade unions and the women's movement simultaneously (see for example, Cullen Owens, 2001, study of Louie Bennett). However, no sustained interpretation of socialist feminism as a fundamental dynamic in the history of the Irish working classes, Irish political history, labour history and intellectual history has yet emerged.[3] In addition, working-class feminist activists have been a critical force in numerous feminist and socialist campaigns and organisations throughout the twentieth century, and generally moved between feminist, socialist and other radical politics.

Mary Daly, in her book *Women and Poverty*, suggested that certain groups of women were by-passed by this current cycle of the women's movement:

> Collectively, women have had significant achievements over the last twenty years... The extent to which the lives of women on low incomes have significantly improved is far from certain, however. Class and gender forces ensure that general freedoms for women only very slowly affect life in poor communities. (Daly, 1989: 100)

Internationally, the women's movement was predominantly mobilised and led by white, middle-class, college-educated women in the 1960s. However, evidence gathered in this research reveals that in the case of Irish feminism, a class analysis was advanced and socialist feminists clearly aimed to overthrow class as well as gender inequality in Irish society (notably, activists in IWU). *Banshee* documents the extensive socialist feminist debate that raged in IWU, for example. And direct engagement with women in working-class communities is widely evident through the CAP and several other campaigns. Similarly, leading members of the IWLM were involved in campaigns associated with the left in Ireland, such as

Housing Action, as they were in socialist feminist campaigns, such as advocacy of *free* contraception.

Debates about class inequality were a regular source of conflict between liberal and socialist women within radical feminist organisations in the 1970s.[4] In addition, a significant number of college-educated activists were working-class in origin, being the first generation to benefit from state improvements in access to university and the introduction of free secondary-school education in the 1967 in the Republic. The relationship between the women's movement and the left has been neglected in existing studies and more in-depth research is necessary in this area.

Some of the successes of the women's movement to date have had a general but, at the same time, uneven impact on all women across class cleavages. Concrete gains since the 1970s reflect general societal acceptance of the more moderate demands of liberal feminism (mainly in the areas of paid employment and property rights). Several mobilising issues in the 1970s, however, did not categorically impact working-class women – because they may never have had a secure full-time job, for example. The institutionalisation of certain successes of second-wave feminism and, in recent years, the concentration of women in particularly disadvantaged situations (for example, as the vast majority of lone parents) have however, provoked an opportunity to replace the old agenda with neglected issues particular to the working classes and women eclipsed by the gains of second-wave feminism (see McCashin, 1996).

A ground-breaking debate about class did materialize in feminist politics in the 1980s, when prolific locally based women's groups began to emerge in working class urban communities and in some rural communities in significant numbers. Although not all these "new" locally based women's groups openly associated with the mainstream women's movement, a class critique of the established concerns of second-wave feminism has emerged within established Irish feminist politics as a consequence. In addition, leading members of locally based women's groups have infiltrated prominent feminist groups (in particular, the National Women's Council of Ireland) and in some cases taken charge of them. For example, Noreen Byrne and Gráinne Healy became NWCI chairpersons in the 1990s. Both were experienced in the left and radical feminist politics as well as locally-based women's groups.

Since the 1980s, the orientation of diverse locally based women's groups in Ireland has provoked fresh debate about feminism and social class, and about rural and urban bias, in the established women's movement. For some commentators, a new kind of feminism embedded in community development and in the praxis of locally based women's groups has consolidated a new third wave of feminism in Ireland. However, the alternative and less optimistic view that the movement of community-based women has little or no association with feminism and the established women's movement has also materialised.

Photograph of Ballymun Community Play Group n.d. (BL/F/AP/1130/6, Attic Press Archive)

Locally-Based Women's Groups

Community development and adult education activities spread rapidly in Ireland in the 1980s and consolidated a new and significant phenomenon in civil society. The numerous locally based women's groups that formed were a significant force in this wider development. Fundamentally, the community sector by its very existence has the potential to challenge the class bias of the practices and concerns of the established women's movement; but the focus of this diverse movement is not at all clear. Generally, community women's groups exercised the non-hierarchical, autonomous and participatory goals and structures that were typical of the broad community development movement that consolidated in that period.

In terms of structures and methods of organisation, at face value the locally based groups of women that appeared in the 1980s resembled the small group, consciousness-raising, radical women's sector which had emerged in the previous decade (see Collins, 1992).[5] However, the question of identification with the women's movement and academic feminism remains controversial in locally based women's groups. Noreen Byrne writes:

> Women's groups operating at community level should in my view claim their space in the
> women's movement. The women's movement does not belong to any class or group – it is
> a social movement made up of women who have decided to take action to own their lives
> and bodies either by themselves or with others. Irrespective of what group or category
> women belong to, we must be clear that we are seeking change from those who continue

"together we stand"

The Constitution of Ireland, drawn up more than 40 years ago and still very much in use today, is the basis for all Ireland's laws. Many of these laws discriminate against women. So does this mean that the very ideas and principles which run through our Constitution are sexist and out of date?

This booklet provides a good case for a radical change to be made to the Constitution, for a new look to be taken at some of our laws, and for a completely new attitude to replace many of the old-fashioned views still held by politicians, law-makers and churchmen in Ireland today.

By covering most of the laws concerning women in the areas of work, marriage, social welfare, health and children and by examining whether they protect or discriminate against women, this pamphlet gives you the information you need either to obtain your rights where these are recognised and provided, or to fight for them where they are not.

"IF WE WANT THE EQUAL PAY AND EMPLOYMENT EQUALITY LAWS TO HELP IRISH WOMEN ASSERT THEIR RIGHTS TO EQUALITY IN EMPLOYMENT, THE FIRST STEP IS TO MAKE SURE THAT EVERYONE GETS THE RIGHT INFORMATION AND THE CONFIDENCE TO USE IT.

CATHIE CHAPPELL'S PAMPHLET WILL BE A BIG HELP IN THIS TASK AND I CONGRATULATE HER AND THE DISTRI-BUTORS, THE "BOTTOM DOG", FOR SPONSORING THIS PROJECT."

SYLVIA MEEHAN,
CHAIRPERSON,
EMPLOYMENT EQUALITY AGENCY.

"I FOUND THIS BOOKLET VERY COMPREHENSIVE AND IN-FORMATIVE. I WOULD CONSIDER IT A MUST FOR ANY WOMAN SEEKING AN UNDERSTANDING OF HER LEGAL RIGHTS AND SOCIAL WELFARE ENTITLEMENTS. THE SECTION ON HEALTH IS PARTICULARLY GOOD. IT GIVES, IN SIMPLE, STRAIGHT-FORWARD, LAY-PERSON'S TERMS, ALL THE KNOWLEDGE WE WOMEN NEED IF WE ARE TO TAKE RESPONSIBILITY FOR OUR OWN HEALTH AND FERTILITY."

ANNE CONNOLLY,
WELLWOMAN CENTRE.

Bread and Roses, magazine of UCD Women's Liberation Group n.d. (BL/F/AP/1517, Attic Press Archive)

by and large to control the structures which will bring about fundamental change. (Byrne in Smyth, 1996: 26)

Class was, of course, a live issue in the early days of the women's movement. Maura Richards (formerly Maura O'Dea, founder of Cherish) was invited to a women's liberation group in Dalkey and observed the following (1998: 47–8):

> Women's liberation had decentralised about this time and branches were being set up everywhere... I don't know what I expected, but what I got was a bunch of very middle-class women talking in very academic terms about unmarried mothers. My working-class background is never very far away and strangely at that time, now I realise, I had very little contact with the "real" middle-class, so probably it was just as much my fault that there was no great meeting of minds between us. Nevertheless I joined the group and it's to my shame that I stuck it out for at least four or five meetings, listening to what I considered to be a lot of rubbish without having the guts to open my mouth... Nevertheless it was because of that group that I eventually met the other women who formed the core that finally became Cherish.

Recent publications have advanced a debate about class in Irish feminist studies (see Dorgan and McDonnell, 1997 and O'Neill, 1999). Whether or not community-based networks pose a challenge to the middle-class bias of the women's movement in Ireland is being explored both in new writing and in the praxis of locally based women's groups. While this is a debate that is still consolidating, a number of general observations can be made. Locally based women's groups display more diversity in terms of social class composition than initially realised in mainstream analysis, and while there is no universal "feminist" orientation in the wider movement of women's community groups, a clear feminist project is apparent and being named at least within *some* groups and networks (see Connolly, 2003b).

Women's community groups were clearly also being formed by middle-class women in the new suburban areas in the 1980s in significant numbers – a phenomenon that has yet to be fully addressed. Equally, the reality that the community women's movement also emerged with vigour in rural Ireland has been obscured by the urban bias of the debate so far.

A survey of locally based women's groups (rural and urban/suburban) was produced by the NWCI in 2001. The growth of the suburbs in Celtic Tiger Ireland has received much attention by sociologists, for example, but the role of women's groups and community politics has not been emphasised. Studies conducted so far suggest that the term "locally based women's groups" is too broad to encompass the diversity of ideas, strategies, politics and activities that seems to characterise this female sector. Some studies of how locally based women's groups are interconnected and networked with the wider community development movement, and have linked their goals to the state/EU-funded programmes (such as the NOW programme, the Social Partnerships, Combat Poverty Agency, and Department of Social Welfare schemes) have been conducted (see Connolly and Ryan, 1999).

Further studies of the diverse educational goals and achievements of women's educational projects have also emerged. In all these studies, it is clear that some thousands of women's organisations in Ireland engage in a wide variety of activities, meeting important social, educational and support needs in the lives of local women. Many groups have co-operated with each other and formed regional networks in the last decade. Furthermore, in recent years greater co-operation between women in the universities, the national feminist networks and locally based women's groups is increasingly apparent. The recent histories of locally-based women's groups are still emerging, and archives are not yet fully available to document the extensive mobilisation of this sector. However, as this sector demonstrates, a vibrant debate has emerged among women within the community sector which is having an impact on mainstream feminism. The next chapter will develop these points in more depth.

Rural Women

For the greater part of the twentieth century, Ireland was a predominantly rural society. Historically, rural women's organisations have always worked for the practical and immediate concerns of disadvantaged women, especially through campaigns for the provision of running water, electricity and housing (see Clear, 2000 and Daly, 1997a). Although the Irish women's movement was seriously constrained in the post-independence period, a politically moderate but large and effective network of rural women continued to mobilise both at the national and local levels. Veteran campaigners dismissed as conservative, religious and moderate by contemporary feminists had long claimed a space in the women's movement that survived in the period from the foundation of the state until the emergence of second-wave feminism.

Women primarily engaged in production consolidated the largest organisation of women in Ireland, the Irish Countrywomen's Association (ICA), from 1910 onwards.[6] According to Heverin (2000: 185): "The ICA did much to improve conditions and give rural women independence through education and income-generating projects." The ICA had close ties with other women's organisations, especially the Irish Housewives Association (IHA), which was a predominantly urban-based group.[7] The ICA as the largest women's organisation in Ireland and one of the oldest rural movements in Europe was a very important accomplice to the IHA (Tweedy, 1992: 112; Ferriter, 1994; Heverin, 2000). Both the ICA and IHA were active in the 1940s and continued to mobilise when the second wave of feminism emerged, from the late 1960s on.

The IHA developed extensive links and alliances with international feminist organisations, which linked Irish feminists to critical international events and developments in the 1950s and 1960s especially. In the ICA, the task of improving the lives of women was frequently combined with generating change in the wider community. Whether or not the organisation was feminist, therefore, has been widely contested. For many ICA members, feminism was not an acceptable slogan and the resurging radical women's movement was generally viewed with scepticism in the 1970s.

Ferriter (1994: 1) argues that because the ICA encompasses the experiences of a large majority of women in rural Ireland in the twentieth century, its importance for Irish history cannot be underestimated:

> Given that the ICA has been more representative of Irishwomen than any other, it is essential that the progression of the society be examined as this progress has been essential to the social and cultural evolution of Independent Ireland. (Ferriter, 1994: 1)

By the 1970s, the ICA was engulfed by debates about radical feminism that went well beyond the long-established parameters set down by the original organisation established in 1910 and "...the ICA was being challenged by other women, a situation they were unused to" (Ferriter, 1994: 58). The new debates about contraception, rape, sexuality, employment inequality and other feminist issues that had never been openly discussed politically in Ireland challenged the consciousness of the ICA. Yet, as a member of the *ad hoc* committee on women's rights, which came together in 1968 to lobby for the First National Commission on the Status of Women and went on to establish the Council for the Status of Women (CSW), the ICA were implicated in the expansion of a key sector of the second wave of the women's movement from the outset.

The tensions that arose between rural women leaders, whose aspirations were originally shaped and formed in a vastly different period and political climate, and new urban-based feminist organisations, who were mobilising in a more radical period of political protest and activism, reflect the transformation of Irish women's lives by 1970. Irish society was fundamentally transformed by urbanisation and economic modernisation in the 1960s. Mamo McDonald, President of the ICA, highlighted the effect of this in a colourful speech in 1985 (see Ferriter, 1994: 60 and Connolly, 2003b):

> ... who speaks for Irish women? – the militants demanding contraception had made their point, she said, but in 1910 Poultry and not the Pill had been foremost on the minds of the Irish countrywomen, and as far back as this, the ICA has been there to assist: for all the publicity which our more militant sisters can generate, the ICA has a more revolutionary and direct bearing on the vast majority of Irish women.

With a 90-year history and over 1,000 guilds nationally, the ICA is the oldest and largest women's organisation in the country. While the ICA is still a vibrant organisation today, the emergence of adult education and community development initiatives nationally in the 1980s led to other important developments for women in rural Ireland. For example, both the Western Women's Link and the recently established Women's Regional Policy Project, which operates in the Sligo, Cavan, Donegal, Monaghan, and Leitrim regions and aims to strengthen the basic community-based women's infrastructure, have developed strong profiles.

Established in 1995, WEFT (Women Educating for Transformation) is one of the most recent examples of a national women's project, engaged in cross-border/cross-cultural partnership work and strategic policy work. WEFT succeeded in establishing the Women's Regional Policy Project in 2001 under the Equality for Women measure in the National Development Plan 2000–2006, which addresses the needs of women's networks in Ireland.

Speaking at the launch of the NWCI *Framing the Future* document, in 2001, Gráinne Healy highlighted the fact that rural women's groups are often providing vital counselling, support and crisis service for women in the absence of any existing services. Services for women (such as refuges, family-planning clinics and rape crisis centres) have operated primarily in large urban centres since the 1970s, providing restricted access for rural women. The number of rural women's organisations and networks has increased significantly in the last two decades in Ireland. These groups are engaged in a wide variety of activities, meeting important social, educational and support needs in the lives of local women and in the rural development co-operatives and networks that operate in Ireland more generally.

Marian Flannery, project director of Women of the North West network, a Co. Mayo-based women's group stated at the launch of "Framing the Future": "Our challenge is about fighting for recognition of rural women; it is about valuing a rural way of life" (quoted in the *Irish Examiner*, 20 November 2001). The extensive activism of women in rural communities today is integral to any general account of community-based politics in Ireland.

Press Release NWCI

Monday 19 November 2001
Launch of:
Framing the Future
An Integrated Strategy to Support Women's Community and Voluntary Organisations
Buswells Hotel Dublin

Gráinne Healy, National Women's Council of Ireland (NWCI) Chairwoman, thanked Mary Wallace TD, Minister for Justice, Equality and Law Reform, for launching the Framing the Future Report. She also thanked the other speakers and went on to explain that Framing the Future is a research study commissioned by the NWCI and conducted by Kelleher Associates. The brief of the study was to investigate the number and activities of women's community and voluntary organisations in Ireland and to identify a strategy for supporting this sector. "The national database compiled for the study indicates that there are 2,631 women's organisations in the 26 counties of Ireland. These organisations cater for up to 75,000 women annually" declared Ms. Healy. "79% of locally based and community women's groups and 65% of women's organisations and projects generally, operate on less than £1,000 per annum" she continued. "There is a clear and urgent need for a defined strategy by the Government to provide realistic funding for these organisations and groups, many of which are providing vital counselling, support and crisis services for women" stated Ms. Healy. "We are calling on Minister Wallace today to lobby her cabinet colleagues to support the vital work of women's groups" she added.

"Women's organisations engage in a wide variety of activities, meeting important social, educational and support needs in the lives of local women and play a vibrant and invaluable role in the broader community" said Ms. Healy. "Women's groups serve the needs of a diverse range of women including urban women, women living in rural areas, disabled women, women experiencing violence, lone parents, lesbians, minority ethnic women, Traveller women, widows and older women" she declared. Ms. Healy pointed to the fact that the number of organisations in the sector has increased significantly in the last 10 years, with 43 per cent of organisations established in the last five years and 60 per cent established in the last 10 years. If the guilds of the Irish Countrywomen's Association (ICA) are excluded, 76 per cent of organisations were established between 1990 and 2000.

"The publication of Framing the Future poses a challenge to the NWCI and the Government to take note of the needs of women's groups and support their work" stated Ms. Healy. "The NWCI intends to respond to this challenge by supporting this sector of women's groups to achieve the levels of funding they require to build their organisational capacity in providing services and supports to so many women at grassroots level" she added.

"We expect the Government, to respond by creating a budget line, which is accessible to local women's groups and to support the NWCI to build the capacity of the sector through the creation of a support unit for women's groups" concluded Ms. Healy.
The major findings of *Framing the Future*.

- There are 2,631 women's organisations in the 26 counties of Ireland;
- 79% of locally-based/community women's groups and 65% of women's organisations/projects generally operate on less than £1,000 per annum;
- Women's organisations engage in a wide variety of activities, meeting important social, educational and support needs in the lives of local women;
- Women's organisations play a vibrant and invaluable role in the broader community;
- The majority of women's organisations are seriously under-funded and lack resources;
- A defined scheme of assistance for women's groups needs to be established by the Department of Social, Community and Family Affairs;
- A programme of cross-departmental funding must be established for women's organisations;
- The NWCI should establish a technical support unit for women's groups;
- The NWCI should lobby for greater resources for the sector;
- The NWCI should have a greater regional presence.

Source: www.nwci.ie

Anti-racism protest in London, *Wicca* magazine n.d. (BL/F/AP/1498/1, Attic Press Archive)

Conclusion

Developments in community politics in the 1980s created a new critique of the class and urban bias of the second-wave women's movement in Ireland. However, in tandem with the general mainstreaming of feminism, the community-based sector has also undergone a transformation and degree of professionalisation in recent years. Furthermore, feminist analysis today displays an awareness that issues concerning poverty and class intersect with other hierarchies which frame women's lives in Ireland, such as race, ethnicity, disability, and sexuality. Indeed, use of the very term "Irish woman" or "Irish women's movement" without qualification of its meaning is now considered problematic.

The women's movement in Ireland has only recently developed a debate about how second-wave feminism "othered" and eclipsed some groups of women. Voices routinely excluded from mainstream feminist agendas, such as Irish Traveller women and disabled women, came forth with a rigorous political analysis of their situation in the 1990s and they too have claimed a space in the established women's movement in Ireland alongside working-class and rural women.[8] In the new millennium, given the increase in immigration in Ireland, it is likely that women in ethnic minorities will also claim their space in the women's movement in the not too distant future.

For some, prioritising the plurality of differences and inequalities that exist among Irish women runs the danger of fragmenting the collective identity that propelled feminism forward in the first place, in the 1970s. At the same time, these developments are moving beyond the widespread mainstreaming of second-wave feminism and symbolise a broadening of the original concerns of the women's movement. New organised groups of women in Ireland, some of whose felt sense of belonging to the category "Irish" has had no legal guarantee and little social acceptance, are emerging in the new century. Recent focus on difference in Irish feminism has, in practice, significantly expanded the constituency that first mobilised the women's movement in the 1970s and then mainstreamed feminism in the 1980s. In the process, fixed definitions of "Irish womanhood" and Irishness are being challenged. Whether these developments will lead to the fragmentation or a healthy proliferation of feminism/s in Ireland, therefore, is a still developing story.

Notes

1 Files BL/F/AP/1–83, of the Attic Press Archive, relate to the personal involvement of Róisín Conroy and the extensive development of women's rights in the Irish labour movement.

2 Several publications by the ESRI and the Combat Poverty Agency have analysed data which documents the extent and experience of women's poverty in Ireland. See, for example, McCashin (1996) and Watson and Nolan (1991).

3 See Beaumont (1997: 185–6) for a discussion.

4 File BL/F/AP/1178, Attic Press Archive: includes IWU discussion paper "Feminism and Socialism" (c.1975–6). Articles in *Banshee* also reviewed feminist socialist campaigns and issues extensively (file BL/F/AP/1515, Attic Press Archive). File BL/F/AP/1142, Attic Press Archive, contains material on socialist women's groups, including: "History behind Bread and Roses: Women's Lib UCD 1976". File BL/F/AP/1497, Attic Press Archive, contains "Women's Voice. Women's Magazine of the Socialist Workers Party" nos. 5, 8, 51, 65. File BL/F/AP/1517, Attic Press Archive, contains copies of "Bread and Roses. UCD Women's Liberation Group", nos. 1, 3–6.

5 Files BL/F/AP/1226–1239, Attic Press Archive: include several items concerning an early campaign to establish a Women's Centre in Dublin (1976–1984).

6 The Society of United Irishwomen was founded in 1910 as the women's arm of the co-operative movement. The first branch was formed in Bree, Co. Wexford by Annita Lett. The name of the organisation was changed in 1935 to the Irish Countrywomen's Association due to the political climate at that time. Today with over 16,000 members in over 1,000 active guilds, the ICA is represented in every county in Ireland. See: www.ica.ie for further information.

7 Files BL/F/AP/1202–1205, Attic Press Archive, contains material relating to the Irish Countrywomen's Association (ICA) (1980–1983). The ICA itself has accumulated extensive archives, which have not been catalogued as an open collection to date. For an account of the organisation's history, using ICA archives, see Ferriter (1994). Tweedy (1992) provides a history of the IHA. File BL/F/AP/1540, Attic Press Archive, contains a tape of an interview of Hilda Tweedy, founding member of the IHA, by Pat Kenny.

8 File BL/F/AP/1368, Attic Press Archive: contains circular letter from the Dublin Travellers Education and Development Group (September 1987) seeking support for a march to highlight issues affecting the Traveller community in Ireland. File BL/F/AP/1550 is a recorded interview with Traveller woman Christina Moore.

Chapter 8
Education and Feminist Studies

Protest organised by the Disabled People's Action Group, Dublin, 22 November 1979. photo: Derek Spiers/reproduced in *Wicca* 13, BL/F/AP/1498, Attic Press Archive)

Feminism is of itself an educational project. When feminist activists in the early 1970s questioned the status quo, they began to unpick their own socialisation, read against the grain, challenge hegemonies, and reconstruct the world from women's own perspectives.[1] Early initiatives in feminist studies tended to be based in voluntarily run women's centres, or located within small networks of friends who set up reading groups and consciousness-raising groups, or as they were called in the USA "rap groups", where a group of women would come together to "rap", or discuss, a particular issue. Women's studies came together in a similar way, as collectives were set up "where each woman agrees to share the responsibility for planning the course, initiating discussion, gathering material and ensuring that every member gets her fair chance to participate" (Steiner-Scott, 1985: 286). For Steiner-Scott, women's studies programmes emerged as "informal groups, that is, those organised outside of traditional educational structures".

As interest grew, groups were set up in more formal ways, such as the "Women in Learning" group in Dublin. A flyer from the group stated:

> WIL is a women's studies group set up by women from diverse areas of interest. All the women
> express dissatisfaction with the education system and its failure to meet the needs of women.
> WIL women ... do not simply want to "put on" courses, but also want to learn for themselves
> and seek out alternative possibilities for education for women ... our own experiences as
> women will be seen as relevant to courses – unlike usual academic courses – where only male-
> defined experiences are seen as valid – all others are rejected as "personal" and "irrelevant".
> (BL/F/AP AP 1415, Attic Press Archive)

Two of the courses listed by WIL were "Our Bodies Ourselves" and "Women and
Children First". WIL was committed to a policy of facilitating women learners, as
is evident from the postscript to its flyer: "n.b. if you have any problems, i.e. finan-
cial/bringing children along etc. please let us know and we will do whatever we can
to help you sort them out". It clearly saw itself as part of the feminist movement at
the time, and talk about "working in co-operation with other groups and sharing
resources and ideas".

From the early 1980s on, women's education projects began to develop
throughout the country, many of them as part of broader adult and community
education programmes, but some also developed independently by local women's
groups.

Apart from course-oriented learning, it is clear that those women in a position
to travel to the various feminist conferences could avail of the opportunity to network with other women from all over the country. This list of women's conferences was drawn up for the IFI Diary and Guidebook 1985, and gives an indication of the number of such events held in the late 1970s:

2 Feb 1975	International Women's Year held in Dublin
19 Mar 1976	International Women's Day Meeting
8 June 1976	CAP [Contraception Action Plan] Meeting in Central Hotel
27 Jan 1978	2nd National Women's Liberation Conference
15 May 1978	Conference on Lesbianism in Dublin
25 May 1978	Galway National Women's Conference on Violence
October 1978	3rd National Women's Liberation Conference Belfast
9 June 1979	All Ireland Women's Conference Dublin
18 June 1983	Women's Conference, Crescent Arts Centre Belfast
6 April 1984	National Women's Conference – Rutland St. Dublin

These conferences provided a forum for women to learn and to develop feminist
practice in workshop sessions. A review of the National Women's Liberation
Conference held in Belfast in 1978 reinforces this point:

> I didn't know there were so many Feminists in Ireland. Didn't know that it was possible to spend
> a weekend at a conference with over 100 women from all over the country and take as assumed
> ideas that I usually have to defend vigorously... The way the conference operated was, for me,
> one of its most interesting aspects. It was part of the attempt by the Women's Movement to

develop a new way of organising and discussing … We used small workshops with about 10 women in each as the basis of the conference. (*Anima Rising* Galway Women's Collective newsletter 1978 (BL/F/AP/1139/17, Attic Press Archive)

The introduction of small group workshops, now a central feature of much education and development work, derived from the small-group consciousness-raising elements of the women's movement. More recent initiatives in feminist learning have adopted the same approach. For example, the Lesbian Education and Awareness/NOW programme in the late 1990s provided training for a group of members of lesbian communities from various parts of the country, with the aim that this trained group of women would then pass on the skills and training they had learned to members of their own organisations. During the programme, an information and resource pack was produced, which continues to be used in a variety of educational settings throughout the country, both within the LGBT communities, and the wider community.

Other less formal ways in which feminists developed their own learning programmes included reading groups and women's libraries, such as the library in the Women's Space at the Quay Co-Op in Cork, and the Women's Centre Shop at 27 Temple Lane, Dublin. Women's centres like these carried catalogues from the women's presses, as well as making available a wide range of feminist reading material. The Women's Library in Cork published a newsletter, which reviewed new books and articles relevant to their readership. Making a wide range of materials available either on loan or at reduced second-hand prices made feminist theories and publications accessible to a wider number of people.

Materials found in the libraries and bookshops included periodicals such as *Banshee* and *Spare Rib*, as well as pamphlets and books relating to a wide range of political and social issues. Pamphlets on women's health matters, including abortion, were also made available cheaply or on loan. Much of this material was imported from abroad, which is an interesting comment on the thinking and ideologies of early Irish feminism, as we discussed earlier. Underlining this point, Róisín Conroy points out in the preface to a bibliography on "Images of Irish Women":

> Although I was asked to compile a bibliography dealing with the subject of women in Ireland, I found that there is such a dearth of Irish material, both factual and theoretical, on topics such as Health and Sexuality that the "Irish only" criteria has little or no relevance. Much of the theory, certainly, that has influenced Irishwomen has been written and published abroad. (*Crane Bag* 4.1 1980)

The establishment of women's studies programmes and centres over the intervening twenty years would change this, and ensure that Irish feminists would begin to publish and read Irish material. In a 1987 paper, Ailbhe Smyth drew attention to the need for women's studies programmes which would be culturally and socially specific, and pointed up two key issues for women's studies in Ireland, stating that it should:

Poster advertising the Women's World Congress held in Dublin, 1987 (BL/F/AP/982/4, Attic
Press Archive)

(a) maintain and develop its relationship with the women's movement; its usefulness and accessibility to all women; create dialogue between researchers and teachers, and institutional and non-institutional programmes and activities;

(b) bring about irreversible change in the ways in which knowledge is constructed and disseminated – in research policies, agendas and methodologies, in curriculum content and pedagogy.[2] (Quoted from a conference paper, "The Emergence and Development of the Women's Movement in Ireland" held in BL/F/AP/1414/26, Attic Press Archive)

Writer June Levine at Women's World Congress, Dublin, 7 July 1987 (photo: Clodagh Boyd)

Women's Studies and the Academy

The establishment of a women's studies programme at Trinity College Dublin in 1983 and the Women's Studies Forum at University College Dublin in 1987 marked the beginning of a new era in Irish feminist education.[3] Both were integral to the establishment and wider acceptance of women's studies in the Irish third-level education system.[4]

The Women's Studies Forum at UCD was a collective which organised academic events, rather than a series of taught programmes. Reflecting on this group, Smyth describes it as: "a space for discussion and exchange, between women in the university, and between women in the university and the community".[5] The Women's Education, Research and Resource Centre (WERRC) was founded in UCD in 1990, and although it initially operated out of a tiny administrative office in the library building, and had no full-time staff members, the enthusiasm for the project of women's studies was infectious.

Byrne *et al* (1996) document the experience in University College Galway. In 1987 a group of students, academics and administrative staff collectively voiced their concern about the lack of attention to gender issues within UCG. They high-lighted the deficiency of women's studies courses on the undergraduate academic curriculum and the absence of equality policies in the workplace. The UCG Women's Studies Centre was established in order to promote contact between staff and students with an interest in these issues and to provide a forum in which to engage in discussion, exchange information and be a source of collective support.[6]

Looking at the development of women's studies in the intervening period, Pat O'Connor points out:

> By the early 1990s, there were approximately 40 Women's Studies courses in existence (Drew, 1993; Ní Charthaigh and Hanafin, 1993) with all the universities in Ireland having Women's Studies at undergraduate and/or postgraduate level … At its best … the existence and vitality of Women's Studies is a radical challenge to the structure and ethos of these institutions. (O'Connor, 1998: 77)

Early women's studies groups in universities discussed the tensions that might arise in the effort to locate the teachings of an activist movement in a traditional academic setting. At a women's studies conference in San Francisco in 1988, Smyth addressed the question of the relationship between the women's movement and women's studies, pointing out that the women's movement was by then becoming more diffuse, and that many of the women coming to women's studies might have no history of activism. She saw this as a challenge for women's studies educators, as they endeavoured to maintain a basis of political activism in their teaching and research. Describing the way in which Irish universities in Ireland in the 1980s were often cut off from the wider community, she emphasised the importance of accessibility and links with community groups. In 1995, Byrne reflected back on these concerns:

> The earlier debates in the women's movement concerned the threat of deradicalisation of women's studies once it became a component in the formal educational system, as carried out by gendered institutions, such as universities. Women's studies has struggled with the dilemma of becoming part of the institution so that the feminist agenda of empowerment and liberation can be carried out within the walls, while at the same time seeking to change the very institution which provides a home for academic feminism. (Byrne, 1995: 26–27)

Thus, it is clear that many members of women's studies projects see the political and educational goals of women's studies as organically linked to the history and aims of the women's movement:

> Establishing women's studies in educational institutions embraces many issues: the production of feminist scholarship, developing feminist research methodologies, creating teaching pro-grammes, curricula and feminist media, liaising and negotiating with institutional bodies and committees, setting up Women's Studies centres and departments, looking for long-term fund-ing, negotiating research contracts, networking and liaising with women's groups, providing

Ailbhe Smyth at Women's World Congress, Dublin, 7 July 1987 (photo: Clodagh Boyd)

support for campaigns and social and political issues. And as the work develops, the list of activities grows. (Byrne, 1995: 26–27)

A more recent development is that for some women in "mainstream" academic departments, "gender studies" have become part of their career trajectory, an area which women are simply expected to teach. For some, a theoretical focus on activist political movements such as the feminist movement is one which tends to be kept at an "objective" remove. The danger here is that teaching feminist studies can become just another aspect of academic specialisation, with no investment in the political or social implications of feminist politics. In contrast, those working on dedicated women's studies programmes tend to see feminism within academe as a form of activism, of institutional and scholarly resistance.[7]

Many women's studies programmes in Ireland operate within the university structure, and are for the most part under-resourced and voluntarily maintained (Connolly, 2003b). Smyth addresses the difficulties posed to women's studies, and a range of other non-traditional subjects, by the compartmentalisation of academic departments:

If you want to do regional studies, or Women's Studies, or Equality Studies, or if you want to move in a pluridisciplinary or cross-disciplinary way it's incredibly difficult because this is seen as being totally subversive ... so it is structurally very difficult to do something like Women's

Women's Liberation Conference 9 September 1979, Trinity College Dublin, where the decision to form the 32 County Feminist Federation was taken (photo: Clodagh Boyd)

"Reflections on the Irish Women's Movement" panel, Women's World Congress, Dublin, 7 July 1987 (photo: Clodagh Boyd)

Some titles from the LIP series of feminist pamphlets published by Attic Press

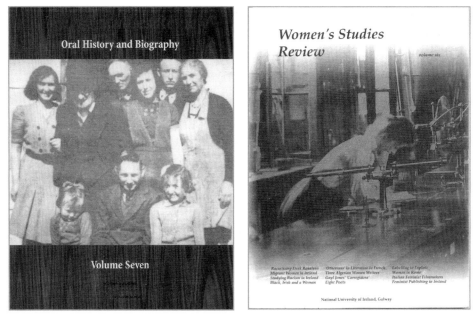

Covers of the journal *Galway Women's Studies Review*

Studies, but a whole lot of other kinds of cross-cultural approaches to knowledge that you might want to develop are also completely impossible in our system.

In dialogue with Deborah Rosenfelt. San Francisco 1988. (BL/F/AP 1566/3. Sound Recording. Attic Press Archive)

Roseneil makes some pertinent observations on the propensity of many feminist academics to move continuously between and across the boundaries of their own discipline and women's studies. She points out that they teach mainstream courses that are compulsory elements of undergraduate and postgraduate disciplines and in addition they teach, in a relatively autonomous way, option courses within their disciplines and within women's studies programmes (1995: 191–205). Roseneil contends that the integration/separation tension results partly from the location of feminism at the margins of mainstream academe and the fact that few lectureships are appointed entirely within women's studies.

A recent funding intervention on the part of an Irish-American trust has enabled some women's studies centres to move away from their dependence on support from within the academy. This external funding has altered the status of women's studies departments and staff at NUIG and the University of Limerick (UL), among others, where full-time posts have been funded on an interim basis. However, this funding is contingent on the host university agreeing to maintain such posts at the end of a fixed period of time, and this has meant that some women's studies departments have not been able to avail of the funding, in the absence of institutional backing. Thus, while it is possible to say that funding initiatives have altered the situation for some women's studies centres, the overall picture is still one of voluntary management and teaching across the field of Irish women's studies.

Today, a wide variety of themes and experiences underpin the remit of women's studies, which is not exclusively confined to academe. Women's studies are undertaken in a variety of contexts, particularly in adult and community education settings. Outreach programmes are maintained by several university-based women's studies centres, with students based in a variety of communities. These courses are run in co-operation with community projects; for example, WERRC has developed links with groups such as the SAOL Project, Ballymun Women's Resource Centre and L.INC. Through its methods, based on principles of consciousness raising and empowerment, Irish women's studies seek to validate knowledge through women's experiences both within and outside of the walls of the university.

Women's Community Education

Smyth's programme for women's studies mentioned earlier, called on feminist educators to maintain and develop a relationship with the women's movement, and to maintain the usefulness and accessibility of women's studies to all women (1987). Bríd Connolly (2002) describes locally based feminist activism as: "the engagement of ordinary women with the Women's Movement, extending the ownership of the movement from purely academic and public arenas, into the everyday lives of ordinary women". The impetus for women's community education in this country has come from locally based women's groups, as discussed in the previous chapter, often working in tandem with larger organisations, such as Aontas, NUI Maynooth's Adult and Community Education Centre, WERRC, the Irish Countrywomen's Association (ICA), local VECs and others. Thus, the issues and concerns of locally based women's groups are inextricably linked with community education carried out in their areas. Access to continuing education has long been highlighted as an issue for locally based women's groups, which see the provision of ongoing education for women as a way to counter women's isolation from each other, and to build community identities. Community education has also moved into the arena of accredited education and training programmes, as a strategy to break the cycle of disadvantage as well as to develop tools to challenge/disrupt the *status quo*.

Daytime education courses began to spring up in the mid-1980s, run by groups such as Clondalkin Adult Morning Education (CAME), Maynooth Adult Daytime Courses (MADE) and the Churchfield Women's Group in Cork. By the early 1990s there were over 100 such groups. Connolly and Ryan (2000) outline the development of daytime education groups in the greater Dublin area. They point out that community-based courses in the 1980s were run by group members themselves, who took on the responsibility for organising childcare facilities, employing tutors and, most importantly, selecting the subjects for study. Women's studies were one of the early components of many of these courses, as local groups began to address

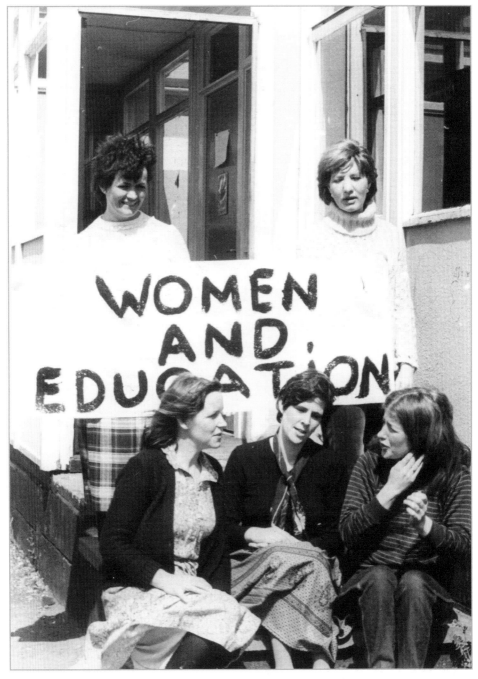

Women's Education Group (BL/F/AP/1129/1, Attic Press Archive) (n.d.)

Doing It For Themselves

Over the past ten years, working class women have become increasingly active in education, and in personal and community development. *Kathleen Maher* reports on a recent initiative in Dublin

PRIOR TO THE 1980s most women in working class communities spent their time isolated in their homes looking after their families. Apart from this, women spent a considerable amount of time queuing for basic services such as welfare, bringing their children to school, shopping, waiting for buses, in fact doing everything except stopping for a moment to look after their own needs as women and human beings.

Article by Kathleen Maher in the *Irish Reporter* 8 (1992)

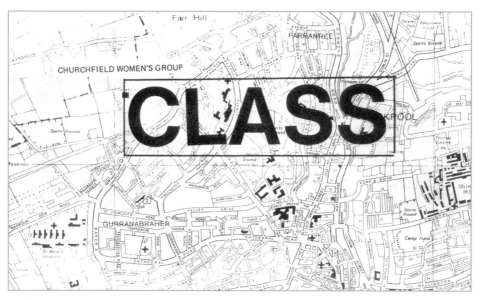

Heading from an article by Churchfield Women's Group on women's rights and gay rights, *Quare Times*, spring 1984 (Irish Queer Archive)

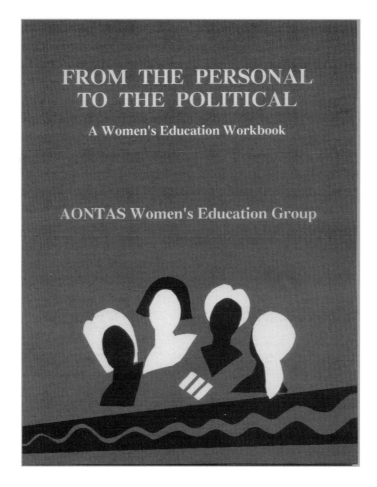

Aontas Women's Education Group Workbook (1991)

the kinds of learning simultaneously being introduced by feminists in the academy. The parallels between this way of organising local women's studies courses and the efforts of early feminist activists working out of women's centres are clear. However, unlike the pioneers of earlier feminist education initiatives who were devising materials from scratch, locally based groups in the late 1980s could draw on the body of feminist material which had emerged during the earlier activist period, together with radical social theories which they adapted for Irish community contexts.

We tend to think of women's community education as a field whose primary investment is in urban working-class women's community development and activism. However, this is not uniformly the case. In itself, extrapolating the differences between adult education, community education and lifelong learning is by no means straightforward. Today, the number and range of courses available (some of which have roots in external educational institutions, are community-led, are accredited by external bodies, or are not accredited at all) does not lend itself to an easy analysis, or an overall picture of this field. This leads to difficulties

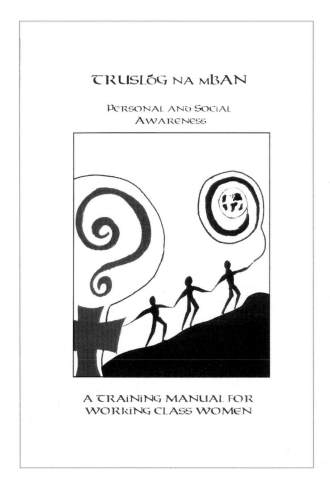

Cork Women's Education Initiative (CWEI) Training Manual (1998)

in assessing the investment in feminist principles across a wide range of groups and courses categorised as "women's community education". For example, at least one-fifth of the 1,000 groups currently listed under the heading "women's community education" are connected with the Home-School Liaison system, which is rooted in the needs of the school system rather than the self-defined needs of the groups, or the (mostly women) members involved (Ní Dhubhda, 2002: 54).

One of the persistent questions thrown up by community activists and practitioners of women's community education is that of an interrogation of class structures within feminism. Noting the increasing numbers of women in working-class communities who participated in community education courses in the 1980s and 1990s, the Cork Women's Education Initiative (CWEI) points out that much of the material covered in such courses has a particular class bias:

> Most of these [courses] have focused on hobby activities or personal development and assertiveness. Almost all have been very individualistic – emphasising how women can change themselves, rather than looking both at the structures that keep women in their place and ways

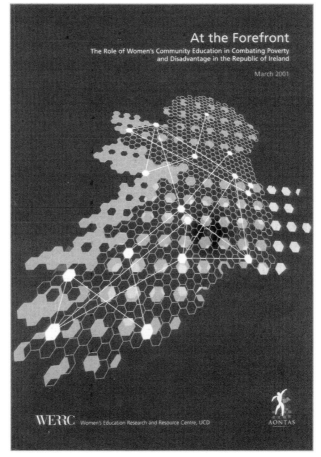

WERRC/Aontas Report on Women's Community Education (2001)

to challenge these structures collectively. Feminism may have been sometimes included, but issues around class were rarely considered relevant to working class women's lives. (1998)

While it is crucial that the class bias of feminist studies is continually scrutinised, such an assessment of the personal-development activities and, consequently, the politicising effects of locally based women's groups, requires further examination. Arguably, consciousness raising is an equally necessary strategy to that of challenging state structures in tackling women's disempowerment. Social change *also* operates at a cultural level, through activities such as personal-development courses and second-chance education. Thus, raising the consciousness of a wider constituency of women who do not have the resources, childcare and time for other activist or community development work is also a critical element of feminist empowerment. As Anne B. Ryan (2001) has argued, personal development *is* important in women's community education; but it needs to be grounded in feminist principles rather than relying on mainstream psychology.

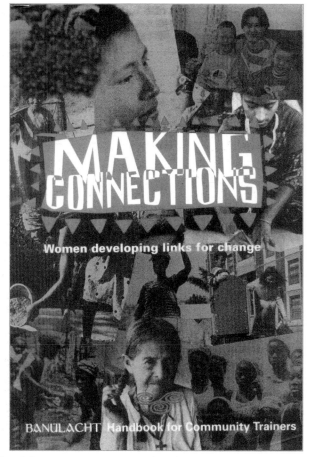

Banúlacht Handbook for Community Trainers (1994)

In the period 1993 to 2003, the number of women's community education groups has increased tenfold (Inglis et al, 1993; WERRC/Aontas, 2001: 27). European funding initiatives in the 1990s such as New Opportunities for Women (NOW), and the Women's Educational Network Development Initiative (WENDI), alongside community development initiatives at local level, have been instrumental in the growth of this sector. Yet, from the perspective of the wider educational picture, this is still a field which receives little attention or resources. The WERRC/Aontas report *At the Forefront* (2001) isolates the lack of childcare and transport support as being among the most significant barriers to women's participation in continuing education. In the absence of core funding in this area, the availability of premises for daytime courses continues to pose problems.

New challenges are posed by the entry of feminist or community-focused courses into the mainstream provision of Adult Education. Ní Dhubhda (2002) refers to the dangers of a "mainstreaming without meaning, or a meaning radically altered but unacknowledged":

At local, community and formal sites of learning, there are an ever-increasing range of courses with the tag "community", or "women's", or both. But just because courses are run specifically for women, are located in a community, or are part of third-level compensatory models of Adult Education, this does not make them women's community education. This education model is not based on the recipe "add and stir". We need to keep reclaiming the right to be political, not just popular. (Ní Dhubhda, 2002: 61)

Nonetheless, despite the continuing challenges presented to educators within women's community education, it is clear that this is an area of education that is going from strength to strength. Furthermore, those coming through these pro-grammes are now in a position to critically challenge power structures in the pub-lic domain:

The slow, gradual, but very significant changes made in areas such as education under female ministers, the activities of women active in community groups, in adult education, and in vol-untary organisations have created a supportive infrastructure or "submerged networks" (Melucci, 1998:248). They have generated an informed woman-centred constituency. (Mahon, 1995: 704)

Mahon refers to the strength of this lobby in mainstream political terms, recently reflected in the effect of this constituency in the elections of women politicians such as Marion Harkin and others, who may not be specifically feminist candi-dates but whose agendas resonate in some ways with women voters.

The Irish Journal of Feminist Studies 2003; 1996

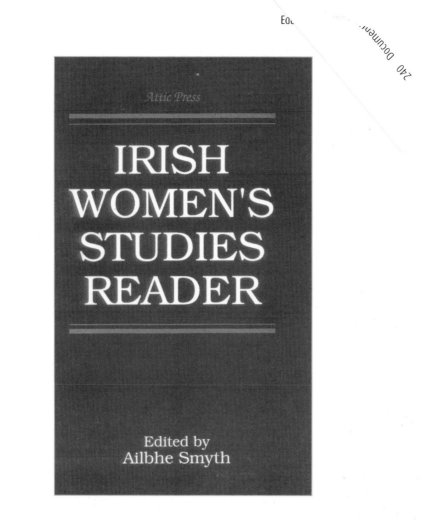

The *Irish Women's Studies Reader* (1993) was published by Attic Press to provide a foundation text in Irish feminism for use in women's studies classrooms

Conclusion

Today, there are many ongoing links between women's community education and women's studies programmes, and some useful alliances have been developed on the ground between locally based women's groups and university departments. The recognition that feminism can be expressed as activism within the institutions, as well as within the wider society, is central. This is specifically the case within academe, where feminists work collectively to challenge institutional and academic values, or improve conditions on behalf of women colleagues and students. Furthermore, the growing number of community-based feminist activists and development workers participating in third-level courses as learners, educators and researchers has enhanced the links between community-based and academic feminism. Cathleen O'Neill has underlined the importance of such cooperation between different kinds of groups:

The women's movement has been the most important movement of this century and it has been crucial to my life and development. It has been instrumental in the development of community-led women's groups. To quote Mary Robinson, there is a "shared leadership, and a quite, radical, continuing dialogue between the individual woman and the collective women". I believe that we need a more active dialogue that will question where the women's movement is going; and we need to set and agree our priorities for the new millennium. There is a huge need to develop a cohesive co-ordinated women's movement because there is much work to be done. (O'Neill, 1999: 42)

Despite these intersections, there remains a tendency to view the academy and community sectors within feminism and other activism as distinct camps with nothing to offer each other. As discussed in Chapter 7, existing research has provided valuable insights into clear divergences between feminist goals and activities of locally based women's group (Ward and O'Donovan, 1996; Costello, 1999). Yet, there are also numerous examples of positive co-operation between women's studies programmes and community groups. A national study of the experience of women involved both in academic women's studies and women's community education would be helpful in enabling an overall picture, and in furthering co-operative work.

Notes

1 See File BL/F/AP/1176, Attic Press Archive, for an early discussion of sexism and sexual inequality in education, where there is a pamphlet entitled "Education Widens the Gap between the Sexes" published by the Education Workshop, Irishwomen United, Dublin (1975, 21pp.). Files BL/F/AP/1341–1351, Attic Press Archive, contain various articles and booklets on the issues of sexism in education.

2 Smyth, "Women's Studies in Ireland: Growth and Change", National Women's Studies Association Conference, 1987.

3 Files BL/F/AP1407–1417, Attic Press Archive, contain various documents concerning the development of a forum and courses in Irish women's studies (1978–1987).

4 File BL/F/AP/1413, Attic Press Archive, details activities of the UCD Women's Studies Forum (1984–5).

5 Paper given at the Visions and Voices Conference, San Francisco State University, 1988.

6 The stated aims and objectives of the Women's Studies Centre are (Byrne, 1996: 84): to provide students with an understanding of women's studies and as an academic discipline; to introduce students to feminist theory as a conceptual and analytical framework; to introduce students to alternative teaching methods; to demonstrate the importance of personal experience in learning and problem-solving; to introduce students to a wide range of study and learning skills; to provide students with a thorough understanding of the position of women in diverse cultures and periods in history; to gain insights into the construction of inequality and the oppression of women; and to explore the representation of women in literature, in art and the media from Ireland and abroad.

7 Anne Byrne and Ronit Lentin have recently conducted a survey of feminist academics. See Byrne (2000).

Bibliography

Andersen, Margaret (1983; 1993). *Thinking About Women: Sociological and Feminist Persepectives*. New York: Macmillan.

Anzaldúa, Gloria (1987). *Borderlands = La Frontera: The New Mestiza*. San Francisco: Spinsters/Aunt Lute.

AONTAS Women's Education Group (1991). *From the Personal to the Political: A Women's Education Workbook*. Dublin: Attic Press.

Aretxaga, Begona (1997). *Shattering Silence: Women, Nationalism and Political Subjectivity in Northern Ireland*. Princeton NJ: Princeton University Press.

Banks, Olive (1981). *Faces of Feminism*. Oxford: Martin Robertson.

Barry, Ursula (1986). *Lifting the Lid*. Dublin: Attic Press.

Barry, Ursula (1988). "The Contemporary Women's Movement in the Republic of Ireland." In Ailbhe Smyth (ed.), *Feminism in Ireland. Women's Studies International Forum*, 11, 4. New York: Pergamon, 317–322.

Barry, Ursula (1992). "Movement, Change and Reaction: The Struggle over Reproductive Rights in Ireland." In Ailbhe Smyth (ed.), *The Abortion Papers: Ireland*. Dublin: Attic Press.

Beale, Jenny (1986). *Women in Ireland*. Dublin: Gill & Macmillan.

Beaumont, Catriona (1997). "Women and the Politics of Equality: The Irish Women's Movement, 1930–1943." In Mary O'Dowd, and Maryann Gialanella Valiulis (eds.), *Women and Irish History*. Dublin: Wolfhound, 185–205.

Beaumont, Catriona (1999). "Gender, Citizenship and the State in Ireland, 1922–1990." In Scott Brewster, Virginia Crossman, Fiona Becket, and David Alderson (eds.), *Ireland in Proximity: History, Gender, Space*. London and New York: Routledge, 94–108.

Becker, Susan (1981). *The Origins of the Equal Rights Amendment: Feminism Between the Wars*. Westport, CT: Greenwood Press.

Bielenberg, Andy (ed.) (2000). *The Irish Diaspora*. London: Longmans.

Blackwell, John (1989). *Women in the Labour Force*. Dublin: Employment Equality Agency.

Bock, Gisela (1991). "Challenging Dichotomies: Perspectives on Women's History." In Karen Offen, Ruth Roach Pierson and Jane Rendell (eds.) (1991), *Writing Women's History: International Perspectives*. London: Macmillan, 1–23.

Boland, Eavan (1989). *A Kind of Scar: The Woman Poet in the National Tradition*. LIP Pamphlet Series. Dublin: Attic Press.

Boland, Eavan (ed.) (1979) *The Wall Leader and Other Stories*. Dublin, Arlen House.

Boland, Eavan (1995). "The Minds and Voices of Modern Irish Women." In Joan Hoff and Moureen Coulter (eds.), *Irish Women's Voices Past and Present*. Indiana: Indiana University Press, 6–9.

Bolger, Pat (1986). *And See Her Beauty Shining There: The Story of the Irish Countrywomen*. Dublin: Irish Academic Press.

Bouchier, David (1983). *The Feminist Challenge: The Movement for Women's Liberation in Britain and the USA*. London: Macmillan.

Bourke, Joanna (1993). *From Husbandry to Housewifery: Women, Economic Change and Housework in Ireland 1890–1914*. Oxford: Clarendon Press.

Boyd, Clodagh, Declan Doyle, Bill Foley, Brenda Harvey, Annette Hoctor, Maura Molloy and Mick Quinlan (1986). *Out for Ourselves: The Lives of Irish Lesbians and Gay Men*. Dublin: Dublin Lesbian and Gay Men's Collectives and Women's Community Press.

Boyle Haberstroh, Patricia (1996). *Women Creating Women: Contemporary Irish Women's Poets*. Dublin, Attic Press.

Bradley, Anthony and Maryann Gialanella Valiulis (eds.) (1997). *Gender and Sexuality in Modern Ireland*. Massacusetts: University of Massacusetts Press.

Breen, Richard, Damian F. Hannan, David B. Rottman and Christopher T. Whelan (eds.) (1990). *Understanding Contemporary Ireland: State, Class and Development in the Republic of Ireland*. Dublin: Macmillan.

Brennan, Pat (1979). "Women Organise in Dublin." *Magill*, January.

Brown, Heloise (1998). "An Alternative Imperialism: Isabella Todd, Internationalist and 'Good Liberal Unionist'." *Gender and History*, 10, 3: 358–380.

Bulbeck, Chilla (1998). *Re-Orienting Western Feminisms: Women's Diversity in a Postcolonial World*. Cambridge: Cambridge University Press.

Byrne, Anne (2000). "Researching One An-other". In Anne Byrne, and Ronit Lentin (eds.), *(Re)searching Women: Feminist Research Methodologies in the Social Sciences in Ireland*. Dublin: IPA, 140–166.

Byrne, Anne, Pat Byrne and Anne Lyons (1996). "Inventing and Teaching Women's Studies: Considering Feminist Pedagogy." *Irish Journal of Feminist Studies*, 1.1: 78–99.

Byrne, Anne, and Madeleine Leonard, (eds.) (1997). *Women and Irish Society: A Sociological Reader*. Belfast: Beyond the Pale.

Byrne, Noreen (1996). "The Uneasy Relationship Between Feminism and Community." In Smyth, Ailbhe (ed.), *Feminism, Politics, Community, WERRC Annual Conference Papers*. Dublin: UCD, 24–27.

Cairns, David and Shaun Richards (1988). *Writing Ireland: Colonialism, Nationalism and Culture*. Manchester: Manchester University Press.

Candy, Catherine (1994). "Relocating Feminisms, Nationalisms and Imperialisms: Ireland, India and Margaret Cousin's Sexual Politics". *Women's History Review*, 3, 1.

Carden, Maren Lockwood (1974). *The New Feminist Movement*. New York: Russell Sage Foundation

Carden, Maren Lockwood (1989). "Social Movement Continuity: The Women's Movement in Abeyance." *American Sociological Review*, 54: 761–773.

Central Statistics Office (2000). *That was Then, This is Now: Change in Ireland, 1949–1999*. Cork: CSO.

Chaftez, Janet Saltzman and Anthony Gary Dworkin (1986). *Female Revolt: Women's Movements in World and Historical Perspective*. Totowa, NJ: Rowman and Allanheld.

Clancy, Mary (1990), "Aspects of Women's Contribution to the Oireachtas Debate in the Irish Free State, 1922–37." In Maria Luddy and Clíona Murphy (eds.), *Women Surviving: Studies in Irish Women's History in the 19th and 20th Centuries*. Dublin: Poolbeg, 206–232.

Clancy, Patrick and Sheelagh Drudy, Kathleen Lynch and Liam O'Dowd (eds.) (1986). *Ireland: A Sociological Profile*. Dublin: IPA.

Clancy, Patrick and Sheelagh Drudy, Kathleen Lynch and Liam O'Dowd (eds.) (1995). *Irish Society: Sociological Perspectives*. Dublin: IPA.

Clear, Catriona (1997). "No Feminine Mystique: Popular Advice to Women of the House in Ireland 1922–1954." In Mary O'Dowd, and Maryann Gialanella Valiulis (eds.), *Women and Irish History*, Dublin: Wolfhound, 189–205.

Clear, Catriona (1987). "Walls Within Walls: Nuns in Nineteenth-Century Ireland." In Chris Curtin, Pauline Jackson, and Barbara O'Connor (eds.), *Gender in Irish Society.* Galway: University College Galway, 134–151.

Clear, Catriona (1990). "The Limits of Female Autonomy: Nuns in Nineteenth-Century Ireland." In Maria Luddy, and Clíona Murphy (eds.), *Women Surviving: Studies in Irish Women's History in the 19th and 20th Centuries.* Dublin: Poolbeg, 15–50.

Clear, Catriona (1995), "'The Women Cannot be Blamed': The Commission on Vocational Organisation, Feminism and 'Home-makers' in Independent Ireland in the 1930s and '40s." In Mary O'Dowd and Sabine Wichert (eds.), *Chattel, Servant or Citizen: Women's Status in Church, State and Society.* Belfast: Institute of Irish Studies, 179–186.

Clear, Catriona (2000). *Women of the House: Women's Household Work in Ireland 1922–1961.* Dublin: Irish Academic Press.

Collins, Tom (1992). "Power, Participation and Exclusion." In *Conference of Major Religious Superiors, New Frontiers for Full Citizenship.* Dublin: CMRS, 86–105.

Connelly, Alpha (ed.) (1993). *Gender and the Law in Ireland.* Dublin: Oak Tree Press.

Connolly, Bríd and Anne B. Ryan (eds.) (1998). *Gender and Education in Ireland*, Vol. I, Maynooth: MACE.

Connolly, Bríd and Anne B. Ryan (eds.) (1999). *Gender and Education in Ireland*, Vol. II, Maynooth: MACE.

Connolly, Clara, Catherine Hall, Mary Hickman, Gail Lewis, Anne Phoenix and Ailbhe Smyth (eds.) (1995). *The Irish Issue: The British Question. Feminist Review*, 50.

Connolly, Linda (1996). "The Women's Movement in Ireland: A Social Movements Analysis 1970–1995." In Dolores Dooley and Liz Steiner-Scott (eds.), *Irish Journal of Feminist Studies*, 1, 1. Cork: Cork University Press, 43–77.

Connolly, Linda (1997). "From Revolution to Devolution: The Contemporary Women's Movement." In Anne Byrne and Madeleine Leonard (eds.), *Women and Irish Society: A Sociological Reader.* Belfast: Beyond the Pale, 552–573.

Connolly, Linda (1999a). "'Don't Blame Women': An Exploration of Current Challenges Facing Feminist Academics." In Connolly, Bríd and Ryan, Anne B. (eds.), *Gender and Education in Ireland*, Vol. II. Maynooth: MACE, 109–120.

Connolly, Linda (1999b). "Feminist Politics and the Peace Process." *Capital and Class*, 69, Autumn.

Connolly, Linda (1999c). "Feminist Scholarship and Contemporary Ireland." In Joep Leerssen, (ed.), *the Irish Review*, no. 24, Autumn. Cork: Cork University Press, 157–161.

Connolly, Linda (2002). *The Irish Women's Movement: From Revolution to Devolution.* London and New York (Hardback): Macmillan.

Connolly, Linda (2003a). "Theorizing Ireland? Social Theory and the Politics of Identity." *Sociology*, vol. 37, no. 2:173–179.

Connolly, Linda (2003b). *The Irish Women's Movement: From Revolution to Devolution.* Dublin (Paperback): Lilliput.

Connolly, Linda (2004). "The Limits of 'Irish Studies': Culturalism, Historicism, Paternalism." *Irish Studies Review*, vol. 12, no. 2: 139–162.

Connolly, Linda and Niamh Hourigan (eds.) (forthcoming, 2005). *Social Movements and Ireland.* Manchester: Manchester University Press.

Conrad, Kathryn (2004) *Locked in the Family Cell: Gender, Sexuality & Political Agency in Irish National Discourse.* Wisconsin: Wisconsin University Press.

Conroy, Róisín (1980) "Images of Irish Women". *Crane Bag* 4.1.

Cork Women's Education Initiative (CWEI) (1991). *Response to Green Paper on Adult Education in an Era of Lifelong Learning.* Cork: CWEI.

Cork Women's Education Initiative (CWEI) (2001). *Truslóg na mBan Personal and Social Awareness: A Training Manual for Working Class Women.* Cork: CWEI.

Costello, Marie (1999). "Challenges Posed by the Integration of Local Development and Local Government: Implications for women's community education." In Bríd Connolly and Anne B. Ryan (eds.), *Gender and Education in Ireland, Vol. II.* Maynooth: MACE, 69–88.

Cott, Nancy F. (1987). *The Grounding of Modern Feminism.* New Haven, CT: Yale University Press.

Coulter, Carol (1993). *The Hidden Tradition: Feminism, Women and Nationalism in Ireland.* Cork: Cork University Press .

Coulter, Carol (1995). "Feminism, Nationalism, and the Heritage of the Enlightenment." In Timothy P. Foley, Lionel Pilkington, Sean Ryder, Elizabeth Tilley (eds.), *Gender and Colonialism.* Galway: Galway University Press, 195–209.

Coulter, Carol (1998). "Feminism and Nationalism in Ireland." In David Miller (ed.), *Rethinking Northern Ireland.* London: Longman Addison Wesley, 160–178.

Craig, Gary, and Marjorie Mayo (1995). "Rediscovering Community Development: Some Prerequisites for Working 'In and Against the State'." *Community Development Journal,* 30.2: 105–109.

Crilly, Anne. Interview. *Slí na mBan/The Way of Women.* 10 July 2003. http://www.tallgirlshorts.net/ marymary/anne.html

Crone, Joni (1988). "Lesbian Feminism in Ireland." In Ailbhe Smyth (ed.), *Feminism in Ireland, Women's Studies International Forum,* 11, (4). New York: Pergamon, 343–347.

Crone, Joni (1995). "Lesbians: The Lavender Women of Ireland". In Íde O'Carroll and Eoin Collins (eds.), *Lesbian and Gay Visions of Ireland,* London: Cassell, 60–70.

Crossley, Nick (2003). *Making Sense of Social Movements.* Manchester: Open University Press.

Cruikshank, Margaret (1992). *The Gay and Lesbian Liberation Movement.* New York and London: Routledge.

Cullen, Mary (1985). "How Radical was Irish Feminism between 1860 and 1920?" In P.J. Corish (ed.), *Radicals, Rebels and Establishment,* Belfast: Appletree Press.

Cullen, Mary (1987) (ed.). *Girls Don't Do Honours: Irishwomen in Education in the Nineteenth and Twentieth Century.* Dublin.

Cullen, Mary (1990). "Breadwinners and Providers: Women in the Household Economy of Labouring Families 1835–6." In Maria Luddy and Clíona Murphy (eds.), *Women Surviving: Studies in Irish Women's History in the 19th and 20th Centuries,* Dublin: Poolbeg, 85–116.

Cullen, Mary (1991). "Women's History in Ireland." In Karen Offen, Ruth Roach-Pierson and Jane Rendell (eds.) (1991). *Writing Women's History: International Perspectives,* London: Macmillan, 429–441.

Cullen, Mary (1994). "History Women and History Men: the Politics of Women's History." In Daltún O Ceallaigh (ed.), *Reconsiderations of Irish History and Culture.* Dublin: Learmhas, 113–133.

Cullen, Mary (1997). "Towards a New Ireland: Women, Feminism and the Peace Process." In Mary O'Dowd and Maryann Gialanella Valiulis (eds.), *Women and Irish History.* Dublin: Wolfhound, 260–277.

Cullen, Mary, and Luddy, Maria (eds.) (1997). *Female Activists: Irish Women and Change 1900–1960.* Dublin: The Woodfield Press.

Cullen-Owens, Rosemary (1984). *Smashing Times: A History of the Irish Women's Suffrage Movement 1889–1922.* Dublin: Attic Press.

Cullen-Owens, Rosemary (1997). "Women and Pacifism in Ireland, 1915–1932." In Mary O'Dowd and Maryann Gialanella Valiulis (eds.), *Women and Irish History.* Dublin: Wolfhound, 220–239.

Cullen-Owens, Rosemary (2001). *Louie Bennett.* Cork: Cork University Press.

Curnoe, Lynda (11 December 1989). "CWMA: A Description and Evaluation". *Feminist.*

Curtin, Chris, Pauline Jackson and Barbara O'Connor (eds.) (1987). *Gender in Irish Society.* Galway: Galway University Press.

CWEI (1998). Truslóg na mBan: A Training Manual for Working Class Women. Cork: CWEI.

Dahlerup, Drude (1986). "Is the New Women's Movement Dead? Decline or Change of the Danish Movement." In Drude Dahlerup (ed.), *The New Women's Movement: Feminism and Political Power in Europe and the US.* London: Sage, 217–244.

Daly, Mary (1989). *Women and Poverty.* Dublin: Attic Press.

Daly, Mary E. (1995). "'Fanaticism and Excess' or 'The Defence of Just Causes': the International Labour Organisation and Women's Protective Legislation in the Inter-War Years." In Mary O'Dowd and Sabine Wichert (eds.), *Chattel, Servant or Citizen: Women's Status in Church, State and Society,* Belfast: Institute of Irish Studies, 215–227.

Daly, Mary E. (1995). "Women in the Irish Free State, 1922–1939: The Interaction between Economics and Ideology." In Joan Hoff and Moureen Coulter (eds.), *Irish Women's Voices Past and Present,* Indiana: Indiana University Press, 99–116.

Daly, Mary E. (1997). "'Turn on the Tap': The State, Irish Women and Running Water." In Mary O'Dowd and Maryann Gialanella Valiulis (eds.), *Women and Irish History.* Dublin: Wolfhound, 206–219.

Daly, Mary E. (1997). "'Oh, Kathleen Ni Houlihan, Your Way's a Thorny Way!'": The Condition of Women in Twentieth-Century Ireland." In Maryann Gialanella Valiulis and Anthony Bradley (eds.) (1997), *Gender and Sexuality in Modern Ireland.* Massachusetts: University of Massachusetts Press, 102–126.

Daly, Mary E. (1997). "Women and Work in Ireland." *Studies in Irish Economic and Social History,* 7.

Delmar, Rosalind (1994). "What is Feminism?" In Juliet Mitchell and Anne Oakley (eds.), *What is Feminism?* Oxford: Blackwell Publishers, 8–33.

Department of Education and Science (2000). *Learning for Life: White Paper on Adult Education.* Dublin: Government Publications, 2000.

Descarris Belanger, Francine and Shirley Roy (1991). *The Women's Movement and Its Currents of Thought: A Typological Essay.* Canadian Research Institute for the Advancement of Women. Ottawa: CRIAW.

Donoghue, Emma (1995). "Noises from Woodsheds". In Íde O'Carroll and Eoin Collins (eds.), *Lesbian and Gay Visions of Ireland.* London: Cassell, 158–170.

Donoghue, Freda, Rick Wilford and Robert Miller (1997). "Feminist or Womanist? Feminism, the Women's Movement and Age Difference in Northern Ireland." *Irish Journal of Feminist Studies*, 2, 1. Cork: Cork University Press, 86–105.

Donovan, Brian L. (1995). "Framing and Strategy: Explaining Differential Longevity in the Woman's Christian Temperance Union and the Anti-Saloon League." *Sociological Inquiry*, 65, 2: 143–155.

Dorcey, Mary (1995). Interview. In Ide O'Carroll and Eoin Collins (eds.), *Lesbian and Gay Visions of Ireland*. London: Cassell, 25–44.

Dorgan, Máire and Orla McDonnell (1997). "Conversing on Class Activism: Claiming Our Space in Feminist Politics." *Irish Journal of Feminist Studies*, 2, 1: 67–85.

Drudy, Sheelagh and Kathleen Lynch (1994). *Schools and Society in Ireland*. Dublin: Gill and Macmillan.

Dublin Lesbian and Gay Men's Collectives (1986). *Out for Ourselves: The Lives of Irish Lesbians and Gay Men*. Dublin: Dublin Lesbian and Gay Men's Collectives and Women's Community Press.

Duncan , William (1982). *The Case For Divorce*. Dublin: ICCL.

Egerton, Linda (1985). "Public Protest Domestic Acquisence." In Rosemary Ridd and Helen Calloway (eds.), *Caught up in Conflict*. London: Macmillan.

Evans, Mary (ed.) (1994). *The Woman Question*. London: Sage.

Evans, Sara (1980). *Personal Politics: The Roots of Women's Liberation in the Women's Movement and the New Left*. New York: Vintage Books.

Evason, Eileen (1991). *Against the Grain: The Contemporary Women's Movement in Northern Ireland*. Dublin: Attic Press.

Evening Press, 14 September 1978. "Prostitution Charge is Withdrawn".

Evening Press, 28 July 1974. "Bikini Lib Girls' Fifth Attack".

Fahey, Tony (1995). "Family and Household in Ireland." In Patrick Clancy, Sheelagh Drudy, Kathleen Lynch and Liam O'Dowd (eds.), *Irish Society: Sociological Perspectives*. Dublin: IPA.

Fahey, Tony and Whelan, Christopher (1994). "Marriage and the Family." In Christopher T. Whelan (ed.), *Values and Social Change in Ireland*. Dublin: Gill and Macmillan, 45–81.

Faludi, Susan (1992). *Backlash: The Undeclared War Against Women*. London: Vintage.

Farley, Fidelma (2000). *Anne Devlin*. London, Flicks Books.

Fennell, Caroline (1993). "Criminal Law & the Criminal Justice System: Women As Victim"; "Criminal Law and the Criminal Justice System: Women As Accused." In Alpha Connolly (ed.), *Gender and the Law in Ireland*. Dublin: Oak Tree Press, 151–171

Fennell, Nuala and Mavis Arnold, (1987). *Irish Women Agenda for Practical Action: A Fair Deal for Women, December 1982–1987, Four Years of Achievement*. Department of Women's Affairs and Family Law Reform. Dublin: The Stationery Office.

Ferree, Myra Marx and Beth B. Hess (1985). *Controversy and Coalition: The New Feminist Movement*. Boston, MA: Twayne.

Ferriter, Diarmaid (1994). *Mothers, Maidens and Myth: A History of the Irish Countrywomen's Association*. Dublin: ICA.

Finch, Janet (1981). "It's Great to Have Someone to Talk to: The Ethics and Politics of Interviewing Women." In Helen Roberts (eds.), *Doing Feminist Research*. London: Routledge, 70–87.

Finlay, Fergus (1990). *Mary Robinson: A President with a Purpose*. Dublin: The O'Brien Press.

Fitzpatrick, David (1987). "The Modernisation of the Irish Female." In Patrick O'Flanagan (ed.), *Rural Ireland: Modernisation and Change 1600–1900.* Cork: Cork University Press, 162–80.

Fitzpatrick, David (1991). "Women, Gender and the Writing of Irish History." *Irish Historical Studies*, 27, 107: 267–73.

Fogarty, Anne (2002). "The Horror of the Unlived Life: Mother-daughter Relationships in Comtemporary Irish Women's Fiction." In Adalgisa Giorgio (ed.), *Writing Mothers and Daughters: Renegotiating the Mother in Western European Narratives.* New York: Berghahn, 85–118.

Foley, Timothy P., Lionel Pilkington, Sean Ryder and Elizabeth Tilley (eds.) (1995). *Gender and Colonialism.* Galway: Galway University Press.

Forde, Kathleen, Joan Byrne and Cathleen O'Neill (1996). "A New Deal Through SAOL." *The Adult Learner*: 17–21.

Freeman, Jo (1975). *The Politics of Women's Liberation: A Case Study of an Emerging Social Movement and its Relation to the Policy Process.* New York: Longman.

Fritz, Leah (1979). *Dreamers and Dealers: An Intimate Appraisal of the Women's Movement.* Boston, MA: Beacon Press.

Galligan, Yvonne (1998). *Women and Contemporary Politics in Ireland: From the Margins to the Mainstream.* London: Pinter.

Galligan, Yvonne, Éilis Ward and Rick Wilford (eds.) (1998). *Contesting Politics: Women in Ireland, North and South.* Colorado: Westview Press/Political Studies Association of Ireland.

Gayford, JJ (1975). "Wife Battering: A Preliminary Survey of 100 Cases." *British Medical Journal*: 194–197.

Gilligan, Ann Louise (1998). "Education Towards a Feminist Imagination". In Bríd Connolly and Anne B. Ryan (eds.) *Gender and Education in Ireland, Vol. I,* Maynooth: MACE, 201–213.

Garber, Linda (2001). *Identity Poetics.* New York: Columbia University Press.

Garvin, Tom (1988). "The Politics of Denial and Cultural Defence: The Referenda of 1983 and 1986 in Context." *The Irish Review*, 3: 1–7.

Gelb, Joyce (1986). "Feminism in Britain: Politics Without Power?" In Drude Dahlerup (ed.), *The New Women's Movement: Feminism and Political Power in Europe and the US.* London: Sage, 103–119.

Gillespie, Elgy (2003). *Changing the Times: Irish Women Journalists 1969–1981.* Dublin: Lilliput Press.

Gilvarry, Emer (2002). "How the Gender Gap is Changing." *Sunday Business Post,* 24 November.

Girvin, Brian (1996). "Ireland and the European Union: The Impact of Integration and Social Change on Abortion Policy". In Marianne Githens and Dorothy McBríde Stetson (eds.), *Abortion Politics: Public Policy in Cross-Cultural Perspective,* New York and London: Routledge, 165–188.

Gray, Breda (2000). "From 'Ethnicity' to 'Diaspora': 1980s Emigration and 'Multicultural' London." In Bielenberg, Andy (ed.), *The Irish Diaspora.* London: Longmans, 65–88.

Gray, Breda (2004). *Women and the Irish Diaspora.* London: Routledge.

Gray, Breda, and Louise Ryan (1997). "(Dis)locating 'Woman' and Women in Representations of Irish National Identity". In Anne Byrne and Madeleine Leonard (eds.), *Women and Irish Society: A Sociological Reader.* Belfast: Beyond the Pale, 517–534.

Gray, Jane (1995). "Gender Politics and Ireland." In Joan Hoff and Moureen Coulter (eds.), *Irish Women's Voices Past and Present*, Indiana: Indiana University Press, 240–249.

Giugni, Marco (1999). "How Social Movements Matter: Past Research, Present Problems, Future Developments." In Marco Giugni, Doug McAdam and Charles Tilly (eds.), *How Social Movements Matter*. Minnesota: University of Minnesota Press, xiii-xxxiii.

Hackett, Claire (1995). "Self-Determination: The Republican Feminist Agenda." *Feminist Review*, 50.

Harding, Sandra (1987). *Feminism and Methodology*. UK: Open University Press.

Hayes, Alan, and Diane Urquhart (eds.) (2001). *The Irish Women's History Reader*. London: Routledge.

Hayes, Liz (1990). *Working for Change: A Study of Three Women's Community Groups*. Report Research Series, 8. Dublin: Combat Poverty Agency.

Heron, Marianne (1993). *Sheila Conroy: Fighting Spirit*. Dublin: Attic Press.

Hesketh, Tom (1990). *The Second Partitioning of Ireland*. Dublin: Brandsma Books.

Heverin, Aileen (2000). *The Irish Countrywomen's Association: A History 1910–2000*. Dublin: ICA.

Hickman, Mary J. and Bronwyn Walter (1995). "Deconstructing Whiteness: Irish Women in Britain." In *The Irish Issue: The British Question. Feminist Review*, 50: 5–19.

Hinkson, Pamela (1991/original 1937). *Seventy Years Young: Memories of Elizabeth, Countess of Fingall*. Dublin: Lilliput Press/London: Collins.

Hoff, Joan (1997). "The Impact and Implications of Women's History." In Mary O'Dowd and Maryann Gialanella Valiulis (eds.), *Women and Irish History*. Dublin: Wolfhound, 15–37.

Holmes, Janice and Diane Urquhart, (1994). *Coming into the Light: The Work and Politics of Women in Ulster 1840–1940*. Belfast: Institute of Irish Studies.

hooks, bell (1981). *Ain't I a Woman: Black Women and Feminism*. Boston, MA: South End Press.

hooks, bell (1994). *Teaching to Transgress: Education and the Practice of Freedom*. London: Routledge.

Hoy, Sue Ellen and Margaret MacCurtain (1994). *From Dublin to New Orleans: The Journey of Nora and Alice*. Dublin: Attic Press.

Hug, Chrystel (1999). *The Politics of Sexual Morality in Ireland*. New York: St. Martins.

Humm, Maggie (ed.) (1992). *Feminisms: A Reader*. London: Harvester Wheatsheaf.

Hussey, Gemma (1990). *The Cutting Edge: Cabinet Diaries 1982–87*. Dublin: Gill and Macmillan.

Inglis, Tom (1998). *Moral Monopoly: The Rise and Fall of the Catholic Church in Modern Ireland*. Dublin: UCD Press.

Inglis, Tom (2003). *Truth, Power and Lies: Irish Society and the Case of the Kerry Babies*. Dublin: UCD Press.

Inglis, Tom, Kay Bailey and Christine Murray. *Liberating Learning: A Study of Daytime Education Groups in Ireland*. Dublin: AONTAS, 1993.

Irish Independent, 3 May 1969. "Whatever Happened to The Women's Centre?" Jean O'Keefe.

Irish Independent, 11 October 1977. "Rape Crisis Centre to Open Shortly." Inga Saffron.

Irish Independent, 13 January 1983. "A Feminist in Power – But can Minister Fennell Work Wonders for Women?" Liz Ryan.

Irish Independent, 16 May 1979. "Preparing the Ground for a Women's Collective." Mary Anderson.

Irish Independent, 16 September 1975. "Cosgrave in Angry Walk-Out over Women's Lib." Frank Byrne.

Irish Independent, 19 May 1978. "ICA Probe on Family Planning 28,000 Women to State Views."

Irish Independent, 25 September 1980. "Government Pledges Aid to Promote 'Natural' Contraception." Joseph Power.

Irish Press, 5 April 1978. "Bishops Put Birth Case."

Irish Press, 6 September 1975. "Taoiseach Walks Out of Meeting."

Irish Press, 14 October 1978. "4,000 in City Anti Rape March."

Irish Times, 3 November 1978. "The Northern Experience of Contraception and Abortion." Elgy Gillespie.

Irish Times, 4 May 1979. "How the Women's Movement keeps Women in a State of Inequality. "Bernadette Barry.

Irish Times, 5 May 1976. "Nine Women on Jury."

Irish Times, 6 January 1979. "IMA to Discuss Bill with Haughey."

Irish Times, 7 April 1981. "FG Pledges Review of Law on Contraception." Renagh Holohan.

Irish Times, 8 April 1979. "Contraception. Letters to the Editor."

Irish Times, 9 March 1971. "Women's Liberation." Mary Maher.

Irish Times, 11 April 1981. "Irish NUJ Hits Abortion Move."

Irish Times, 13 November 1975. "Hecklers Disrupt Contraception Rally." Geraldine Kennedy.

Irish Times, 15 December 1978. "Details of Haughey's Health (Family Planning) Bill, 1978, Are Outlined." Dr David Nowlan.

Irish Times, 15 December 1978. "Haughey Bill Allows Sale of Contraceptives on Prescription." Dick Walsh.

Irish Times, 15 September 1978. "State Withdraws Charge of Being a Prostitute."

Irish Times, 16 September 1975. "Surprise Women's Rights Speaker Follows Taoiseach." David McKittrick.

Irish Times, 17 February 1983. "Taoiseach Hears Case of Amendment Group." Olivia O'Leary.

Irish Times, 17 February 1983. "The Abortion Referendum. Letters to the Editor."

Irish Times, 18 May 1978. "Nurses Oppose Some Contraceptives." Dr David Nowlan.

Irish Times, 18 October 1980. "Labour to Press for Divorce Bill." Denis Coghlan.

Irish Times, 19 February 1993. "45% Opted for Abortion after IFPA Counselling." Padraig O'Moráin.

Irish Times, 20 April, 1979. "A Voters' Switch from Pig to Sow Chauvinism will not Change the Record of Women in Politics." Geraldine Kennedy.

Irish Times, 22 March 1976. "Feminist Group Seeks Law Changes."

Irish Times, 22 September 1980. "Cardinal Stopping Reform Say Gays."

Irish Times, 22 September 1980. "Leader of Widows Group Hits Out Over Neglect."

Irish Times, 22 September 1980. "Rome Synod to Seek Ways of Strengthening the Family." Patrick Nolan.

Irish Times, 23 September 1980. "Family Planning Act. Letters to the Editor."

Irish Times, 27 July 1978. "Haughey's Prescription. Editorial."

Irish Times, 27 September 1980. "Abortion. Letters to the Editor."

Irish Times, 27 September 1980. "Conference Told of Abortion Dangers." Patrick Nolan.

Irish Times, 27 September 1980. "Woods Sets Out Abortion View." David Nowlan.

Irish Times, 28 November 1980. "Forward to the family. Interview with Betty Friedan." Mary Maher.

Irish Times, 29 September 1980. "Therapeutic Termination Distinct from Abortion."

Irish Times, 30 October 1975. "Picket on Archbishops House."

Irish Times, 31 October 1980. "After 15 years Demanding our Rights What do we Get?" Mary Maher.

Irish Women's Liberation Movement (IWLM) (1971). *Irishwomen: Chains – or Change?* Dublin: IWLM.

Jackson, Pauline (1986). "Women's Movement and Abortion: The Criminalisation of Irish Women." In Drude Dahlerup (ed.), *The New Women's Movement: Feminism and Political Power in Europe and the US.* London: Sage, 48–63.

Jackson, Pauline (1987). "Outside the Jurisdiction: Irish Women Seeking Abortion." In Chris Curtin, Pauline Jackson and Barbara O'Connor (eds.), *Gender in Irish Society.* Galway: Galway University Press, 203–223.

Kaplan, Gisela (1992). *Contemporary Western European Feminism.* London: Allen and Unwin.

Katzenstein, Mary Fainsod (1987). "Comparing Feminist Movements of the United States and Western Europe: An Overview." In Fainsod Katzenstein, Mary and McClurg Mueller, Carol (eds.), *The Women's Movements of the United States and Western Europe: Consciousness, Political Opportunity and Public Policy,* Philadelphia, PA: Temple University Press, 3–20.

Kelly, Kate and Triona Nic Giolla Choille(1990), *Emigration Matters for Women.* Dublin, Attic Press.

Kelly, Kate and Triona Nic Giolla Choille(1995), "Listening and learning: Experiences in an Emigrant Advice Agency." In Patrick O'Sullivan (ed.), *Irish Women and Irish Emigration.* Leicester: Leicester University Press, 168–191.

Keeling, Nikki (2001). "Herstory". *L.Inc* 1.3: 4–5.

Kelleher, Margaret (2003). "The Field Day Anthology and Irish Women's Literary Studies." *Irish Review,* no. 30, Spring/Summer: 82–94.

Kennedy, Finola (1986). "The Family in Transition." In Kieran A. Kennedy (ed.), *Ireland in Transition: Economic and Social Change Since 1960.* Cork: Mercier Press, 91–100.

Kennedy, Stanislaus (1981). *One Million Poor? The Challenge of Irish Inequality.* Dublin: Turoe Press.

Kennedy, Finola (2001). *Cottage to Crèche: Family Change in Ireland.* Dublin: Institute of Public Administration.

Kennedy, Patricia (2002). *Maternity in Ireland: a woman-centred perspective.* Dublin: The Liffey Press.

Kennedy, Patricia (ed.) (2003). *Motherhood in Ireland: creation and context.* Cork: The Mercier Press.

Kiely, Liz, Máire Leane and Rosie Meade. "Basic Education in the Community: Women's Experiences". In Bríd Connolly and Anne B. Ryan (eds.) (1999). *Gender and Education in Ireland, Vol. II.* Maynooth: MACE, 131–152.

Kiely, David M. (1999). *Bloody Women: Ireland's Female Killers.* Dublin: Gill and Macmillan.

Lagerkvist, Amanda (1997). "To End 'Women's Night': A Restance Discourse of the Irish Housewives Association in the Media in 1961–62." *Irish Journal of Feminist Studies,* 2, 2: 18–34.

Ledger, Sally, Josephine McDonagh and Jane Spencer (eds.) (1994). *Political Gender: Texts and Contexts.* London: Harvester Wheatsheaf.

Lee, J.J. (1978). "Women and the Church Since the Famine." In Margaret MacCurtain and Donnchadh O Corráin (eds.), *Women in Irish Society: The Historical Dimension.* Dublin: Arlen Press: 37–45.

Lentin, Ronit (1993). "Feminist Research Methodologies – A Separate Paradigm? Notes for a Debate." *Irish Journal of Sociology,* 3: 119–138.

Lentin, Ronit (1998). "'Irishness,' the 1937 Constitution and Citizenship: A Gender and Ethnicity View." *Irish Journal of Sociology,* 8: 5–24.

Lentin, Ronit (ed.) (1995). *In From the Shadows: The UL Women's Studies Collection.* Limerick: Women's Studies Centre, University of Limerick.

Lentin, Ronit and Anne Byrne (eds.) (2001). *(Re)Searching Women.* Dublin: IPA.

Lerner, Gerda (1979). *The Majority Finds its Past: Placing Women in History.* Oxford: Oxford University Press.

Levine, June (1982). *Sisters: The Personal Story of an Irish Feminist.* Dublin: Ward River Press.

Longley, Edna (1991). *From Cathleen to Anorexia: The Breakdown of Irelands.* LIP Pamphlet Series. Dublin: Attic Press.

Luddy, Maria and Clíona Murphy (1990). "'Cherchez la Femme' The Elusive Woman in Irish History." In Maria Luddy and Clíona Murphy (eds.), *Women Surviving: Studies in Irish Women's History in the 19th and 20th Centuries.* Dublin: Poolbeg, 1–14.

Luddy, Maria and Clíona Murphy (eds.) (1990). *Women Surviving: Studies in Irish Women's History in the 19th and 20th Centuries.* Dublin: Poolbeg.

Luddy, Maria (1995a). *Women in Ireland 1800–1918: A Documentary History.* Cork: Cork University Press.

Luddy, Maria (1995b). *Women and Philanthropy in Nineteenth Century Ireland.* Cambridge: Cambridge University Press.

Luddy, Maria (1997). "Women and Politics in Nineteenth-Century Ireland." In Mary O'Dowd and Maryann Gialanella Valiulis (eds.), *Women and Irish History.* Dublin: Wolfhound, 89–108.

Lúibhéid, Eithne (1997). "The Pink Tide: Narrating Ireland's Lesbian & Gay Migrations." *Journal of Commonwealth and Postcolonial Studies,* 7.1: 149–68.

Lynch, Kathleen (1999). *Equality in Education.* Dublin: Gill & Macmillan.

MacCurtain, Margaret (1978). "Women, the Vote and Revolution." In Margaret MacCurtain, and Donnchadh O Corráin (eds.) (1978), *Women in Irish Society: the Historical Dimension.* Dublin: Arlen Press: 46–57.

MacCurtain, Margaret (1990). "Fullness of Life: Defining Female Spirituality in Twentieth-Century Ireland." In Maria Luddy and Clíona Murphy (eds.) (1990), *Women Surviving: Studies in Irish Women's History in the 19th and 20th Centuries. Dublin:* Poolbeg, 233–263.

MacCurtain, Margaret (1995). "Late in the Field: Catholic Sisters in Twentieth Century Ireland and the New Religious History." In Mary O'Dowd and Sabine Wichert (eds.), *Chattel, Servant or Citizen: Women's Status in Church, State and Society.* Belfast: Institute of Irish Studies, 34–44.

MacCurtain, Margaret (1997). "Godly Burden: The Catholic Sisterhoods in Twentieth-Century Ireland." In Maryann Gialanella Valiulis, and Anthony Bradley (eds.), *Gender and Sexuality in Modern Ireland,* Massachusetts: University of Massachusetts Press: 245–256.

MacCurtain, Margaret and Donnchadh O Corráin (eds.) (1978). *Women in Irish Society: the Historical Dimension.* Dublin: Arlen Press.

MacCurtain, Margaret and Mary O'Dowd (1992). "An Agenda for Women's History in Ireland." *Irish Historical Studies,* xxviii, 109.

Maguire, Anne (1995). "The Accidental Immigrant". In Ide O'Carroll, and Eoin Collins (eds.), *Lesbian and Gay Visions of Ireland.* London: Cassell. 200–211.

Maher, Kathleen (1996). "Straight Talking: Feminist Community Activism." In Ailbhe Smyth (ed.), *Feminism, Politics, Community,* WERRC Annual Conference Papers. Dublin: UCD, 28–33.

Maher, Kathleen (1992). "Doing it for Themselves." *Irish Reporter,* 8, 6–7.

Maher, Mary (1982). "Five Reasons Against a Referendum." In Mavis Arnold and Peader Kirby (eds.), *The Abortion Referendum: The Case Against.* Dublin: Anti-Amendment Campaign, 9–12.

Mahon, Evelyn (1994). "Feminist Research: A Reply to Lentin." *Irish Journal of Sociology,* 4: 165–169.

Mahon, Evelyn (1995). "From Democracy to Femocracy: The Women's Movement in the Republic of Ireland." In Patrick Clancy et al (eds.), *Irish Society: Sociological Perspectives.* Dublin: Institute of Public Administration, 675–708.

Mahon, Evelyn, Catherine Conlon and Lucy Dillon (1998). *Women and Crisis Pregnancy: A Report Presented to the Department of Health and Children.* Dublin: The Stationery Office.

Malcolm, Elizabeth (1999). "'Troops of Largely Diseased Women': VD, the Contagious Diseases Acts and Moral Policing in late Nineteenth-Century Ireland." *Irish Economic and Social History,* Vol. xxvi, 1999: 1–14.

Martin, Biddy (1991). *Women and Modernity: The (Life)Styles of Loue Andreas-Salome.* New York: Cornell.

Marja, Talvi (1996). "The Role of Adult Education in the Process of Integration into Europe." *The Adult Learner.* 50–55.

Mauthner, Natasha S., Odette Parry and Kathryn Backett-Milburn (1998). "The Data are Out There, or are They? Implications for Archiving and Revisiting Qualitative Data." *Sociology,* 32, 4: 733–745.

Meaney, Gerardine (1991). *Sex and Nation: Women in Irish Culture and Politics.* LIP Pamphlet Series. Dublin: Attic Press.

Meehan, Paula (1991). *The Woman Who was Marked by Winter.* Meath: Gallery Press, 40–42.

Merck, Mandy, Naomi Segal, and Elizabeth Wright (1998). *Coming Out of Feminism?* London: Blackwell.

McAdam, Marie (1994). "Hidden from History: Irish Women's Experience in Emigration." *The Irish Reporter,* 13: 12–13.

McCafferty, Nell (1985). *A Woman to Blame.* Dublin: Attic Press.

McCafferty, Nell (2004). *Nell.* Dublin: Penguin.

McCashin, Tony (1996). *Lone Mothers in Ireland – A Local Study.* Dublin: Oak Tree Press/Combat Poverty Agency.

McDonagh, Rosaleen (1999). "Nomadism, Ethnicity and Disability: A Challenge for Irish Feminism." *f/m,* 3: 30–31.

McWilliams, Monica (1993). "The Church, the State and the Women's Movement in Northern Ireland." In Ailbhe Smyth (ed.), *Irish Women's Studies Reader.* Dublin: Attic Press.

McWilliams, Monica (1995). "Struggling for Peace and Justice: Reflections on Women's Activism in Northern Ireland." In Joan Hoff and Moureen Coulter (eds.), *Irish Women's Voices: Past and Present,* Indiana: Indiana University Press, 13–39.

McWilliams, Monica and Avila Kilmurray, (1997). "Athene on the Loose: The Origins of the Northern Ireland Women's Coalition." *Irish Journal of Feminist Studies,* 2, 1: 1–21.

McWilliams, Monica and McKiernan, Joan (1993). *Bringing it out in the Open: Domestic Violence in Northern Ireland.* University of Ulster/HMSO: Centre for Research on Women:

Meaney, Geraldine (2004). *Nora, Ireland into Film Series.* Cork: Cork University Press.

Mitchell, Juliet and Anne Oakley (1999). *Who's Afraid of Feminism.* London: Penguin.

Mitchell, Juliet and Anne Oakley (eds.) (1986; 1994). *What is Feminism?* Oxford: Blackwell.

Mitchell, Paul and Rick Wilford (eds.) (1999). *Politics in Northern Ireland*. Oxford: Westview Press.

Morgan, Valerie, and Kathleen Lynch, (1986). "Gender and Education: North and South." In Patrick Clancy, Sheelagh Drudy, Kathleen Lynch and Liam O'Dowd (eds.), *Ireland a Sociological Profile*. Dublin, IPA, 529–592.

Moane, Geraldine (2001). "Colonialism and the Celtic Tiger: Legacies of History and the Quest for Vision". In Mike Cronin, Luke Gibbons and Peader Kirby (eds.), *Reinventing Ireland: Culture, Society and the Global Economy*. London: Pluto.109–123.

Moane, Geraldine (1999). *Gender and Colonialism: A Psychological Analysis of Oppression and Liberation*. London: Macmillan.

Moane, Geraldine (1996). "Legacies of Colonialism for Irish Women: Oppressive or Empowering?" In Dolores Dooley and Liz Steiner-Scott (eds.), *Irish Journal of Feminist Studies*, 1.1. Cork: Cork University Press.

Moane, Geraldine (1997). "Lesbian Politics and Community." In Anne Byrne and Madeleine Leonard (eds.), *Women and Irish Society: A Sociological Reader*. Belfast: Beyond the Pale, 431–446.

Mulholland, Marie and Ailbhe Smyth (1999). "A North-South Dialogue." *f/m*, 3: 10–17.

Mulvey, Cris (1992). *Changing the View: Summary of the Evaluation Report on the Allen Lane Foundation's Programme for Women's Groups in Ireland 1989–1991*. Dublin: Allen Lane Foundation.

Murphy, Clíona (1989). *The Women's Suffrage Movement and Irish Society in the Early Twentieth Century*. London: Harvester.

Murphy, Clíona (1992). "Women's History, Feminist History or Gender History?" *The Irish Review*, 12: 21–26.

Murphy, Clíona (1997). "A Problematic Relationship: European Women and Nationalism, 1870–1915." In Mary O'Dowd and Maryann Gialanella Valiulis (eds.), *Women and Irish History*. Dublin: Wolfhound, 144–158.

Murphy-Lawless, Jo. (1998). *Reading Birth and Death: A History of Obstetric Thinking*. Cork: Cork University Press.

National Adult Literacy Agency (2001). *Submission in Response to the White Paper on Adult Education: Learning for Life*. Dublin: NALA.

National Women's Council of Ireland (NWCI) Millennium Project (2001). *Knowledge is Power: Women and Education*. Dublin: NWCI, 2001.

Ní Chuileanáin, Eiléin (ed.) (1985). *Irish Women: Image and Achievement*. Dublin: Arlen House.

Ní Dhubhda, Siobhán (2002). "From Accidental Activists to Borderland Radicals: Radicalising Community Women's Education in Ireland." Unpublished dissertation, National University of Ireland, Maynooth.

O'Carroll, Íde (1990). *Models for Movers: Irish Women's Emigration to America*. Dublin: Attic Press.

O'Carroll, Íde and Eoin Collins (eds.) (1995). *Lesbian and Gay Visions of Ireland*. London: Cassell.

O'Carroll, J.P. (1991). "Bishops, Knights and – Pawns? Traditional Thought and the Irish Abortion Referendum Debate of 1983." *Irish Political Studies*, 6: 53–71.

O'Connor, Pat (1998). *Emerging Voices: Women in Contemporary Irish Society*. Dublin: IPA.

O'Connor, Pat (1995). "Understanding Continuities and Changes in Irish Marriage: Putting Women Centre Stage." *Irish Journal of Sociology*, 5: 135–163.

O'Dowd, Liam (1987). "Church, State and Women: The Aftermath of Partition." In Chris Curtin, Pauline Jackson and Barbara O'Connor (eds.), *Gender in Irish Society.* Galway: University College Galway, 3–33.

O'Dowd, Mary (1997). "From Morgan to MacCurtain: Women Historians in Ireland from the 1790s to the 1990s." In Mary O'Dowd and Maryann Gialanella Valiulis (eds.), *Women and Irish History.* Dublin: Wolfhound, 38–56.

O'Dowd, Mary and Sabine Wichert (eds.) (1995). *Chattel, Servant or Citizen: Women's Status in Church, State and Society.* Belfast: Institute of Irish Studies.

O'Neill, Cathleen (1992). *Telling It Like It Is.* Dublin: Combat Poverty Agency.

O'Neill, Cathleen (1999). "Reclaiming and Transforming the (Irish) Women's Movement." *f/m*, 3: 41–44.

O'Reilly, Emily (1988). *Masterminds of the Right.* Dublin: Attic Press.

O'Toole, Tina. (2003). "Moving into the Spaces Cleared by Our Sisters: Lesbian Community Activism in Ireland and Canada". In Meryn Stuart and Andrea Martinez (eds.), *Out of the Ivory Tower: Taking Feminist Research to the Community,* Toronto: Sumach Press.

O'Sullivan, Patrick (ed.) (1995). *Irish Women and Irish Migration.* London: Leicester University Press.

Oakley, Anne (1981). "Interviewing Women: A Contradiction in Terms." In Helen Roberts (ed.), *Doing Feminist Research.* London: Routledge & Kegan Paul.

Pettit, Lance (2000). *Screening Ireland: Film and Television Representation.* Manchester: Manchester University Press.

Phelan, Shane (1989). *Identity Politics: Lesbian Feminism and the Limits of Community.* Philadephia: Temple UP.

Pugh, Martin (1997). "The Rise of European Feminism." In Martin Pugh (ed.), *A Companion to Modern European History 1871–1945.* London: Blackwell, 155–174.

Randall, Vicky and Joni Lovenduski (1993). *Contemporary Feminist Politics: Women and Power in Britain.* Oxford: Oxford University Press.

Rath, Anne (1999). "Coming to Know in Community: Voice, Metaphor and Epistemology". In Bríd Connolly and Anne B. Ryan (eds.) (1999). *Gender and Education in Ireland, Vol. II.* Maynooth: MACE, 45–66.

Reinharz, S. (1992). *Feminist Methods in Social Research.* New York: Oxford University Press.

Richards, Maura (1998). *Single Issue.* Dublin: Poolbeg.

Riddick, Ruth (1993). "Abortion and the Law in the Republic of Ireland: An Overview 1861–1993." Addresss to the New England School of Law, Boston, Massachussets.

Riddick, Ruth (1994). *The Right to Choose: Questions of Feminist Morality.* Lip Pamphlet Series. Dublin: Attic Press.

Riordan, Patrick (1992). "Abortion: the Aftermath of the Supeme Court's Decision." *Studies,* 81, 323, 293–302.

Roberts, Helen (ed.) (1981). *Doing Feminist Research.* London: Routledge & Kegan Paul.

Robertson, Hilary (2000). "Disruptive Women Artists: An Irigarayan Reading of Irish Visual Culture." *Irish Studies Review,* 8,1.

Robertson, Hilary (1995). "Irish/Woman/Artist: Selective Readings." *Feminist Review,* 50: 89–110.

Robinson, Mary (1988). "Women and the Law in Ireland." In Ailbhe Smyth (ed.), *Feminism in Ireland, Women's Studies International Forum,* 11, 4. New York: Pergamon, 351–355.

Rooney, Eilish (1995). "Political Division, Practical Alliance: Problems for Women in Conflict." In Joan Hoff and Moureen Coulter (eds.), *Irish Women's Voices: Past and Present*, Indiana: Indiana University Press, 40–48.

Rooney, Eilish (1999). "Critical Reflections and Situated Accounts." *Irish Journal of Feminist Studies*, 3, 1: 97–106.

Rooney, Eilish (2000). *Difference Matters*. In Carmel Roulston and Celia Davies (eds.), *Gender, Democracy and Inclusion in Northern Ireland*, Basingstoke: Palgrave.

Rose, Catherine (1975). *The Female Experience: The Story of the Woman Movement in Ireland*. Galway: Arlen House.

Rose, Kieran (1994). *Diverse Communities: The Evolution of Lesbian and Gay Politics in Ireland*. Cork: Cork University Press.

Roseneil, Sasha (1995). "The Coming of Age of Feminist Sociology." *British Journal of Sociology*, 46, 2: 191–205.

Ross, Becki. (1995). *The House That Jill Built*. Toronto: University of Toronto Press.

Roulston, Carmel (1999). "Feminism, Politics and Postmodernism." In Yvonne Galligan, Éilis Ward and Rick Wilford (eds.), *Contesting Politics: Women in Ireland, North and South*. Colorado: Westview Press/Political Studies Association of Ireland, 1–17.

Roulston, Carmel and Celia Davies (eds.) (2000). *Gender, Democracy and Inclusion in Northern Ireland*. Basingstoke: Palgrave.

Rowbotham, Sheila (1989). *The Past is Before Us: Feminism in Action Since the 1960s*. London: Penguin.

Rowley, Rosemary (1989). "Women and the Constitution." *Administration*, 37, 1: 42–62.

Ryan, Anne B. (1997). "Gender Discourses in School Social Relations." In Anne Byrne and Madeleine Leonard (eds.), *Women and Irish Society: A Sociological Reader*. Belfast: Beyond the Pale, 26–39.

Ryan, Anne B. (2001). *Feminist Ways of Knowing: Towards Theorising the Person for Critical Adult Education*. Leicester: NIACE.

Ryan, Anne B. and Bríd Connolly (2000). "Women's Community Education in Ireland: The Need for New Directions towards 'Really Useful Knowledge'." In Jane Thompson (ed.), *Stretching the Academy: The Politics and Practice of Widening Participation in Higher Education*. Leicester: NIACE. 94–110.

Ryan, Barbara (ed.) (2001). *Identity Politics in the Women's Movement*. New York: New York University Press.

Ryan, Barbara (1992). *Feminism and the Women's Movement: Dynamics of Change in Social Movement Ideology and Activism*. New York/London: Routledge.

Ryan, Louise (1995). "Traditions and Double Moral Standards: the Irish Suffragists Critique of Nationalism." *Women's History Review*, 4.4.

Ryan, Louise (1996). *Irish Feminism and the Vote: An Anthology of the Irish Citizen Newspaper 1912–1920*. Dublin: Folens.

Ryan, Louise (1997). "A Question of Loyalty: War, Nation and Feminism in Early Twentieth Century Ireland." *Women's Studies International Forum*, 20, 1: 21–32.

Sales, Rosemary (1997). *Women Divided: Gender, Religion and Politics in Northern Ireland*. London: Routledge.

Segal, Lynne (1999). *Why Feminism?* Oxford: Blackwell.

Shorthall, Sally (1991). "The Dearth of Data on Irish Farm Wives: A Critical Review of the Literature." *Economic and Social Review*, 22, 4: 311–32.

Slattery, Helen. (2001) "Herstory". Interview. *LINC* 1, 2: 5.

Smyth, Ailbhe (1985). "Women and Power in Ireland: Problems, Progress, Practice." *Women's Studies International Forum*, 8, 4: 255–262.

Smyth, Ailbhe (1987). "Women's Studies in Ireland: Growth and Change". Unpublished paper presented at National Women's Studies Association Conference, Dublin.

Smyth, Ailbhe (1988). "The Contemporary Women's Movement in the Republic of Ireland." In Ailbhe Smyth (ed.), *Feminism in Ireland. Women's Studies International Forum*, 11, 4. New York: Pergamon, 331–342.

Smyth, Ailbhe (1988). "Visions and Voices Conference." Unpublished plenary lecture, San Francisco State University.

Smyth, Ailbhe (1993). "The Women's Movement in the Republic of Ireland 1970–1990." In Ailbhe Smyth (ed.), *Irish Women's Studies Reader*. Dublin: Attic Press, 245–69.

Smyth, Ailbhe (ed.) (1988). "Feminism in Ireland." *Women's Studies International Forum*, 11, 4. New York: Pergamon.

Smyth, Ailbhe (ed.) (1992). *The Abortion Papers: Ireland*. Dublin: Attic Press.

Smyth, Ailbhe (ed.) (1993). *Irish Women's Studies Reader*. Dublin: Attic Press.

Smyth, Ailbhe (ed.) (1996). *Feminism, Politics, Community*. Dublin: WERRC Annual Conference Papers, UCD.

Smyth, Ailbhe (1997). "Dodging Around The Grand Piano: Sex, Politics and Contemporary Irish Women's Poetry." In Vicki Bertram (ed.), *Kicking Daffodils: 20th Century Women's Poetry*, Edinburgh: Edinburgh University Press.

Smyth Ailbhe (ed.) (1997) Introduction. *Wildish Things, an Anthology of New Irish Women's Writing*. Dublin, Attic Press.

Staggenborg, Suzanne (1991). *The Pro-Choice Movement: Organization and Activism in the Abortion Conflict*. Oxford: Oxford University Press.

Stanley, Liz and Sue Wise (1993). *Breaking Out Again: Feminist Ontology and Epistemology*. London: Routledge.

Stationery Office (1970). *Report of the First Commission on the Status of Women*. Dublin: Government Publications Office.

Stationery Office (1985). *Irish Women: Agenda for Practical Action*. Working Party on Women's Affairs and Family Law Reform. Dublin: Government Publications Office.

Stationery Office (1993). *Report of the Second Commission on the Status of Women*. Dublin: Government Publications Office.

Stationery Office (1999). *Green Paper on Abortion*. Dublin: Government Publications Office.

Stationery Office (1998). *Report of the National Commission on the Family*. Dublin: Government Publications Office.

Steiner-Scott, Liz (ed.) (1985). *Personally Speaking: Women's Thoughts on Women's Issues*. Dublin: Attic Press.

St. Peter, Christine (2000). *Changing Ireland: Strategies in Contemporary Women's Fiction*. London, Palgrave.

Sunday Independent, 3 December 1978. "Birth Control March."

Sunday Independent, 21 January 1979. "The Politics of Contraception." Joseph O'Malley.

Sunday Press, 13 July 1975. "Girls 'Invade' Fitzwilliam."

Sunday Press, 28 July 1971. "Round 2 at the Forty Foot."

Sunday Tribune, Magazine, 21 May 1995. "Feminism is the Radical Notion that Women are People: 25 years on, what has changed for Irish women?"

Sunday World, 1 December 1978. "New Moves Planned as the Battle over Birth Control Rages On." Eamonn McCann.

Tansey, Jean (1984). *Women in Ireland: A Compilation of Relevant Data.* Dublin: Council for the Status of Women.

Taylor, Verta (1986; 1989). "The Future of Feminism in the 1980s: A Social Movement Analysis." In Laurel Richardson and Verta Taylor (eds.), *Feminist Frontiers: Rethinking Sex, Gender and Society,* Reading, MA: Addison-Wesley, 434–51.

Taylor, Verta (1989). "Social Movement Continuity: The Women's Movement in Abeyance." *American Sociological Review,* 54: 761–774.

Taylor, Verta and Nancy Whittier (1992). "The New Feminist Movement." In Laurel Richardson and Verta Taylor (eds.), *Feminist Frontiers III: Rethinking Sex, Gender and Society.* US: MacGraw Hill, 533–548.

Thirsk, Joan (1995). "The History Women." In Mary O'Dowd and Sabine Wichert (eds.), *Chattel, Servant or Citizen: Women's Status in Church, State and Society.* Belfast: Institute of Irish Studies, 1–11.

Thompson, J.L. (1988). "Adult Education and the Women's Movement." In Tom Lovett (ed.), *Radical Approaches to Adult Education: A Reader.* London: Routledge.

Thompson, Jane (ed.) (2000). *Stretching the Academy: The Politics and Practice of Widening Participation in Higher Education.* Leicester: NIACE.

Tweedy, Hilda (1992). *A Link in the Chain: The Story of the Irish Housewives Association 1942–1992.* Dublin: Attic Press.

Tynan, Jane (1996). "Redefining Boundaries: Feminism, Women and Nationalism in Ireland." *UCG Women's Studies Centre Review,* 4: 21–30.

Urquhart, Diane (1996). "In Defence of Ulster and the Empire: The Ulster Women's Unionist Council, 1911–1940." *UCG Women's Studies Centre Review,* 4, 31–40.

Urquhart, Diane (2000). *Women in Ulster Politics, 1890–1940.* Dublin: Irish Academic Press.

Valiulis, Maryann Gialanella (1997). "Engendering Citizenship: Women' Relationship to the State in Ireland and the United States in the Post-Suffrage Period." In Mary O'Dowd and Maryann Gialanella Valiulis (eds.), *Women and Irish History.* Dublin: Wolfhound, 159–172.

Walby, Sylvia (1990). *Theorizing Patriarchy.* London: Blackwell.

Wallace, Ruth (ed.) (1989). *Feminism and Sociological Theory.* UK: Sage.

Walsh, Deirdre (2000). "My Personal History of Cork". *LINC,* 1.1: 6.

Walsh, Eileen (1996). "Travellers, Inclusion and Adult Education." *The Adult Learner.* 42–48.

Walsh, Louise (1995). "Artist-Activist". In Íde O'Carroll and Eoin Collins (eds.), *Lesbian and Gay Visions of Ireland.* London: Cassell, 171–180.

Ward, Eilis and Orla O'Donovan (1996). "Networks of Women's Groups and Politics: What (Some) Women Think." *UCG Women's Studies Review.* 4, 1–20.

Ward, Margaret (1989). *Unmanageable Revolutionaries: Women and Irish Nationalism.* London: Pluto.

Ward, Margaret (1991). *The Missing Sex: Putting Women into Irish History.* Dublin: Attic Press.

Ward, Margaret (1991). "The Women's Movement in Northern Ireland: Twenty Years On." In Sean Hutton and Paul Stewart, (eds.), *Ireland's Histories.* London: Routledge.

Ward, Margaret (1995). *In Their Own Voice: Women and Irish Nationalism.* Dublin: Attic Press.

Ward, Margaret (1997). "Nationalism, Pacifism, Internationalism: Louie Bennett, Hanna Sheehy-Skeffington, and the Problems of "Defining Feminism." In Maryann Gialanella Valiulis and Anthony Bradley (eds.), *Gender and Sexuality in Modern Ireland.* Massachusetts: University of Massachusetts Press, 60–84.

Ward, Margaret (1998). "National Liberation Movements and the Question of Women's Liberation: The Irish Experience." In Clare Midgley (ed.), *Gender and Imperialism.* Manchester: Manchester University Press.

Women's Information Network (1993). "Choosing Abortion: A Practical Guide to Abortion and Other Options for Women with Crisis Pregnancies." Dublin: Women's Information Network.

Women's Education, Research and Resource Centre (1999). *A Study of Feminist Education as an Empowerment Strategy for Community-Based Women's Groups in Ireland.* Dublin: WERRC.

Women's Education, Research and Resource Centre/Aontas (2001). *At The Forefront: The Role of Women's Community Education in Combating Poverty and Disadvantage in the Republic of Ireland.* Dublin: AONTAS.

Wills, Clair (1993). *Inproprieties: Politics and Sexuality in Northern Irish Poetry.* Oxford: Clarendon.

Yuval Davis, Nira (1997). *Gender and Nation.* London: Sage.

Chronology

1898	Local Government vote granted to women.
1900	1 October, first meeting of Inghinidhe na hÉireann (Daughters of Éireann)
1908	5 May, Irish Women's Franchise League founded.
1909	National University of Ireland established and open to women.
1910	Society of the United Irishwomen founded, which became the Irish Countrywomen's Association (ICA) in 1935.
1911	5 September, Irish Women Workers Union established.
1912	November, 71 members of the Irish Parliamentary Party vote against the Women's Suffrage Bill and Women's Suffrage amendments to the Home Rule Bill.
1914	5 April, Cumann na mBan founded (the women's branch of the Irish Volunteers). Became involved in the 1916 Rising and the War of Independence.
1918	Franchise granted to Irish women over 30. Countess Markievicz elected the first woman to the first Dáil Éireann.
1919	1 April, Countess Markievicz appointed Minister for Labour of the first Irish Republican government.
1921	6 women elected to the second Dáil.
1922	Suffrage for all adults over 21 introduced under the first Free State Constitution. 2 women elected to the 3rd Dáil, 4 women elected to the Senate.
1923	5 women elected to the 4th Dáil.
1925	4 women elected to the Seanad.
1927	The Juries Act declared that juries in criminal and civil cases would be drawn from ratepayers, almost a total exclusion of women from jury service. 4 women elected to the 5th Dáil. 1 woman elected to the 6th Dáil.
1928	5 women elected to the Seanad.
1929	Censorship of Publications Act provided for a mandatory ban on books or periodicals advocating "the unnatural prevention of conception."
1930	Women's Social and Progressive League founded. Later it pointed out the negative implications for women in the newly written 1937 Constitution.
1931	31 July, Louie Bennett became the first woman President of the Irish Trade Union Congress.
1932	2 women elected to the 7th Dáil.
1933	3 women elected to the 8th Dáil.

1935   The Joint Committee of Women's Societies and Social Workers founded to campaign on important issues affecting women.
The Criminal Law (Amendment Act) prohibited the sale, advertising or importation of contraceptives.

1937   The 1937 Constitution introduced and defined a particular role for women.
Article 41.3.2 enshrined a prohibition on divorce.
2 women elected to the 9th Dáil.

1938   Dublin Club of the Soroptimists founded to improve social conditions.

1942   The Irish Housewives Association founded and later set up the Consumers Association.

1943   3 women elected to the 11th Dáil, 3 women elected Senators.

1944   4 women elected to the 12th Dáil, 3 women elected Senators.

1948   4 women elected to the 13th Dáil, 4 women elected Senators.

1951   5 women elected to the 14th Dáil, 3 women elected Senators.
"Mother and Child Scheme" Bill introduced by Dr. Noel Browne, Minister for Health but, withdrawn after pressure from the Catholic hierarchy.

1953   Health Act provided free medical, surgical, midwifery and hospital maternity services.

1954   6 women elected to the 15th Dáil, 4 women elected to the Senate.

1957   5 women elected to the 16th Dáil, 4 women elected to the Senate.
Married Women's Status Act, giving married women control of their own property.

1958   Garda Síochána Act provided for the employment of bean garda (women police).

1959   ICTU Women's Advisory Committee established.

1961   4 women elected to the 17th Dáil, 3 women elected to the Senate.

1964   Guardianship of Infants Act, giving women guardianship rights equal to those of men.

1965   The Succession Act passed, it abolished distinctions between the rights of inheritance of males and females. The rights of widows to a just share of their husbands' estate were increased and clarified.
Irish Federation of Women's Clubs founded.
5 women elected to the 18th Dáil, 4 women elected to the Senate.

1967   National Association of Widows founded following a public meeting held in the CIE Hall, Dublin.

1968   An ad hoc committee representative of several long-standing women's groups presented a memorandum to the Taoiseach calling for the establishment of a National Commission on the Status of Women.

1969   3 women elected to the 19th Dáil, 5 women elected to the Senate.

1970   Government set up First Commission on the Status of Women, Chaired by
          Thekla Beere.
        First meeting of the IWLM.

1971   *Chains – Or Change?* published by the Irish Women's Liberation Movement
        Late Late Show appearance.
        IWLM protest at Pro-Cathedral. Picket placed at Archbishop's residence.
        Women's Progressive Association formed by Margaret Waugh (later re-named the
          Women's Political Association).
        Commission on the Status of Women publish Interim Report on Equal Pay.

1972   AIM established.
        Cherish established.
        Report of the Commission on the Status of Women published.

1973   Council for the Status of Women established.
        Civil Service (Employment and Married Women) Act 1973: Removal of the
          Marriage Ban in the Civil Service, Local Authorities and Health Boards.
        Social Welfare Act provides for Deserted Wives and Unmarried Mothers
          Allowance.
        ADAPT founded.
        Mary Robinson introduces Private Members Bill to the Seanad (Senate) to amend
          the 1945 Criminal Law (Amendment) Act and the Censorship of Publication
          Acts 1929 and 1945.

1974   Women's Representative Committee set up by Minister for Labour to implement
          the recommendations of the Report of the Commission on the Status of
          Women.
        Supreme Court ruling in favour of Mary McGee, finds the ban on the
          importation of contraceptives for private use unconstitutional. Supreme Court
          recognises the existence of a constitutional right to marital privacy.
        Máirín de Burca and Mary Anderson take a case to the Supreme Court, claiming
          the 1927 Juries Act unconstitutional.
        Anti-Discrimination (Pay) Act passed.
        Social Welfare Act grants payment of Children's Allowance to mothers.
        Provision for payment of an allowance to single women over 58 years and to the
          wives of prisoners.
        Maintenance Orders Act provided for a reciprocal enforcement of maintenance
          orders between Ireland and the UK.
        Women's Aid opens its first refuge.
        Irishwomen United was established.
        Irish Gay Rights Movement set up

1975   International Women's Year.
        IWU holds its first public meeting at Liberty Hall and adopts ICTU Working
          Women's Charter.
        UN Decade for Women inaugurated at Mexico.
        Arlen House (publishing house) established in Galway
        Banshee magazine is published by the IWLM.

1976   CAP (Contraceptive Action Programme) launched by Irishwomen United.
        European Commission rejects Irish Government's application for derogation
          from Commission's Directive on Equal Pay.

1976   Juries Act passed following de Burca/Anderson case, which deemed conditional
       exclusion of women from jury lists to be unconstitutional.
       IWU invade the 'male only' forty-foot bathing area at Sandycove.
       Family Law (Maintenance of Spouses and Children) Act passed.
       Family Home Protection Act passed, to prevent family home being sold without
       family's consent or without the prior consent of the other spouse.

1977   First Rape Crisis Centre opened in Dublin.
       6 women elected to the Dáil – First preference votes for women increase from
       42,268 to 81,967.
       6 women elected to the Senate.
       Employment Equality Act, resulted in establishment of the Employment Equality
       Agency.
       Unfair Dismissals Act passed.
       Wicca magazine's first publication.

1978   "Women against violence against women" march to protest against rape and
       sexual assault.
       Irish Feminist Information (IFI) is set up.
       (May) First Irish Conference on Lesbianism held at Trinity College Dublin.
       (August) Marie McMahon case hits the headlines.

1979   2 women elected to the European Parliament.
       Maire Geoghan Quinn appointed to the Cabinet, the first woman since
       Constance Markievicz in 1919.
       Health (Family Planning) Act passed restricting sale of contraceptives to *bona
       fida* couples only.
       Women's Right to Choose Group formed.
       Campaign for an Irish Women's Centre launched.

1980   First Irish Pregnancy Counselling Centre established.
       Status Conference and magazine launched.
       Opening of Dublin Women's Centre.
       Joni Crone appears on the *Late Late Show*

1981   Beginning of Pro-Life Amendment Campaign.

1982   Murder of Declan Flynn in Fairview Park.

1983   Open Door Counseling established in Dublin following Irish Pregnancy
       Counseling Centre's financial collapse.
       Abortion referendum results in Article 40.3.3 of the Constitution of the Irish
       Republic, guaranteeing the "right to life of the unborn."
       Irish Feminist Information (IFI) established.
       KLEAR women's group established.
       Anti Reagan demonstration by Woman against Disarmament.
       Attic Press established.
       UCD Women's Studies Forum established.
       (August) Demonstrations in response to the judgment on Fairview Park murder.

1984   Attic Press, feminist publishing house, is established in Dublin.
       Co-Operation North grant to Lesbian Lines north and south.

1985   UN Global Women's Conference at Copenhagen.

1985   Róisín Conroy's High Court case and repeal of the Social Welfare Code
        Campaign.

1986   Nuala Fennell appointed Minister of State for Women's affairs.
        Divorce Referendum.
        Interdisciplinary Congress held in Dublin.

1988   Supreme Court ruling on abortion information.

1990   Mary Robinson elected President of Ireland.
        WERRC established at UCD.

1992   X Case.
        Abortion Information and Right to Travel referenda.
        20 women elected to Dáil Éireann.
        Report of the Second Commission on the Status of Women published.
        Decriminalisation of Homosexuality.
        First legal case to award custody of her children to a lesbian mother.

1993   Visit to Áras an Uachtaráin by a delegation from the Irish lesbian and gay
        communities.

1995   Divorce referendum passed.
        Regulation of Information Act introduced.

Index

Page numbers in italics are illustrations and captions